25⁰⁰

D0849183

The Philadelphia Quakers

The Philadelphia Quakers
in the Industrial Age
1865-1920

PHILIP S. BENJAMIN

Temple University Press   PHILADELPHIA

Temple University Press, Philadelphia 19122

© 1976 by Temple University. All rights reserved

Published 1976

Printed in the United States of America
International Standard Book Number: 0-87722-086-7
Library of Congress Catalog Card Number: 76-22967

Support for this publication was provided by
The Barra Foundation, Inc. and friends of Philip Benjamin

Contents

Introduction

By the middle of the nineteenth century the American nation was a loose collection of disparate, autonomous, and frequently isolated communities. While it had progressed considerably toward national unity from the extreme localism of the colonial period, the nation and its nearly thirty-six million people remained divided by the regional and local identities of individual communities with their own traditions and ways of dealing with social problems. But in the decades that followed the Civil War the forces of technological change eroded this distinctiveness. Rail transportation, industrialization, urbanization, and business combination all worked to nationalize the social order.[1] The homogeneous secular culture that emerged perpetuated many of the norms that the Protestant churches had made part of the American value system since the colonial period. But because of other changes taking place in the half century after Appomatox, this culture was less and less susceptible to church influence.

One of the few unifying elements in American life at the time of the Civil War was the widespread conviction that a Christian civilization had come into being on these shores. Both sides in that tragic internal conflict claimed to be fighting to uphold a Protestant America. Despite the absence of an established church, Americans frequently equated their own nationality with Protestantism. And while denominations competed for church members under a system of religious voluntarism, they found grounds for agreement in the notion that theirs was a Christian nation. But when the nation emerged from its first global war five and a half decades later, the old surety about its religious purpose was missing. Social change had eroded the spiritual depth and direction that had once prevailed at every level of the social structure. By 1920 the population had soared to three times its size during the Civil War. A flood of European immigrants—primarily Roman Catholics and Jews—had brought the old Protestant consensus to an end. What had emerged was a pluralist society far more diverse than the denominational mosaic of previous generations. Not only were Protestants having to share the nation with other faiths, they were facing a challenge from irreligious materialism encouraged by the nation's obvious prosperity.[2]

Thus, in five decades the sources of unity and divisiveness in the nation had been completely reversed. The geographic pluralism of diverse autonomous communities had given way to a religious and ethnic pluralism. And in the process of developing a homogeneous national culture, this transformation "profaned" or secularized religious norms and values. The new values included an atomizing individualism, competitive pursuit of wealth and social status, a faith in endless progress, an often belligerent ethnocentrism, an intense commitment to political processes, and a dynamic changeability which involved Americans in evanescent enthusiasms. As William Clebsch has pointed out, religions have summoned "energies for sanctifying the arenas of common life in America," only to find that the spoils of their victories went to the society at large, not to the churches. Once this secularized culture reached its maturity, it became an engine of considerable social force, permitting little deviance from its national norms. It sought to temper the ethnic and religious pluralism by halting the influx of immigrants and attempting to Americanize them.[3]

To better understand the process of cultural homogenization and the secularization of religious norms, we need to know more about the influence that the changing social patterns of these years had upon specific segments of the population. The Quakers constituted a small proportion of Philadelphia's population in the industrial age, but as members of the boards of the city's banks, corporations, and social agencies, they exercised an important influence upon its development. Both the group and the city have roots deep in the American past, and their importance during the colonial period has received considerable scholarly attention. But because the Religious Society of Friends consigned itself to minority status and failed to grow, historians of post–Civil War America have been interested only in its pacifist stand since 1917. Their neglect of nineteenth-century America's second largest city is less understandable. Philadelphia's only major multivolume history was published in 1884. Its modern development has only now begun to receive the scholarly attention it deserves.[4]

Much of American religious history has focused on theology, a good deal of it special pleading by church leaders. Written to explain the growth of the Social Gospel movement among the larger Protestant bodies, the standard religious studies of the period from 1865 to 1920 ignore other religious concerns.[5] Because the questions we have asked about the Friends in these years differ from those asked in usual denominational histories, it has been difficult to develop the kind of comparative perspective which would help us to view the subject most clearly. We have used scattered data from other groups when applicable. More general conclusions about urban religious developments must await similar studies of other religious bodies.

Quakers have always characterized themselves as a people apart from the cultural mainstream. In the 1860s they were governed by a Quietism which accentuated their aloofness from the rest of American society. Despite their Protestant origins Friends became openly critical of the major tenets of the growing national culture. We shall see how their response to industrialization and urbanization as well as their outlook toward politics, reform, philanthropy, and minorities were part of their attempt to chart a distinctive course for themselves. But like any religious group which has chosen not to isolate itself geographically, the Quakers were influenced by secular pressures for conformity. Those pressures bear an important relation to the decline in their Quietism in the new century and their willingness to deal more vigorously with worldly problems in the industrial city. For Friends, as for most Americans, these years determined their development in the twentieth century.

The Philadelphia Quakers

CHAPTER 1 | Division and Declension

In mid-April 1871, as had been their custom for generations, members of the Religious Society of Friends from Philadelphia and its surrounding rural towns gathered at the large meetinghouse at Fourth and Arch Streets for what they called the "Yearly Meeting." In the week-long sessions that followed, this body—the most authoritative in local Quakerism's organizational structure—met first in silent worship, and then to debate church priorities and fund programs. The gathering of Friends for this annual event served to remind other Philadelphians of the existence in their midst of this "island community" which differed markedly in values and behavior from the majority of the city's population. In their lapelless plain coats, broad-brimmed hats, and somber gray, the Quakers provided a strikingly rustic anomaly to the observer in the spring of 1871. To most citizens, Friends appeared a bit odd; yet their reputation as a reserved and tranquil people had won them a certain awe and respect. Their ancestors had, after all, founded this port city on the Delaware River one hundred ninety years earlier, which earned them the kind of reverential treatment accorded historical artifacts. What the average Philadelphian did not realize in 1871 was that the religious health of this island community had deteriorated seriously. Weakened by division and declension, Quakerism had fallen into a stagnancy in which a focus on rules superseded spiritual vitality.

Measuring their religious well-being by their ability to attract new members, most Protestant churches in the Gilded Age could declare themselves healthy indeed. Serious membership losses, however, prompted Quakerism to an increasingly defensive adher-

3

ence to tradition. Most American churches were giving less and less thought to their past. As Sidney Mead points out, they operated with a freedom devoid of historical perspective. Acting upon the voluntary principle basic to American religion, these denominations turned interest in revivalism and missionary enterprises into a competitive struggle for new members. Friends, on the other hand, did not look outward from their meetinghouses in search of converts. Rejecting the American ideal of endless growth, they looked inward to the maintenance of "true religion." Proselytizing usually involved compromise, and this most Quakers were unwilling to hazard. The only element of religious life they shared with other churches was a growing pietism, which marked the retreat from Enlightenment rationalism. But they never indulged in the emotional excesses which frequently accompanied that retreat for revivalists. Despite their growing alienation from mainstream religion, they shunned a total withdrawal "from the world" which had led sects such as the Mennonites into rural seclusiveness.[1]

The Quaker community suffered from more than a serious declension. Like many minorities, it was wracked with internal divisions. Anyone venturing into the Arch Street meetinghouse during the Yearly Meeting in April 1871 would have witnessed behavior which mocked Friends' tradition of tranquility. Contending parties argued bitterly over church matters. To make matters worse, an even larger secessionist group of Friends with rival claims of legitimacy met for its Yearly Meeting in May in a meetinghouse on Race Street, several squares away. Between these "Hicksites," who had separated in 1827, and the Arch Street "Orthodox" there reigned a silence far more ominous than the recriminations of the April Yearly Meeting. Theological issues had played a major part in the 1827 Separation; these were only beginning to fade from some memories in the seventies. Superseding them were intense social jealousies and growing differences over the proper relationship between Friends and the larger culture. This issue had lain at the root of the "Lamb's War" which George Fox and his original followers had waged in their attempt to transform English society in the 1650s. These early Quakers had fought for simplicity, equality, community, and peace with the strangest of weapons: peculiar patterns of behavior. After their failure to convert all England to their beliefs, they clung to those patterns, thereby perpetuating their estrangement from "the ways of the world." These patterns finally gained codification in early eighteenth-century Pennsylvania when the Yearly Meeting issued the first of a series of "Disciplines."[2] As the nineteenth century brought troubled times, the primary issue within both branches was how far Friends would enforce their Disciplines in defending their distinctiveness against the assimilative pressures of American culture.

After integrity and hard work brought the first few generations of English and American Quakers a solid prosperity, they learned the attractions of worldly culture. The simultaneous demands of the secular and religious worlds have maintained an uneasy tension among them ever since. Most denominations have accommodated themselves rather easily to secular norms, but cultural ambivalence comes close to defining the Quaker personality. Gary Nash has noted this ambivalence in describing the difficulties William Penn and his successors had in establishing a viable political authority in early Pennsylvania. Friends displayed both collective and atomistic tendencies in those years; they were restrained and community-oriented, at the same time professing egalitarianism, nonconformity, and individualism. Among the Quaker merchants of eighteenth-century Philadelphia, Frederick Tolles finds a similar conflict between "inward and outward plantations": as Quakers moved into society through commercial and civic activities, they built "hedges" around their religious life. Those hedges provided "the necessary conditions for a culturally insulated and autonomous existence" once their domination of the commonwealth ended. H. Richard Niebuhr also points to this ambiguity by describing the Society of Friends as something between a worldly church which accommodates its ethics to those of civilization and a sect which prefers isolation to ethical compromise. Modern Quakerism, he notes, has shown a greater affinity for the churchly concept of "Christ as a representative of culture" than the sect-like view of Christ as the antithesis of culture.[3] In the years after the Civil War, sect-type Quakers then in the majority battled the worldly-church type for the future of their island community.

The organization of the Society of Friends reflected a marriage of democratic and hierarchical principles. Each Quaker held his membership in a Monthly Meeting which met to conduct its business twelve times a year. One of these sessions featured "queries" into the members' behavior, answers to which were recorded in the minutes. The Meeting dealt with violators of the Discipline, accepted new members, supervised marriages, and organized committees to deal with its financial and educational activities. Each Monthly Meeting chose representatives to attend a district Quarterly Meeting, which examined answers to the queries submitted to it, heard appeals, and sent representatives to the regional Yearly Meeting. This authoritative body determined the standards of the Discipline, provided support for benevolent causes, and issued statements on public affairs. It also carried on correspondence with other Quaker bodies in England and the United States. In the 1750s, Philadelphia Yearly Meeting had created an executive body to deal with the problems caused by the French and Indian War. This "Meeting for Sufferings" dealt with problems which arose when the Yearly Meeting was not in session and prepared recommendations on questions referred to it for study. In all these Meetings, Friends openly discussed matters and required near unanimity to make a decision, a method they called "the sense of the Meeting." Lacking a paid professional ministry, they required only a clerk to preside over business meeting sessions. Small branches of the Monthly Meeting—called "Preparative" or "indulged"— served particular neighborhoods as houses of worship.[4]

Friends met together for worship several times a week, even at midday and in the evening. The worship was silent save for those moments when individual members were moved to give verbal expression to their thoughts. Only a small proportion ever spoke in meetings for worship, and those few who grew articulate in this spontaneous preaching won recognition of that talent. Meetings designated Friends of sustained eloquence and maturity as "ministers," although this carried no professional connotation and they continued in their regular occupations. Meetings also chose Friends "of solid judgment, prudence and experience" as elders to oversee the ministers and assist them in nurturing a proper religious spirit among the members. Thus was the prophetic side of Quakerism balanced by the priestly. Constituting a leadership group within the faith, ministers and elders had their own Preparative and Quarterly Meetings. To deal with breaches of the Discipline, each

Monthly Meeting appointed overseers who labored arduously with violators of Quaker standards. They sought to induce acknowledgments of error and conformity to norms established by the Discipline. If these efforts were unavailing and the Meeting determined the transgressor to be an "irreclaimable offender," excommunication from the Society—most frequently called "disownment"—followed. The disowned party could always appeal, first to the Quarterly and finally to the Yearly Meeting. The rate at which Philadelphia Meetings expelled members varied considerably over time. In the post-Civil War decades they disowned a very small proportion of the membership—nothing like the years 1755 to 1774, when several thousand were expelled.[5]

After the Hicksite Separation of 1827, both branches issued separate but nearly identical Disciplines. Both continued to describe this code of behavior as "an exterior hedge of preservation to us, against the many temptations and dangers, to which our situation in this world exposes us." The language and intent of the Orthodox and Hicksite Disciplines published in 1869 differed little from eighteenth- and early nineteenth-century editions. By reprinting sections of the rules written as early as 1711 and 1719, the Yearly Meetings reinforced the emphasis older leaders sought to place on tradition. Dated language gave an imperishable quality to the Quaker testimonies of pacifism, simplicity, community, and equality. Perhaps the most distinctive of these deplored all resorts to violence among men. The Disciplines instructed Meetings to arbitrate between contentious members and threatened disownment for those who provoked conflict by defaming their neighbors or using hearsay evidence to accuse others. They permitted no participation in military service and urged Friends to "sincerely labor to experience a settlement [of disputes] on the alone sure foundation of pure unchangeable Truth." They included strictures against payment of taxes for any aspect of warlike activity and against business profiteering in wartime. The Disciplines even prohibited members from accepting the return of surplus funds originally taken in distraint during time of war.[6]

In support of a testimony nearly as significant, the Disciplines enjoined Quakers to adopt a plainness and simplicity in speech, apparel, furniture, salutations, and conversation. "Scriptural names" of days of the week and months of the year ("first," "second," etc.) were preferred to the pagan ones of common usage. The rules urged Friends to avoid ostentatious displays at weddings and funerals and in celebrating public and religious holidays. They warned the young against "vain fashion, bad company, and other excesses" for which they and their parents could suffer disownment. The same fate awaited those who made intemperate use of alcohol, gambling, dancing, music, novel reading, and lotteries, or attended stage plays, horse races, and "other vain sports." Behind these strictures lay the belief that the attainment of Christian Truth was possible only for those whose minds remained clearly focused on reality and not distracted by unnatural activity.[7]

To preserve the Quaker community the Disciplines imposed rules of exclusivity. They threatened disownment for those who failed to attend meetings for worship or who attended marriages performed by a minister or priest. The Orthodox required strict endogamy, even barring their members from marrying Hicksite Friends or attending their marriage ceremonies. While the Hicksites warned of the possibility of disownment for those who "married out of Meeting," they evidenced a willingness to supervise marriages with non-Friends under certain circumstances. Not only did Friends eschew proselytizing, but they made the process by which outsiders could gain membership a prolonged period of examination by overseers and elders. The Hicksites were warned against joining secret societies such as the Masons. Both Disciplines encouraged families to worship together and to engage in interfamily visiting with other members. To assure that the young would be brought up in the faith, they required each Monthly Meeting to provide a school where a Quaker teacher offered a "guarded education." They urged parents to send their children to these institutions out of what the Orthodox called "a religious concern of primary obligation." The Disciplines also assigned special responsibilities for the care of indigent members to each Monthly Meeting. Friends' primary concern was clearly their own membership. The rules of the Discipline attempted to preserve the integrity of the Quaker community by keeping outside influences at arm's length.[8]

Seventeenth-century Quaker protest had included a pioneering egalitarianism, and the Disciplines continued to support this testimony. They acknowledged the equality of men and women, making both eligible for the positions of minister and elder. Separate Women's Meetings sought to assure autonomy for both sexes in all Meeting business. Strictures against a paid ministry and the belief in unanimous decisions both attested to the democratic spirit of the faith. Those who did not deal justly with all men or failed to repay their creditors equally ran the risk of Meeting censure. As a reminder of their early abolitionist activity, the Disciplines continued to reprint injunctions against slaveholdng and participation in the slave trade, even after passage of the Thirteenth Amendment. They also urged Friends to support schools for Negroes so as to assist them "to become useful members of civil society."[9]

Hedged in by these testimonies, many Friends hoped to preserve their distinctive life from the assimilative power of worldly American culture. But the half-century which followed publication of the 1869 editions of the Discipline witnessed the breaching of those testimonial walls. Increasing numbers of Friends in both branches experienced social discomfort over issues of Quaker peculiarity, including plain dress, marriage, education, and the arts. Their efforts won first a loose enforcement of the rules and eventually major Discipline revision in the interest of social accommodation. Thus, despite their Protestantism, their colonial credentials, and their Anglo-Saxon origins, the Quakers of Victorian Philadelphia were not unlike Catholic and Jewish newcomers from Europe who gradually abandoned elements of their "peculiar peoplehood" to adjust to American ways. Most island communities—rural, urban, native, and foreign, even sects like the Amish—have been unable to resist the assimilative process, despite determined efforts to maintain their separation from "the world." Ethnic and religious minorities, the Society of Friends among them, have always sheltered in their midst those striving to preserve their distinctiveness. Arrayed against them have been those who preferred to sacrifice distinctiveness to cultural unity in the interest of wider social interaction. The confrontation between these elements lies at the core of American social change in the five decades that followed the Civil War.[10]

In some ways, the Orthodox-Hicksite division mirrored the conflict over culture among Philadelphia Friends. The issue of worldliness had joined with theological and social disputes to produce the 1827 Separation. True to its essential ambivalence, early

Quakerism had maintained a synthesis of prophetic and priestly elements. While encouraging individual witness and preaching, it appointed elders and overseers to check the atomistic tendencies of the faith. The synthesis broke down early in the nineteenth century as leading ministers began to emphasize one element to the exclusion of the other. When they acquired personal followings, an open clash resulted. A Long Island Quaker mystic, Elias Hicks, placing emphasis on "the inward light" of God working in every man, believed that men could attain salvation quite independent of Scripture if they but followed the direction of that light. He also questioned Trinitarian doctrines and Christ's divinity. This produced a response from those who called themselves "Orthodox" and who stressed the redemptive power of Christ and the Bible. Reflecting English Methodist and Anglican influences, the Orthodox grew more authoritarian in demanding acceptance of Christ's atonement and dependence on divinely inspired Scripture as the means of salvation. They also adopted the Calvinist view that worldly prosperity conferred the responsibility of religious leadership; while most of the Orthodox were affluent, the Hicksites had lower or declining occupational status. The mystic Hicks demanded a Quietist retreat from the "ways of the world." The Separation, which took place amidst scenes of chaotic disorder in the Yearly Meeting of 1827, sundered Philadelphia families and neighborhoods.[11]

A secular issue—the disposition of the property of a once-unified Quakerism—continued to sustain mutual animosity between the branches long after 1827. Friends fought out questions of property in protracted litigation before the courts. Forty years after the tragic break, both sides continued to press financial matters in a manner ill-calculated to heal their wounds. In 1867 the Orthodox Meeting for Sufferings made public a report estimating the total property losses from meetinghouses kept by the Hicksites at something over $300,000. When some individual Orthodox Meetings attempted to solve financial disputes with local Hicksites by resort to compromise, the Meeting for Sufferings overruled their efforts. As late as 1872 a group of Hicksites went to court in rural Sadsbury, Pennsylvania, to gain possession of fifty-six acres of land belonging to the old Orthodox Meeting there. Hicksite pamphleteer Thomas Speakman, who had rushed into print in 1869 to rebuke "the imperious deportment and defamatory imputations" of the Orthodox, correctly pointed out that the Orthodox had fared better than the Hicksites on the property question. They retained all but one of the city's meetinghouses and had excluded the "Separatists" from the boards of the Westtown School, the Friends' Asylum in Frankford, and the Shelter for Colored Orphans. Children under the care of this last institution were assigned to foster parents of any denomination save Catholics, Unitarians, and Hicksites.[12]

The coupling of Unitarians and Hicksites remained a favorite Orthodox theme, although it was only a half-truth. An evangelical weekly, *The Friends' Review*, concluded that the unhappy division in the Society was far better than forcing "true Friends" to listen to "Socinian preaching." The Orthodox Meeting for Sufferings criticized the Hicksites for establishing "the manifestation of the Spirit of Christ in the heart of man, as being alone his Saviour: independent of the man, Jesus Christ who died on Calvary." It suggested that by substituting mere belief for the actual work of God's grace in man's heart, the Hicksites had encouraged human presumption and undue confidence in man's spiritual safety. As late as 1894, the Orthodox body continued to attack Hicks for attempting to remove Christ from the key role in man's salvation.[13]

In his study of nineteenth-century Friends which appeared in 1875, Thomas Hodgson traced the doctrines of Hicks and his supporters to German rationalism. Hodgson attributed to Hicks the view that "*Reason* is the '*balancing principle*' to detect 'counterfeit' presentations to the mind; so that we are not to be expected 'to believe what we do not understand!' " Considering the intense mysticism of Hicks and his dependence on the inner light, this interpretation is wide of the mark. But it fit nicely with the distrust of reason and intellect which prevailed in conservative Orthodox circles, where Unitarian rationalism and Hicksite views were indistinguishable. As *The Friend* put it in 1881, "when not enlightened by a Divine opening [intellect] cannot comprehend how He who walked among His disciples in an outward body could have all the power of Heaven and earth and be Lord of all." The Orthodox declared that the Bible was something more than a treatise on moral philosophy. They described the study of divinely inspired Scripture as a true spiritual exercise—not merely an intellectual one. By taking these positions, Orthodox Friends allied themselves with other conservative Protestant churches in resisting the liberal theology which had garnered increasing numbers of adherents in the last decades of the nineteenth century.[14]

When they built their separate Meeting structure, Hicksite Friends created in place of the Meeting for Sufferings a mere Representative Committee. This body issued no theological pronouncements in response to the doctrinal condemnations emanating from Arch Street. But controversialists like Thomas Speakman continued to attack the Orthodox, imputing to them "grasping avariciousness and love of power" as well as moral "crookedness." Samuel Janney's scholarly history of the Society of Friends offers welcome relief from such polemics. While admitting that Hicks held views not in strict accord with early Friends' writings, Janney found sufficient precedents for mystical pietism in nascent Quakerism to support the Hicksite position of 1827. He described the Separation as a peaceful response to the attempt of the Philadelphia elders to impose a "creed" upon the Society. This, Janney wrote, violated the tradition of doctrinal freedom fostered by decentralized Quaker organization.[15] The theme of religious liberty remained central to the Hicksite position. They even went so far as to try to practice it themselves.

The Hicksites not only tolerated theological diversity, they embraced it. So imbued with the spirit of liberalism were they that the *Friends' Intelligencer* could assert in 1872 that no man should be permitted to impose his "truth" upon any other. Trinitarians and Unitarians worshipped side by side in their meetinghouses throughout the Philadelphia area. They did disagree over what Hicks' position on Scripture actually had been, some Hicksite Trinitarians fearing the substitution of human for divine strength as much as their Orthodox critics. But Hicksites did not view doctrinal diversity as inimical to spiritual unity because they believed tolerance and charity would preserve the harmony needed for common worship. Those hopes were not to be realized. Race Street Monthly Meeting leaders became so exercised over the want of Meeting unity that they took measures to promote corporate social activity for the entire membership. In 1886 the clerk of the Women's Yearly Meeting abandoned her post with enthusiasm, so difficult had she found the responsibility. Even the democratic means employed to reach decisions seemed to buckle under the strain. Trying to work with "the sense of the meeting," Friends could rely only on the hope that divine power would bring all discordant views into a beautiful harmony.[16]

Theological diversity also affected the relationship between the Hicksite Friends and the larger culture. As a quietist mystic, Hicks had criticized the worldliness of many Friends. His early adherents had described their act of separation as "a quiet retreat" from the scenes of disorder which seemed to plague Quakerism in 1827. But those who followed did so for a multiplicity of reasons, as Robert Doherty has shown, and many did not share the intense quietism of Hicks. Though the Hicksites constituted the less prosperous of the two branches in the 1820s, their diligence in business had erased that difference by the seventies and eighties. This new affluence in part explains the ease with which many were led to conform to aspects of worldly culture at the expense of Quaker distinctiveness. Their liberalism was equally significant. By leaving doctrine to individual promptings and the inner light, the Hicksites exposed even the most important of Friends' testimonies to doubt and questioning. Despite continued evidence of quietism in the Race Street Yearly Meeting at the end of the century, a greater proportion of the Hicksites than of the Orthodox succumbed to cultural compromise. One of the initial differences between the two branches had undergone a remakable reversal.[17]

The two responded quite differently to that thorny question which troubled all religious Victorians—the scientific challenge to faith. The Orthodox labelled Darwinism "a system built upon the deceptive reasoning of fallible man." While the Hicksites showed some admiration for Louis Agassiz's attacks on that system, they often attempted to smooth over differences between science and religion. After a controversial 1874 speech in which the British scientist John Tyndall struggled to define the power of the universe and emerged an agnostic, *The Friend* and the *Friends' Review* attacked Tyndall for his fully developed materialism, while the Hicksite *Intelligencer* lauded him "for the firm and undaunted stand he has taken in defence of truth." By the eighties, the Hicksite weekly reprinted a *Popular Science Monthly* article asserting that religion as sentiment could withstand the challenge of science, but religion formulated into a system of theology could not. By the late nineteenth century their liberalism gave the

Hicksites a unity with a growing number of Protestant denominations. They even joined some of these in support of social causes, something the Orthodox steadfastly refused to do.[18]

While they had learned to communicate with other denominations, the Hicksites remained locked in a consensual silence with their Orthodox cousins through the nineties. Their liberalism and openness did prompt them to make the first moves toward reconciliation, but those efforts awaited an altered climate at the turn of the century. Orthodox fixation on the wounds of separation did more than anything else to sustain the barriers to communication. Logan Pearsall Smith remembered warnings not to play in the street with Hicksite children. An Orthodox Quakeress recalled that " 'Friends of the other branch' seemed sometimes more alien and remote than non-Friends, 'the world's people.' " A handful from each branch attended some of the other's meetings for worship, a few of the Orthodox apparently doing so out of curiosity or to make a religious point. The influential Arch Street minister Joseph Elkinton spoke often in the "Separatist" meetings he attended. Yet others felt a social pressure so keen on this issue that they preferred to keep their visits secret. The animosities of the 1820s died hard. Joshua Baily's urban philanthropy brought him into association with "some Romanists and some Jews," but when asked to sign an 1897 call for a public meeting on international arbitration supported by Hicksite and Orthodox Friends alike, he refused. Curiously, within Orthodox circles Baily was known for his openness and for his criticism of those Friends who dominated the Yearly Meeting, whom he faulted for narrowness and rigidity.[19]

Orthodox Friends realized as little unity on religious doctrine as the Hicksites had, but they dealt with it in a different way. In this branch, the difficulties resulted from the growth of evangelism. Primarily articulated by the English Friend Joseph John Gurney, evangelical views had a profound impact on meetings in the United States a decade after the Hicksite Separation. Gurney's influence in the West was enormous, and in Philadelphia he succeeded in winning a fair number of supporters. Most of these were affluent city Friends who turned the Twelfth Street Meeting into a bastion of Gurneyite evangelism, though they constituted only a minority of the Yearly Meeting. Gurney had struck a responsive chord in many with his emphasis on the "historical Christ" as opposed to

the "inward Christ." He played down the mystical side of Quakerism in favor of a more active role for each individual in his own
salvation. To this end, he encouraged Bible study, a more intellectual approach to religion, and involvement in causes of human
betterment. This had an obvious appeal to the urbane Friends
whose civic and commercial connections in Philadelphia made
them chafe under the restraints of the Quietist Yearly Meeting.
Baily and others at Twelfth Street sought to involve Friends in
social problems which were worldly indeed.[20]

The rise of evangelical doctrines produced a response on the
part of the rural-based traditionalists of Philadelphia Orthodoxy.
They looked for leadership to a Rhode Island Friend, John Wilbur, whose attacks on Gurney caused a split in New England
Yearly Meeting in 1845. These "Wilburites" articulated a quietism
which remained dominant in Philadelphia for the rest of the century. The quietists believed that sinful man could do little for his
own regeneration, but must wait upon the Lord for direction.
Only by quieting human thoughts, appetites, and interests, and
only through passive waiting for divine light, they asserted, could
man prepare the room within his soul for God. There was little
place for intellect in this process—hence the distrust of learning
shown in Orthodox Yearly Meeting attacks on the Hicksites.
Quietism placed a premium on individual religion, for it claimed
that organized spiritual or benevolent activity would hamper God's
particular direction to each man. The Wilburites, or Arch Street
Friends as they were often called, opposed all concerted efforts to
deal with social problems. When the Orthodox in Ohio divided
into Gurneyite and Wilburite bodies in 1854, Philadelphians feared
that the same split would sunder their Yearly Meeting, already
reduced in membership to 7,000. When it came time to correspond
officially with Ohio Friends, a fight developed over which of the
two Orthodox bodies should be recognized. To prevent a threatened Gurneyite departure in 1857, the Yearly Meeting decided to
suspend correspondence with all other Meetings in the United
States and abroad. This suspension was to continue for forty
years.[21]

Visiting Friends who attended the Yearly Meeting in hopes of
delivering epistles from other Quaker bodies met obdurate refusals to accept them. Most of the disputes in the seventies arose

over evangelical Quaker visitors. The Wilburite majority did not recognize them as real Friends, while Gurneyite defense of the visitors naturally opened all the old wounds which had threatened Meeting health for three decades. The resulting public disputes left no one happy. The Wilburites were openly rude to Ohio and Indiana evangelicals; they either interrupted the visitors as they addressed a meeting or kept their hats on during a prayer of supplication. This narrow impoliteness and the repeated attempts by Gurneyites and Wilburites alike to scrap parts of the 1857 compromise brought Philadelphia Orthodoxy to the nadir of its experience in the seventies. It must be admitted, however, that deviations from Quaker practice by many Western Friends revealed what evangelism could do when it exceeded Gurney's definitions. Planned services, congregational singing, a paid ministry, and use of the phrase "Friends' Church" all developed west of the Alleghenies to accommodate increasing numbers of converts from other churches. One zealous Ohio minister went so far as to be baptized by immersion. This was too much for staid Philadelphians: it outraged the Wilburites and embarrassed the Gurneyites. Henry Hartshorne, editor of the evangelical *Friends' Review*, warned the Ohio Quaker that his revivals threatened to interfere with the leadership of Christ.[22]

The Wilburites did draw distinctions between the two types of evangelism, but they thought the Philadelphia Gurneyites naive in failing to see that their doctrines had reaped a whirlwind. Evangelical changes appeared to them to be a surrender of distinctive Quakerism to the false ideal of "comprehensiveness." When Meetings sanctioned Bible classes, First-day schools, and prayer meetings, Arch Street Friends thought it implied "a distrust in our own deeper principles." And they warned that comprehensiveness would never bring unity. "Truth is not a mere matter of opinion, nor are the doctrines of the gospel uncertain or undefined," declared *The Friend* in 1871. The Quietists wanted checks on that atomistic individualism which was producing a "modified Quakerism," and they resisted demands for change in the Discipline, a codification which they saw as originating in "Divine Wisdom." Directing their comments to Twelfth Street, they cited Paul's criticism of "the pride of intellect" as a force which destroyed the unity, simplicity, and humility of the primitive church. The Meetings for Sufferings warned the Gurneyites in 1886 that the committees they demanded for the conduct of religious and philanthropic activity would "lessen our dependence on the immediate government of Christ over His Church."[23]

Because of Arch Street sentiments against organized philanthropy, concerted efforts to deal with social problems had to operate outside the Yearly Meeting structure. An independent Friends' Freedmen Association came into being in 1863 to provide relief and education for the recently freed Southern slaves. Gurneyites provided most of the support, and they created similar associations to aid the Indians and promote peace. By the end of the century, these organizations were holding their annual sessions at the Twelfth Street meetinghouse in the evenings of Yearly Meeting week. Arch Street Friends ignored them. In 1875 the Twelfth Street Meeting, adhering to Gurneyite beliefs in the Atonement and the saving power of Scripture, gave a member permission to conduct Bible classes in the meetinghouse. One of its committees held evening gatherings to stimulate interest in Friends' mission in public life. The Gurneyites founded the Friends' Institute in 1880 to promote education; its classes in history and literature and special talks on current affairs attracted Friends and outsiders alike. Bewailing the paucity of college-trained Quakers, one Gurneyite urged the teaching of "the scientific grounds of our belief and practice." In describing the state of the Orthodox Yearly Meeting in 1894, Isaac Sharpless, president of Haverford College, expressed the fear that quietism could lead to its extinction: "The spiritual development of some members is cramped for want of exercise," he declared. He regarded it as nothing but pettiness on the part of the Wilburites to devote time to criticizing those who abandoned the plain dress or said "December" instead of "Twelfth month."[24]

Narrow and rigid the quietists may have been. Imperious and rude they often were. But the Wilburite leadership of Philadelphia Yearly Meeting was manning the dikes which protected their distinctive faith from the flood of liberal religion and worldly culture. They viewed both Gurneyite evangelism and Hicksite liberalism as defections from essential Quaker faith, and they were correct in seeing those elements as agents of assimilation. The quietists had become defensive and vindictive because they too feared for the future of Quakerism. The late Howard Brinton has observed that the Wilburites were in the best position to reconcile the conflicting elements in the Society of Friends, standing as they did at a theological midpoint between the Gurneyites and the Hicksites. But these were men of limited vision, arguing not so much from the experience of "the light" as from tradition and often using language which did more to rekindle old differences than to restore harmony. Even after the bitterness of the seventies had given way to the more placid eighties, Joseph Walton, clerk of the Yearly Meeting, had the insensitivity to suggest to a prominent Gurneyite that Friends should cultivate a "spirit of submissiveness" to authority. And truly inspired ministry was rare among them. Joseph S. Elkinton, the best-known exception, carried the message of Christ to Friends throughout the United States and Canada, as well as to a wider public, including the Indians and the Doukhobors. Yet, when elected to the board of the interdenominational Christian League in 1895, Elkinton's strict quietism prevented him from serving, despite his agreement with the league's aims. Wilburite scrupulousness and individual isolation tended to limit the influence of Friends outside the faith. Such ways were ill suited to the enormous task of reuniting the Society's divergent branches on the eve of the twentieth century.[25]

During the stormy sessions of the Orthodox Yearly Meeting of 1873, a Friend visiting from Indiana, where conversions were swelling Meeting membership rolls, issued a stark warning: "You may call it prophecy or conjecture, but I believe this Yearly Meeting will continue to decrease untill [sic] there will be none to take the place of those who are now the standard bearers." It was a chilling prediction. Friends who sought accommodation with the larger culture often worried that unless the Discipline was revised such prophecies would indeed come true. Writing in a fatalistic tone in 1881, a Hicksite noted the passing of prominent Quakers: "I can see very few coming forward to fill their places. What is to become of our Society in another generation, I cannot foretell." Two decades later, an Orthodox Friend confided to his diary that the Society was dying out in Philadelphia. As the nineteenth century drew to a close, the accommodationists became more and more vocal on the membership problem. To their warnings the Wilburite weekly, *The Friend*, had a reply: "Quakerism is not a census of numbers, but a consensus of principles. . . . The one census-taker possible for Quakerism is not a counter of heads, but a Searcher of hearts." This was clever idealism, but it reflected an ostrich-like unwillingness to face up to reality which did not bode well for the future of the faith.[26]

Prior to the 1827 Separation, Philadelphia Yearly Meeting—urban and rural quarters included—numbered approximately 26,-000 adherents. Rufus Jones estimated that close to 18,500 became Hicksites, while nearly 7,500 remained Orthodox. The city's population in 1830 was a mere 188,787. Three-quarters of a century later, the branches had declined 38 and 40 percent respectively, while Philadelphia's overall population had risen over 500 percent to 1.3 million. At the end of the nineteenth century only 16,000 Friends remained in the two Yearly Meetings. The grimness of these statistics was heightened by the knowledge that most Quaker bodies had sustained no such decline. Though smaller than the Orthodox group in Philadelphia, New York and New England Yearly Meetings had both enjoyed recent increases. Membership doubled in Baltimore in the three decades after 1865, while it tripled in North Carolina. With the exception of Ohio, no Yearly Meeting west of the Alleghenies had fewer than 10,000 members in the nineties. British Friends showed increases as well; London Yearly Meeting membership rose by a quarter between 1871 and 1901, swelled by a rapidly rising number of convincements. Only the Hicksites posted a decline throughout the United States; by 1890 the Philadelphia group represented half of the national total of 22,000.[27]

An examination of membership statistics in detail sheds further lights on the nature and source of the decline (Tables 1–2). In 1881, when thousands of Americans had already moved into the growing urban industrial centers, some 73 percent of all Friends in the Philadelphia area continued to live outside the city. In the last two decades of the century the Orthodox lost more than a fifth of their membership while the Hicksites lost about a seventh. But the Hicksite losses were more evenly divided between the Quarters than those of the Orthodox. Within these years the Arch Street Yearly Meeting consolidated two sets of faltering Quarterly Meetings in rural areas. Bucks and Burlington, north of the city on opposite sides of the Delaware, sustained the heaviest decline,

while Philadelphia Meetings—distributed between Abington and
Philadelphia Quarters—held their own, sustaining only an insignificant loss. Does this mean that more religious vitality survived
in the city Meetings? The closing of urban meetinghouses would
lead to reverse conclusions. Friends were vacating residential
neighborhoods in the eastern sections of the city, compelling the
discontinuance of Monthly Meetings and requiring the sale of
familiar Quaker landmarks. Both branches had meetinghouses off
Washington Square; the Orthodox closed Orange Street in 1872
and the Hicksites abandoned Spruce Street in 1903. The Orthodox
Northern District Meeting at 6th and Noble Streets had 416 members in 1881, but lost nearly 200 of them by 1899. It was reluc-
tantly "laid down" fifteen years later. The Hicksites transformed
the nearby Green Street meetinghouse into a social settlement in
1913 when the Monthly Meeting moved to Germantown.[28] More
definitive explanations of city membership stability in the eighties
and nineties require a closer look at changes in an individual
Meeting.

Membership turnover in the Twelfth Street Meeting was much
like urban population changes which historians have recently
brought to light. This Orthodox Meeting claimed a membership of
648 in 1882. Thirty years later it had fallen to 602. What these
statistics fail to reveal is that the Meeting received 828 individuals
as new members between 1882 and 1912, while 874 Friends left
the Meeting. The greatest number of these departures resulted
from deaths, and when the number of deaths (357) for this thirty-
year period is set against the number of births (149), the comparison points up the deep difficulties for growth and survival
under which the Meeting operated. Nearly as many Friends transferred out to other Quaker Meetings as died. Changing a Preparative Meeting in suburban Haverford into a Monthly Meeting in
1904 induced many Friends living nearby to transfer their membership there, causing a 20 percent drop at Twelfth Street in the
two years after the change. Had this not happened, the downtown
body would probably have shown a thirty-year increase in 1912.
So Twelfth Street was not as unhealthy as other urban Meetings
caught in the downward spiral. Friends there disowned 51 members during the thirty years—8 percent of the 1882 membership.

In the light of disownments in previous Quaker history, this was a low figure. The disowned parties were guilty of diverse violations: intoxication, habitual attendance at opera and the theater, unethical business activity, and especially marrying out of Meeting. As time passed, rigid enforcement of the rules gave way to gentler procedures, particularly on the marriage issue. More troubling than the disownments were 128 resignations. Yet births more than kept pace with these losses stemming from worldly influences and the attractiveness of other churches. Two members were reinstated after periods outside the Meeting in these years.[29]

Children of mixed marriages gained membership by parental request, and this accounted for 66 of the 828 new members between 1882 and 1912. Only 106 adults entered at their own request. Many of these had Quaker connections through a single parent, and the records do not distinguish between them and converts from other faiths. This low rate of "convincements" shows none of the vitality which sustained Meetings in the Western states and in Britain. Yet, the number of adult convincements rose in each succeeding decade. There were but 23 from 1882 to 1891, but the number had risen to 50 for the period 1902 to 1912. The social and educational programs which Twelfth Street instituted to reach out to its own members and outsiders succeeded in attracting a modest but increasing number of new people into the Society at the very time that some were predicting extinction. This was one of the healthier signs on the Quaker horizon, and it reflected trends which were realized only in the twentieth century. Together births, reinstatements, parental requests, and convincements accounted for less than 40 percent of the new members. A greater influx came from established Quakers who transferred their memberships to Twelfth Street from other Meetings. Of these 505 newcomers, 118 entered from Philadelphia, 66 came from other cities and abroad, but the largest number (321) came from rural areas.[30] These data suggest that the larger rural losses found in the Yearly Meeting statistics reflected urban migration in the eighties and nineties instead of a stagnant Quakerism unique to the countryside. In fact, rural areas continued to nurture faithful communities of Friends whose testimonies clashed less with their surroundings than was the case in the city. Declension was more an urban than a rural phenomenon. But urban economic opportunities had a way of overcoming loyalties to small towns and farms, and they brought many Friends to Philadelphia.

Measuring the ritual and spiritual life of Meeting members is clearly beyond the historian's grasp. Sufficient evidence exists, however, to construct a typology of Friends based on recorded involvement in Quaker institutional life. The core of that life was the activity by which Meetings maintained and cared for the Quaker community. By tracing individual Meeting activity in a sample of the membership of three Center City Meetings, we can determine the commitment to their faith of Friends in Philadelphia for this period.[31] The prime category in the typology can be labelled "Weighty Friends." This was the really active contingent which shouldered the major burden of church work and gained appointment as ministers, elders, overseers, and clerks. Those who never accepted a single assignment from among the multifarious duties of Monthly Meeting business, who failed to provide a guarded education for their children, and who left no financial bequests for Quaker projects can be called "Nominal Friends." Between these two groups were those who left more modest evidence of commitment through institutional support. We shall call this third group "Practicing Friends." This typology first of all affords a means of determining the range of institutional commitment among Friends. When contrasted with other biographical data in the sample, it also provides a means of measuring other influences upon Friends' behavior.

Almost 54 percent of the Quakers studied were Nominal Friends. This is a high proportion when compared with twentieth-century typologies for other denominations. Joseph Fichter has designated only 20 percent of the parishioners in his New Orleans study as "marginal Catholics," while Benjamin Ringer found a comparable group constituted 32 percent of a Northern parish in the Episcopal Church. The inescapable conclusion is that Friends in these years could count on only a small proportion of their members for active participation in Meeting affairs. Yet the Weighty Friends, who constituted 13.2 percent of the membership, made up a somewhat larger group proportionately than Fichter's "nuclear Catholics" and Ringer's most active Episcopalians. The more democratic nature of the organizational structure attracted a greater proportion of Friends into leadership positions than the hierarchical structure of these other more "established" churches. The remaining third of the late nineteenth- and early twentieth-century Meeting members were Practicing Friends.[32]

A breakdown of the Center City Meetings reveals that the one dominated by Quietists had higher rates of active participation than the others (Table 3). Arch Street, which remained a Wilburite preserve, had a far healthier distribution of the three types of Friends than the Gurneyite Twelfth Street Meeting or the Hicksite Race Street Meeting. Quietists developed fewer ties with secular life in Philadelphia, and more of them made the Meeting a center of their active lives. As a smaller Meeting with 200 to 300 members, it also had more success in fostering interest in its corporate life. Many of its members lived in rural towns and growing suburbs with Meetings of their own. The willingness of these members to become religious commuters testifies to their desire to maintain this inner-city Meeting at an historic site. These data also reveal that the Hicksites had a much greater proportion of nominal members than did the Orthodox; Race Street Friends clearly had an edge in embracing worldly culture. The statistics also support the contention that smaller congregations are more effective for a greater proportion of their membership than larger ones.[33]

The data confirm the view that more vital modes of Meeting participation were imported to the city from rural areas, which provided a better environment for this form of religious vitality (Tables 4–5). When the birthplace of subjects in the sample is checked against the typology, it shows that the urban-born produced a significantly higher proportion of Nominal Friends than those born outside the city. Only a tenth of those born in cities became Weighty Friends, while more than a sixth of the rural-born rose to this leadership group. Moreover, the later a Friend arrived in the city, the more likely he or she was to become active in the affairs of the Quaker community, particularly when the Friend moved to Philadelphia after the age of thirty-five. This group boasted the smallest proportion of Nominal Friends, followed closely by those who arrived between the ages of nineteen and thirty-five. Without the support of this rural-born contingent, Quakerism in Philadelphia would have fallen into much sorrier estate than it did.

If further corroboration is needed for the contention that the Society of Friends was in a stagnant period in the last decades of the nineteenth century, the data on active Meeting participation provides it (Tables 6–7). The first-generation Friends—those born in the 1840s—reached what sociologists consider the years of greatest personal church activity in the late seventies and eighties. The second generation—born in the 1860s—reached its peak of involvement after 1900. The first of these generational groups produced a greater proportion of Nominal Friends than the second. The drop in Nominal Friends after the turn of the century was modest, but sufficient to indicate a change in Meeting support. Reductions in the proportion of Nominal Friends after 1900 strengthened both of the Orthodox Meetings, but at Race Street the decrease was insignificant. More Hicksites became Weighty Friends after 1900 than before, but efforts to involve members socially failed to decrease the uninvolved segment of their Meeting from its high three-fifths level. The decision by many city-wide quietist leaders to retain memberships at Arch Street gave that Meeting a remarkably high proportion of Weighty Friends before 1900. As quietism went into a decline, the Meeting could not maintain those high levels and the Weighty proportion fell seven percentage points after the turn of the century. Also, in its quietist period Philadelphia Quakerism was dominated more by women than it was after 1900 (Table 8). Among the 1840s generation, male participation was significantly below that for the 1860s generation. After the turn of the century Quaker men constituted an even higher proportion of Weighty Friends than women. Yet Quaker women retained a uniformly smaller proportion of Nominal Friends both before and after 1900.[34]

Hazarding explanations for these changing patterns in Meeting involvement must await examination of the influence of Philadelphia's secular life upon the two generations of Friends. And we shall first want to analyze the nature of the changes which Quakers made to their Disciplines to alter their relationship to the larger culture. In the frequent self-analyses of the eighties and nineties, the Yearly Meetings concluded that the state of religion was "low" in their island community. But confronted by a declining membership which threatened to extinguish the Society, they could not agree on how to reverse this trend. Preferring to maintain traditional ways, Quietists feared that aggressive efforts to seek converts would require too many compromises with Truth. And the city seemed to hasten their decline; it took pious rural Friends and diverted them from Quaker simplicity and realism, hardening them to worldliness.

By itself, urban life in the industrial age was enough to severely strain the Society of Friends' ability to keep its community intact. But the severity of its internal divisions placed it under an even greater handicap. Abrasive disputes over the cultural question, the theological significance of Christ and Scripture, the recognition of separatist bodies, all tore the Society apart at the very time it needed its resources to preserve the Quaker faith as a meaningful approach to life in industrial society. In the absence of these efforts, members drifted away with frightening regularity. The quietists were tied to a rigid defensiveness of Quaker tradition; the accommodationists were willing to abandon so much of their religious past that it would have crippled essential Quakerism. As controversies raged between them, the hope for reconciliation evaporated. In such a state, the Society could hardly have provided an attractive alternative to those Friends who were subjecting faith and culture to scrutiny, let alone outsiders in search of a new religious home.

CHAPTER 2 | Worldly Ways and the Guarded Education

The seventeenth-century Quaker attempt to humble the proud had led to the formulation of a testimony against elegant fashion and the arts. But what began as an earnest endeavor to persuade all men to reject ostentatiousness and return to the simplicity of early Christianity became in time a badge of identity. Friends in England and America adopted styles of dress and speech which were purposely distinctive. Compliance was widespread; not until the nineteenth century did social pressure to abandon plain styles began to affect the more worldly Quakers. Then, because of its visibility, the simplicity issue became a battleground in the fight over preservation of Friends' distinctiveness. Traditionalists used the argument for simplicity not only to maintain older styles of dress and patterns of speech, but to discourage interest in the arts. Meeting censure of music, literature, theater, and ostentatious building design served as internal controls over members to keep their minds focused clearly on the divine and on the practical. The struggle over these issues in the years after the Civil War reflected the success of trends toward accommodation with the wider culture which were changing the Society of Friends from a sect into a church.

Since it was particularly the young who were influenced by the lures of contemporary fashion and the arts, the Quakers had been quick to create schools which would instill a respect for their own values among the youth of the community. The eighteenth and early nineteenth centuries witnessed the most fruitful years for these institutions, which provided what was called a "guarded education" on the elementary and secondary level. Yet by the

Victorian era many of these schools had disappeared for want of support. No matter how noble their goals, they failed to sustain Quaker traditions against the eroding influence of American culture. As mere extensions of the Meetings they served, they could do no more than reflect the ambivalence toward the standards of American society which characterized the membership itself. Only a few continued to provide that particular "hedge against this world" which supported Friends as a peculiar people.

To shore up these educational defenses Quakers abandoned their hostility to higher learning. In order to create opportunities for training those who would staff their schools, they established college-level institutions outside Philadephia. But if the aim was to strengthen the guarded education of old, it was decidedly unsuccessful. Just as the traditionalist opponents of higher learning feared, Haverford, Swarthmore, and particularly Bryn Mawr were less resistant to the influences of the wider culture than the elementary and secondary schools had been, although they retained some Friendly distinctiveness. The demolition of the rule-bound forms which marked the faith at the time of the Civil War can be attributed in part to younger Friends who were schooled at these collegiate institutions. While helping to undermine the Society of Friends of old, the colleges provided the intellectual and some of the spiritual leadership for its rebuilding in the twentieth century.

The tradition of simplicity was a significant element in the Quaker attempt to return Christianity to its humble beginnings. What governed man's spirit inwardly required outward expression. Their habits of dress and speech not only reinforced the idea of simplicity in Friends but offered outward criticism of contemporary culture. By maintaining attire similar to that worn by the earliest settlers, traditional Friends made themselves rather conspicuous in industrial Philadelphia. Though they had abandoned knickers, they retained broad-brimmed hats and gray coats without lapels. The conservative Wilburites who adhered most strictly to these outward forms dominated Orthodox Meetings in the seventies and eighties and set the image for Orthodox Friends in the city. One of their number, a tailor by trade, refused to make a coat for an influential Indiana Friend because the style he requested was too fashionable.[1] The Wilburites believed that those attired in the fashion of the day "did not have the appearance of Friends." An elderly Orthodox minister once told a younger Friend at Twelfth Street, "Joshua, I wanted to have thee on that committee, but thy coat was in the way."

The more wealthy Gurneyite Friends who received the brunt of this criticism were far from extravagant in their attire. While they admitted that the plain dress had once fostered family feeling, they rejected the view that George Fox had established a Quaker style for all time. One Gurneyite characterized the Wilburites as "conspicuously peculiar as well as plain." This question brought painful disputes to the Orthodox Yearly Meeting in the seventies.[2] The issue was not simplicity itself, but the uniformity of its expression. As part of the city's economic and social elite, many Gurneyites saw no attraction in the rusticity which the more conservative Arch Street Friends wanted to perpetuate. If the Gurneyites were too quick to blur the distinctions between Quakerism and the wider culture, the Wilburites confused outward manifestation with principle in insisting on a uniform plainness for all Friends.

For the Hicksites, dress was never a divisive question. Race Street leaders urged members never to prejudice themselves against others in the Society for their appearance. They believed that Divine direction would produce a rustic plainness in some and prompt others to adopt more fashionable styles. Since pressure for contemporary fashion came often from the young, family harmony dictated compromises with the plain style of the past. While the Hicksites left such matters up to the individual, however, they never forsook their belief in the principle of simplicity. They decried the extravagance of the eighties, which they believed was the product of new wealth and the advancement of trade. But they also saw that some of the outward forms of simplicity had lost their original significance. In 1895 the Yearly Meeting urged Friends to continue the use of plain language among themselves, not as a testimony against social rank, but because "it is the language of love, —of affection, —of the home."[3]

Belief in simplicity produced a harsh practicality among Friends which led to condemnation of the fine arts. The official attitude toward painting and sculpture was negatively critical. In the eighteenth and early nineteenth centuries, when Philadelphia artists were doing some of the finest painting in America, most Friends refused to have their portraits painted or, when they did, insisted that these representations be silhouettes of their profiles. In 1882 the Orthodox denounced the importing of works of art into the United States by the affluent because it represented a "mode of life and a code of morals utterly at variance with the pure teaching of the gospel." They considered arguments about artistic excellence as "a cover" for baser motives, claiming that appreciation of art led to unholy thoughts. So strong was the censure of artistic expression in Quaker tradition that it produced feelings of guilt among those inclined to turn to it as a recreation. Convalescing from an illness in 1866, a Haverford College student had taken up painting, but he worried that he could reconcile himself to the craft only when he had made some money by selling one of his paintings.[4]

Friends who developed artistic talent into a vocation rarely found Quakerism congenial. The contradiction between their Meeting's denunciations of art and their own commitment often drove them from the Society. Stephen Parrish, a birthright member of the Race Street Meeting who abandoned a business career at the age of thirty-one to make painting his fulltime profession, won some success when his works received wide exhibition in Europe and the United States. Never more than a Nominal Friend, Parrish resigned his membership twelve years later, in 1889. His more famous son, Maxfield Parrish, was disowned for marriage by the same Meeeting in 1897. After a few years of study at Quaker Haverford, he went on to become one of the most famous illustrators of the early twentieth century. The rich blue skies, castles, and fairy-tale atmosphere the younger Parrish portrayed were hardly in the spirit of simplicity enunciated by his ancestors.[5]

Yet not all Quakers committed to the arts were alienated from their faith. The architect William L. Price grew up an Orthodox Friend and attended the Westtown School. When he married a Hicksite in 1888, the Arch Street Meeting promptly disowned him. Accepted as a member at Race Street, he became a Practicing Friend there, serving on committees and sending his children to Swarthmore. Meanwhile, Price embraced artistic creation as fully as any man could: he founded a community for artists and writers in suburban Rose Valley, wrote plays, collected objects of art, and sustained an avid love of music. He designed homes for the Philadelphia aristocracy in French Gothic and Renaissance styles, the very antithesis of Quaker simplicity. The best known of these was "Woodmont," which he created for Alan Wood, Jr., the steel manufacturer, in Conshohocken. Like a chateau it dominated a whole hillside and featured interior elements imported from European Gothic structures. Similarly, Price's design for the Jacob Reed clothing store on Chestnut Street (1891) included an Italianate loggia for the fourth story.[6]

As a practical art, architecture seemed to win its practitioners immunity from Meeting criticism. Adherence to styles with plain lines and no ornamentation would have earned them fewer commissions in the Victorian era, and Friends accepted these realities, though they continued to demand simplicity in buildings erected for their own institutions. Addison Hutton, an Orthodox Friend, was the most popular architect of the era for such construction. His commission from Haverford College provided explicit instructions to avoid architectural features suggesting Oxford and Cambridge and to repudiate flamboyance. Haverford's Barclay Hall (1876) and Bryn Mawr's Taylor Hall (1885) fulfilled these objectives, although their subdued Gothic lines and towers suggest some influence of worldly fashion. His success in making form follow function in the school building he designed for Westtown (1886) won the Yearly Meeting committee's comment that the structure "gave the general impression . . . of simplicity combined with solid usefulness, without much attempt to produce results merely striking or ornamental." Yet Hutton's work for others ran the full gamut of Victorian eclecticism. His Ridgway Library on South Broad Street (1875) was late Greek Revival; the Y.M.C.A. Building at 15th and Chestnut (1876) combined ornate Gothic style with a mansard roof; the Girard Trust Company Building (1888) reflected the Romanesque influence made popular by Henry Hobson Richardson.[7] Walter Cope and Thomas Stewardson, who succeeded Hutton as favorite designers among the Quakers, also managed to temper simplicity with ornamental styles. Their dormitories for Bryn Mawr College and the University of Pennsylvania were Gothic and Jacobean in design and, though plain, their school building for Penn Charter on Twelfth Street employed some Gothic lines.

Affluent Friends themselves reflected diverse architectural tastes in the turn-of-the-century suburban residences they ordered built.

Some lived in baronial castles, others chose English half-timber facades, while still others preferred solid structures topped off by mansard roofs. Many who settled in the Powelton section of the 24th Ward in West Philadelphia lived in modest replicas of Italianate villas. Yet the brick row housing of the city—utilitarian in the extreme—provided shelter for more Friends in this era than the ornate creations found in some suburbs. Well suited to Quaker professions of simplicity, row homes on Arch, Vine, and Mount Vernon Streets combined quality, comfort, and practicality.[8]

That aspect of American culture which elicited the most adamant denunciations by traditional Quakers was music. The Discipline clearly enjoined Friends against singing in their worship services, and it forbade the playing of musical instruments for entertainment. But an Orthodox warning in 1873 that stricter enforcement of the rules against music was forthcoming suggests widespread violation of the Discipline on this score. Increased use of hymns in Quaker services in the West also prompted renewed interest in the subject. Time, the Yearly Meeting asserted, was too short to waste upon the vain amusements which music afforded. Eight years later it admonished parents not to allow their children to learn to play instruments. In the same decade the Meeting for Sufferings even denounced the practice of family singing. The conservatives admitted that music in worship services quieted nerves and soothed feelings, but they thought it incapable of producing "any profitable spiritual impressions." Responsive to these pronouncements, some Friends bore individual testimony against music. When an Orthodox banker found that a religious center for young people in Italy to which he had contributed was going to provide "instrumental music for acceptable worship," he withdrew his financial support. Yet in these years Philadelphia Quakerism produced David Bispham, a famous interpreter of Wagnerian roles and a leading baritone at New York's Metropolitan Opera.[9]

Both branches placed a ban on the reading of novels and romances, which were viewed as being inconsistent with Friendly simplicity. Fear of unnatural arousal of the senses played a part in this. Orthodox and Hicksite alike were urged to read only useful books and to shun the sensational. Even the liberal Twelfth Street Meeting accused the Free Library of Philadelphia of circulating pernicious books to the young. The Orthodox Meeting for Sufferings asserted that the literature of adventure, crime, and romance influenced immature minds to view the blessings of family life as tame and uninteresting. Novel reading, it was claimed, destroyed the taste for profitable books, "while a dreamy habit of thought is begotten," making it difficult to face the duties of life.[10]

Friends made exceptions for classic works in their ban on literature, and they viewed poetry as particularly evil, even when written by one of their own. Visiting New England, a Wilburite minister who spent the night in a room used by the Quaker poet John Greenleaf Whittier felt compelled to comment: "All the poetic associations did not prevent me from a good night's sleep." Friends who cultivated an interest in literature found their Meetings rather inhospitable. The urbane broker Morris Longstreth Parrish, a noted collector of first editions who published biographies of novelists Lewis Carroll, Charles Reade, and Wilkie Collins, soon found his way to the Episcopal Church and resigned his birthright membership in the Race Street Meeting in 1913. Through the late nineteenth century the rapidity with which both branches censured writing that might undermine traditional Quakerism shows how fearful they were of the assimilating power of contemporary culture. Both Yearly Meetings scrutinized manuscripts seeking official publication status; many of those submitted failed to win the Quaker imprimatur. And periodicals of other Protestant denominations came in for criticism for fostering an unhealthy skepticism among Quaker readers.[11]

Both branches established libraries offering reading which would guard the young from disturbing notions which clashed with Quakerism. Housed close to Friends' Central and Friends' Select, they served as resources to which students at these institutions could be directed by their teachers. All the volumes in the Orthodox collection on 16th Street were carefully selected by a committee which screened out even those writings of Friends which were viewed as too liberal. Rufus Jones, a prominent Friend, spoke of his being put on "the Quaker Index." In the 16th Street library young Friends in search of imaginative or exciting reading found the closest approximation in books on travel. Those in search of magazines had to look elsewhere; most of the popular periodicals contained fiction, which kept them from the library's shelves.

Most Protestant churches in America took their responsibility for governing social behavior very seriously, never hesitating to press for the imposition of Victorian middle-class standards on the entire population in their towns and cities. Friends travelled a more distinctive route in Philadelphia, concentrating on their own religious community and arguing from their own premises. The denunciations of contemporary dress, painting, music, the classics, and college football made by the traditionalists were not efforts to play a supervisory role over the entire urban populace but attempts to preserve uncompromised the most obvious expressions of Quaker distinctiveness. Their failure testified to Friends' essential ambivalence and the ease with which they were assimilated into the patterns of interest and behavior of "the world's people." In their pursuit of the noble aim of distinctiveness, the traditionalists injured the Quaker cause by insisting on a rigid uniformity. Their willingness to use disownment to maintain that uniformity prompted several departures from the faith and created internal anxieties which were the very antithesis of the community they hoped to foster.

The susceptibility of the young to the attractions of the wider culture prompted Friends to guard their children from its influences in their formative years. In the eighteenth and early nineteenth centuries individual Quakers had created schools in their own homes, while others had founded large academies. Meetings had established their own institutions in both rural and urban settings. In all of these, Quaker teachers tried to instill a love and respect for the Friends' testimonies of community, pacifism, equality, and simplicity. Through subsidies and scholarship aid, the Yearly Meeting attempted to assure all birthright members of what was appropriately called a "guarded education"—practical schooling designed to prepare the young for their confrontation with the economic challenges of the day. The schools employed books written by Friends which remained free of such elements as dramatic or poetic selections, plural forms of address, and descriptions of wars. In such a system of education, Friends believed, lay the assurance that Quakerism would survive as an untainted expression of Christian faith.[12] But by 1920 the number of these Quaker institutions in the Philadelphia area had diminished significantly, and those which had survived retained few of the distinctive patterns of schooling with which they had begun.

The major cause of this failure was no doubt the growth of the public schools, which provided opportunities for increasing numbers of Americans at no charge. Declining membership in the Society of Friends created severe difficulties in financing the small schools associated with Monthly and Preparative Meetings. Not only did the Yearly Meetings provide funds to keep small Friends' schools in operation, but they paid the boarding fees of Quaker children who moved to areas where the guarded education was readily available. As they lost students, the schools were unable to maintain their facilities and retain competent teachers. Thus, they became less attractive. Warnings from Quaker leaders against the evils of the public schools emphasized their lack of religious instruction and the low morals of the pupils. Friends criticized them for failing to prepare the young for their social and civic duties. While Quakers viewed children as innately innocent, they did subscribe to the gospel of hard work as a prerequisite to responsible adulthood. Some Friends believed the public schools were "infected with the spirit of 'learning made easy'" and produced scholars with only the appearance of educational achievement because the true mastery of no discipline was required. Yet the Orthodox Education Committee had to admit in 1876 that improved instruction in the city's schools was one of the prime causes of decreased attendance at Quaker institutions. Renewed interest in maintaining a school system absorbed both the Orthodox and Hicksites in the seventies.[13]

Because of their affluence and their tradition of internal conformity, the Orthodox sustained schools more distinctively Quaker than did the other branch. And they kept a greater proportion of their young people in these schools than the Hicksites did in theirs. In 1887 only 19 percent of the school-age children in the Orthodox Yearly Meeting sought instruction outside the Quaker school system, if the official reports are to be believed. That same year the Hicksites estimated that fully 52 percent of their youth attended public or private schools not under Friends' care. The Hicksite day schools freely admitted students from outside the Quaker fold. This may have helped keep a greater number of schools in operation, but in Orthodox eyes it compromised the principles of the guarded education. Only when financial necessity compelled them did the Philadelphia Monthly Meetings permit the Select Schools to open their doors to "the world's children" in 1877. Once admitted, children from other denominations provided the basis for expansion of several Quaker institutions of learning. Friends found themselves cast in a new role—educators to Philadelphia's upper class. Only the wealthy could afford the rising tuition fees of this period. Eventually a new justification for Quaker education appeared: the schools were described as an influence for good which would expose greater numbers of Philadelphians to Friends' principles. As early as 1890, three-fifths of the students enrolled at the recently consolidated Friends' Select School were from other denominations. Just a block away at the larger Hicksite institution, Friends' Central, the proportion was even higher: four-fifths of its students came from outside the Quaker community.[14]

As the proportion of non-Quaker students in attendance rose, the pressure to abandon Friendly traditions increased commensurately. Instead of the hoped-for influence of Quaker principles upon larger numbers of young people, particular traditions were compromised. Simplicity had always dictated a school calendar which allowed no time to engage in elaborate celebrations of Christmas and other holidays, but the new complexion of the school population compelled the Friends to alter vacation schedules. Even Westtown capitulated in 1903. Pianos and singing soon made their appearance in the Quaker elementary schools. Fifth-day meeting attendance at Arch Street—some twelve blocks distant—by Select School students, which had always served as a link between old and young, fell off as the scholars who were not Friends refused to participate. These gradual changes, while not destroying the guarded education, began a process of alteration which would make these schools very like existing private day schools outside of Quakerism.[15]

Like many other nineteenth-century Americans, Friends viewed urban life as an evil. It is not surprising therefore that Friends founded boarding schools beyond the limits of Philadelphia as a hedge against worldly influence upon the young. Established in 1799 in rural Chester County, the Westtown School attracted the children of Friends far beyond the Philadelphia area. As late as 1919, it accepted as students only those children who could claim both parents as members of Orthodox Meetings. Not until boarding schools became increasingly popular in the East did the Race Street Yearly Meeting open a comparable institution. The George School held its first classes near Newtown in Bucks County in 1893 and limited its student body to those with either one or both parents members of Hicksite meetings. With outside influences at a minimum, both schools hoped to preserve the distinctive culture of Friends in a family-like atmosphere.

With its longer tradition and run by a committee of relatively conservative Friends, Westtown worked more diligently than did George School to maintain the guarded education against the forces of contemporary culture. Its curriculum after the Civil War differed from other boarding schools of the era in its emphasis on practical disciplines; instruction in mathematics and, to a lesser degree, science was rather advanced. Though grammar and writing were required, the reading program excluded poetry, drama, and prose fiction. A quotation from Shakespeare which adorned the copy books was carefully inked out by the teachers before distribution to the pupils. Naturally there were no school plays at Westtown. Music was also absent; one unique form of Westtown student rebelliousness involved whistling or singing at the top of one's lungs in a summerhouse near the school. Even at the end of the century, the principal ordered the custodial staff to burn confiscated mouth organs. Though opposed by a few Friends as pagan intrusions, Latin and Greek had had firm roots in the curriculum since the 1830s, but modern languages did not win a place at the school until the 1890s, when French and German were first offered. History won increasing attention, but the Westtown version omitted past wars in text and discussion.[16]

Most boarding schools founded in the late nineteenth century took as their goal the preparation of Christian gentlemen. They preferred classical courses to less rigorous English courses since most of their students went on to college. With a far smaller proportion of its charges headed for college, Westtown decided to retain both in 1872. Using a modified elective principle, the school demanded a three-year course for both groups within the school. Westtown sought to prepare Christians, not gentlemen. To this end it offered religious instruction. Robert Barclay's *Catechism* and the attempts of other early Friends to define their faith became required reading in the nineteenth century. To charges that the courses in religion violated the Quaker tradition of "Gospel liberty" and provided further evidence of enforced uniformity, defenders argued that Friends did have specific religious beliefs which must be taught. By the end of the century, religious instruction became more sophisticated, involving for the first time the study of biblical history and analytical comparisons between the Old and New Testaments. The school also maintained Quaker standards of simplicity as it applied to dress and speech. This was no easy task. Parents frequently sent their children to Westtown with clothing which school authorities felt compelled to alter because it lacked the required plainness of style. The administration devised countless artful ways to get students to use "thee" instead of "you" without resorting to direct punishments. The Westtown Committee also censured parents for sending large quantities of food to their children at the Christmas season. The simplicity of life and housing conditions at Westtown were not unique. Some New England boarding schools cultivated a Spartan regimen for their affluent charges, who were frequently pampered at home; one historian has called it "corrective salutary deprivation." At Groton, they hoped it would build character; at Westtown they were adhering to religious principle.[17]

Friends were quick to foster programs of physical education when the school grounds permitted it. Westtown opened a new gymnasium in 1899 and had increased opportunities for girls in this field eleven years before. Physical education was one thing; organized athletics was something else again. The violence and extreme competitiveness of the latter made the Quakers less enthusiastic, but they acceded to student demands for extramural baseball contests as early as the 1860s. Rugby football was popular, but the school administration succeeded in phasing it out early in the twentieth century. Soccer and, for a brief time, cricket supplanted the rougher sport. Athletics at George School became a matter of concern to the Hicksite Yearly Meeting only in 1905, when college football caused a national scandal. The Meeting issued a mild warning against "the growing trend of athleticism in the schools," which it hoped that its boarding school could avoid. If other educators of the day could see athletics as a substitute for sex among their pubescent charges, it is likely that Friends had the same reason for tolerating this healthful, if occasionally brutal activity. Quaker traditions which were clearer than the stand on athletics also succumbed to pressures from students, parents, and teachers. Despite the testimony against artistic pursuits, Westtown introduced a course in freehand drawing in 1899. News that George School students were performing in plays caused a storm of controversy in the 1915 Yearly Meeting at Race Street.[18]

More significantly, all the Quaker secondary schools in and out of the city were gradually altering their primary function. Ideally, the guarded education offered all that young Friends needed to shoulder the responsibilities of adult life. Hostility to notions of higher learning had limited the number of Quakers receiving a college education. The successful development of Haverford and Swarthmore changed all that. Despite continued protestations about the primacy of religious goals, the Friends' schools undertook with increasing seriousness to prepare their students for college entrance, not just to the Quaker colleges but to other schools as well. George School principal George L. Maris had enumerated college preparation as a primary goal when the institution first opened its doors in 1893. At the turn of the century J. Henry Bartlett at Friends' Select, J. Eugene Baker at Friends' Central, and William Wickersham at Westtown all made changes in curriculum with an eye more to admission requirements of the colleges than to a consistent upholding of Friends' principles. By 1910, nearly three-quarters of the Westtown graduates were going on to college. As they were to show in the decades that followed, these Friends' schools were in an ideal position to innovate in ways that the bureaucratized public schools and more rigid private institutions could not. But they had moved a great distance from providing a hedge against the world's culture for Quaker youth.[19]

Yet, the essence of the Quaker testimonies survived. Simplicity was not limited to denials of art and literature. And pacifism might still survive the playing fields at Westtown. Dedicated Quaker teachers continued to instill respect and love for these doctrines. Though there was nothing uniquely Quaker about the two boarding schools' self-characterization as large families— Exeter, St. Paul's, and Groton used it as well—the ideal which insisted on low pupil-teacher ratios reinforced the Quaker doctrine of community. The commitment to equality proved durable as well. True, Friends did not open their schools to needy minorities in this period. But in an era which showed little sympathy for coeducation, the Quakers undertook to train the sexes together. Through the early nineteenth century the Orthodox Select Schools had instructed boys and girls at different locations. Westtown operated as two separate schools under a single roof. A screen even divided the sexes as they ate in the Westtown dining room. But in the early eighties the screen came down. Boys and girls were integrated at small tables each headed by a teacher. By the end of the decade nearly all classes were integrated, permitting a more elastic curriculum. When the Select Schools were consolidated into a single structure in 1886, recitations threw boys and girls into the same classrooms. And at Friends' Central and George School, Hicksites had always practiced integration. In an age when the Philadelphia public schools segregated the sexes on the high school level and in many elementary schools, this distinctiveness was significant.[20]

Sufficient alumni records exist for the larger Quaker secondary schools to hazard some tentative conclusions as to the influence of the guarded education in the late nineteenth century. Of the 710 Friends in our sample, one-third attended major Quaker schools in the Philadelphia area (Tables 9–11). While less than a fifth of the Hicksites had the benefit of a guarded education, more than half of the Orthodox did. The Hicksite boarding school did not open until well after these Friends reached adulthood, and many of the Orthodox attended Westtown for brief terms, giving them a mere brush with its religious influence. The Meeting whose members had the greatest exposure to the distinctive schooling was the conservative body on Arch Street. But the greater worldliness of the Hicksites is apparent in these differences. Nearly identical proportions of urban- and rural-born Friends attended the schools. Despite the fact that Quaker education generally became less available in the nineteenth century, a greater proportion of the Friends born in the 1860s attended the schools. The question of the survival of this parochial system became an important issue at the very time that the later generation came of school age. It is noteworthy that women born in the sixties were just as likely to receive a secondary education in Quaker schools as were the men; this had not been the case for the earlier generation. Not only were Friends discussing the school question in the seventies and eighties, but some of them—particularly the Hicksites—also became preoccupied by the issue of equal opportunities for women. The effects of these concerns were reflected in school attendance.[21]

It is also important to determine how effective the Quaker institutions were in fostering loyalty and commitment to the Society of Friends. The data suggests that this early training clearly disposed Friends to take a more active role in its institutional life (Tables 12–14). Fully half the Weighty Friends had attended Quaker schools, while only a quarter of the Nominal Friends had done so. Within the Monthly Meetings a majority of the leadership positions were in the hands of those with Quaker education. It it also clear that the graduates of this parochial system took the rules of endogamy more seriously than other Friends; a greater proportion of the Quaker-trained group "married within Meeting." Having attended these Quaker institutions, Friends were also more likely to see to it that their children were sent there. In the years before Friends' schools began to make compromises with worldly culture, the guarded education did instill a more serious commitment to Quaker institutions than did public and nonsectarian private schooling. This was exactly what its supporters in the Yearly Meetings asked of it.

Compared to most Protestant denominations, the Society of Friends was tardy in creating institutions of higher learning. Lacking a paid ministry and a carefully articulated theology, Quakers felt none of the urgency which prompted the Puritans in Massachusetts to open Harvard College soon after their arrival in the new world. But Friends had other reasons for their hesitancy. If God spoke to men and women directly, would not too much intellectual training—"creaturely notions" some Friends called it—stand in the way of divine revelation? Practical training which prepared men to earn a livelihood never won the Quakers' censure because it did not interfere with the inner light. Though much of this hostility continued through the nineteenth century, Friends in Philadelphia founded three colleges between 1833 and 1884. At the time of the incorporation of each, the declared purposes of the institutions lay within the guidelines for the guarded education. But the goals of the incorporators were from the outset a mixture of Quaker concern and worldly aspiration. In part, Friends sought to educate teachers for the secondary school system they had built. Some have claimed that college building was the direct result of the 1827 Separation—a quest for an articulated religious position. But the founding of Haverford, Swarthmore, and Bryn Mawr colleges were also a response to the success of other denominations in developing institutions of higher learning. Rather than see young Friends go to those colleges, the Quakers created institutions of their own. Older Friends continued to distrust the Quaker colleges. Their distrust was not misplaced, for all three soon became agents of change within the Society.[22]

In the early years of its operation, Haverford was little more than a school. It did not gain the power to grant collegiate degrees until twenty-three years after its founding in 1833, although the level of instruction was always higher than that at Westtown. While Swarthmore always had a distinct college program, more than 85 percent of its students were in the preparatory department when it opened in 1869. In both institutions the Board of Managers exercised rather strict control over student behavior to ensure adherence to Quaker testimonies. The desire of the Boards to decide every detail of college life undermined faculty authority and led to resignations in both. The strict regimen, one manifestation of which was President Edward Magill's "One Hundred Laws of Swarthmore College," also produced a climate of student rebelliousness which sabotaged educational goals. In New England colleges in this period, a similar rebelliousness led to the resignation of several presidents. Wiser administrators altered the strict policy at the Quaker institutions in the eighties. Deans Elizabeth Powell Bond at Swarthmore and Isaac Sharpless at Haverford persuaded their Boards to adopt gentler rules which eventually led to responsible student self-government. By 1903 the preparatory departments in both colleges had been dropped. And the faculties eventually won from their Boards the full responsibility for day-to-day control over students and program. Bryn Mawr never had the aura of a secondary institution; from the outset it was a college which even sustained a graduate program. Its first Dean, M. Carey Thomas, was more concerned about intellectual training than Quaker testimonies.[23]

Compared to other colleges in the Northeast, these Quaker institutions remained quite small. Discounting their preparatory programs, Haverford had but 98 students and Swarthmore 187 by the academic year 1894–95. Then only in its tenth year, more aggressive Bryn Mawr had 283 students, including 49 in the graduate program. The faculty-student ratios compared favorably to other colleges. Bryn Mawr's 1:11 ratio and Swarthmore's 1:10 were close to that at Amherst in the nineties. Haverford's 1:5 ratio put it in a class by itself. As they grew larger in the next twenty years, all three kept their ratios below 1:10. Bryn Mawr and Swarthmore had nearly 450 students each by 1914–15, while Haverford had grown to 179. All three admitted students who were not Friends by the eighties, and the proportion of those outside Quakerism increased. Bryn Mawr, which shed its Quaker affiliation rather quickly, admitted a freshman class in the fall of 1912 in which only 2 percent of the students were Friends. By the eighties Haverford had attracted a considerable number of the sons of wealthy Philadelphians who were not Friends. Upon attaining the presidency of the college in 1887, Isaac Sharpless began a policy of weeding out those whose goals were more social than intellectual, despite the financial losses this entailed. As they protected their own youth and kept a distinct Quaker orientation at the college, the Haverford managers pursued ideals which kept classes small and faculty-student relationships intimate.[24]

If the founders of the three colleges had envisioned them primarily as teacher-training institutions, they were soon disappointed. Under Samuel Gummere and Thomas Chase, Haverford built a commitment to the liberal arts which was so strong that it never developed any courses in education for its all-male student body. This failure prompted the Yearly Meeting to institute Normal instruction at the Westtown School in 1882. It had a firm place in the school's program by 1901 and many Friends were encouraged to enter teaching by this route. Pressure on coeducational Swarthmore to provide teachers for Hicksite schools brought some results. Normal training and a model school were introduced in 1878, but lasted only a brief span of years. President Magill opposed it because he believed it lowered standards. Attempts to revive the program in the nineties under the presidency of Charles DeGarmo, himself a professor of pedagogy, proved abortive. It was not until 1912 that Swarthmore created a department of psychology and education. Bryn Mawr introduced courses in the field early in its development, but also tied them rather carefully to the developing discipline of psychology.[25]

Haverford students in the years following the Civil War were required to take Greek and Latin each of their four years at the college. Electives, so popular in the wake of President Eliot's innovations at Harvard, were permitted on a modified basis for seniors in 1876, when the college established separate requirements for classical and scientific courses. While Greek was required in the former, students in the latter still faced requirements in Latin and a modern language. Thomas Chase rejected demands for less taxing requirements for students intending to go into business. During his thirty-year presidency beginning in 1887, Isaac Sharpless improved the quality of instruction by attracting several important scholars to Haverford's faculty. He also dropped admission by certificate, instituted special examinations for applicants, stiffened the graduation requirements, and later demanded two years' work in each major elective subject. Outside pressure had forced the college to offer engineering as early as the 1870s, though the level of instruction was high, with an emphasis on the theoretical. A scientist himself, Sharpless continued instruction in the subject, but majors were forced to carry half their courses in required offerings in the humanities.[26]

The rigidity with which Haverford clung to tradition in the face of demands for a more popular and applied curriculum reflected its nurture in Philadelphia Orthodoxy. But it was the rigidity and not the curriculum which was Orthodox; the study of Shakespeare, poets, and assorted pagan authors won no plaudits from the facing benches at Yearly Meeting. Important as Sharpless was in Haverford's development, it was Thomas Chase and his brother, Pliny Earle Chase—both Worcester, Massachusetts, Friends trained at Harvard—who rooted the college in the classics and philosophy in the seventies. They achieved this transformation without arousing the ire of Quaker leaders in Philadelphia because in strength of character they approached the Friends' ideal so clearly; Pliny Chase, a logician of wide learning, was as influential in Haverford Meeting as he was in the classroom. It was perhaps the absence of these qualities in another outsider, M. Carey Thomas, which opened Bryn Mawr to so much hostility. Her willingness to look outside Quakerism in assembling a faculty and her strong ties with the Johns Hopkins University, which so epitomized the triumph of German higher education in the United States, led to characterizations of the college as "a victory of secularizing intellectuality over Christian culture." There was no sweetening of the curricular diet she served undergraduates in 1885; two ancient and three modern languages, mathematics, philosophy, and a science were required for graduation. This regimen was modified only slightly in the institution's first thirty years. In those three decades the library grew to 77,000 volumes—larger by 10,000 than Haverford's, which had been building for eighty years. And the graduate school attained national respect.[27]

Ten miles to the south Swarthmore mirrored the greater susceptibility of the Hicksites to the influences of contemporary culture. As early as 1876 it dropped ancient languages as a requirement for the classical course. The male students' preference for science in the early years was very much in tune with Quakerism, although leaders such as Lucretia Mott had warned against the skepticism which its study might breed. But the interest in pure science gave way to applied studies in the eighties. Engineering grew to be the largest department; it offered twenty-two courses in 1907, while its nearest rivals, mathematics and English, offered nine and seven respectively. Slower to win their independence from the Board of Managers, the faculty and President Magill offered little resistance to the demand for practical, technical orientation. Unlike Haverford and Bryn Mawr, Swarthmore accepted on certificate the graduates of Friends' Central, George School, several Hicksites schools in other cities, and some public schools in the Philadelphia area, and it made no move to adopt an entrance exam. Sustained academic leadership was also wanting. Swarthmore had six different presidents in the decade and a half which followed 1888. The first of these, James Magill, who brought to the college traditions nurtured in the Boston Latin School, where he had been a submaster—a far cry from the scholarly Chases, his contemporaries at Haverford—seemed merely to carry out the wishes of the businessmen on the Board of Managers. The last, Joseph Swain, won complete authority over the academic program from the Board as a condition of leaving the presidency of Indiana University, but once in office he merely confirmed the trend toward applied studies, explaining the engineering offerings and developing business courses in the economics department.[28]

No violation of Quaker principle resulted from these curricular trends. It was in social life and recreation that Swarthmore ignored the testimonies of community, equality, and pacifism. Social fraternities, which caused so much internal division in New England colleges in the late nineteenth century, first came to Swarthmore in 1888 replacing earlier literary societies. Twenty-five years later there were five fraternities at the college. While students lived in college dormitories, they assembled in rented rooms in Swarthmore village for social events. Haverford, claiming fraternities destroyed the college's community life and Quaker spirit, severely limited two student-initiated societies in size and function so as to prevent social divisiveness. Between the two colleges a football rivalry developed beginning in 1879; fed by alumni enthusiasm and youthful ardor, it produced un-Quakerly violence on the field and off. More susceptible to pressure to put the college "on the map" through intercollegiate athletics, Swarthmore got larger Ivy League universities on its football schedule, even hiring professionals to strengthen its teams. It turned down a sizeable Quaker bequest in 1907 because it required abandonment of all intercollegiate athletics. When a brutal game with the University of Pennsylvania in 1904 caused a national scandal, the annual Haverford-Swarthmore game was dropped by President Sharpless, not to be resumed until 1914. To counter the football enthusiasm, Sharpless encouraged already popular cricket as a more gentlemanly sport. The Haverford cricket teams toured England five summers between 1896 and 1914.[29]

An examination of the statistical data drawn from our sample reveals that 15 percent of the 710 Friends attended college in an era in which very few did so. Only half of these chose Quaker institutions (Tables 15–17). When those born in the 1840s are compared with those born in the sixties, it is clear that college attendance was on the rise. The increase came primarily in the Quaker colleges, which were expanding. College attendance was more prevalent at the affluent Twelfth Street Meeting, which gave ideological approval to higher education. The college group there displayed the clearest preference for Quaker institutions over non-Quaker ones. The 52 individuals who attended the Quaker colleges included proportionately fewer Weighty Friends and more Nominal Friends than did those who did not receive a collegiate education. More surprising is the fact that Friends attending colleges outside the faith showed a greater commitment to Quakerism than those who went to the Friends' own colleges and those who had no higher education at all. The curriculum of the Friends' colleges was not instilling the loyalty to the religious community it was intended to between 1860 and 1890.

In 1867, Haverford's Board of Managers expressed the hope that the college's educational program "may be marked for its solid worth, its freedom from mere superficial accomplishments, its tendency to foster simplicity and moderation in character and manner, and above all, for subordination to that work of grace in the hearts of the students, without which all intellectual training is in vain." A Thomas Chase or an Isaac Sharpless would have argued that the college adhered to these goals in the years that followed. The Philadelphia conservatives would not have agreed. The students founded a literary society as early as 1834 in which they pursued cultural interests outside the curriculum. Limitations on Haverford's library acquisitions in the field of fiction remained in effect until 1900. But the literary society donated its own 3,800-volume collection to the library in 1888; it contained a good deal of fiction. Moreover, the previous year President Sharpless had brought to the college a fresh product of Harvard and German university training, Francis B. Gummere. Offering courses in English and German literature, Gummere published several studies of English poetry and ballads which won him a national reputation. Student dramatic productions did remain unacceptable until 1910. But for the fifteen years preceding that, class plays much like minstrel shows were performed in Alumni Hall. A glee club had been organized in 1887 and a banjo and mandolin club surfaced two years later. Another four decades passed before music won a place in the curriculum.[30]

Haverford had not directly encouraged these lapses from the Discipline. But the college environment, involving as it did a spirit of inquiry and experimentation, provided fertile soil for their development. Sharpless himself seemed to mediate between the desires of the students and the Yearly Meeting insistence on a strict simplicity. Yet he contributed inadvertently to the deterioration of the religious content of the educational program by appointing first-rank scholars to the faculty. While most of them were Friends, they began to separate their religious commitments from their intellectual ones. The demands of specialization, which fostered compartmentalization of studies, sundered the old unity of faith and learning. This development was not unique to the Friends' colleges; it occurred in institutions with other Protestant affiliation. While requirements for chapel at places like Oberlin and for Fifth-day meeting for worship at Haverford continued, religion became increasingly a personal and individual concern, not a corporate one. The presence on campus of increasing numbers of students from different faiths aided the trend away from the Quaker ideal of community. Once the commitment to specialized scholarly inquiry was made, attempts to turn back the clock always ended in failure. The appointment of former Friends' Central School principal William Birdsall to the presidency of Swarthmore in 1898 was such an attempt. His piety, simplicity, and faithfulness won only scorn from those oriented toward scholarship, and he resigned after four years. What remained at Haverford and Swarthmore was a Friendly influence which prevailed through forceful individuals whose personal witness to Quaker testimonies led many of the students to enrich their faith. Their impact was sufficient to perpetuate many elements of Quaker distinctiveness at the two colleges, but the Friends' ideal of community was beyond recapture.[31]

The erosion of Quaker distinctiveness in these schools and colleges cannot be attributed alone to outside influences. It is, of course, true that these institutions had been forced to admit "the world's children," and they did accommodate themselves to their new student bodies in several ways. But the real push for acculturation came from Friends themselves. Their essential ambivalence toward worldly ways made the guarded education a virtual impossibility. Social and technological change were breaking down the essential differences between America's island communities and molding a national culture. Friends' resistance to this cultural homogenization was exceedingly fragile. Their testimony of simplicity suffered decisive compromises as music, literature, eclectic architectural styles, and fashionable dress won acceptance in many segments of the Quaker community. The broadening horizons of higher education played a major role in introducing worldly ways to Friends. Equally decisive was the influence of the marketplace. As men of business, Quakers had long been exposed to secularizing pressures. But the affluence and social status they enjoyed in the nation's second city made it even more difficult for them to maintain testimonies which appeared increasingly rustic and odd.

| In the
Marketplace

In the summer of 1868 two young men of the Quaker faith combined capital of $54,000 to open a retail dry goods business at the fortuitous juncture of Eighth and Market Streets in Center City Philadelphia. So successful was their store that it became a multimillion dollar business by the end of the nineteenth century. And so enduring was the operation that it continued as a family-controlled department store into our own time. The original partners developed the venture on the principles of the Friends' business ethic. Thus, the same integrity, frugality, and hard work which had turned pious Quaker merchants into "grandees" in colonial Philadelphia seems to have been operative even in the years following the Civil War. Yet the success of Strawbridge and Clothier was far from typical of the experience of Friends who engaged in business in the Gilded Age.[1] The Quakers were definitely prosperous as a group, and some identified with the city's rather self-conscious upper class. They lived in neighborhoods which insulated them from the working-class immigrants who manned the growing industrial enterprises of this manufacturing city. But Philadelphia also attracted a good number of rural Quakers of modest means in the late nineteenth century. In the highly competitive urban economy of the period, these Friends held their own, but they made less dramatic gains than did the dry goods merchants at Eighth and Market. As the size of business organizations grew in the new century, Friends began to eschew the entrepreneurial role which they had played in previous generations.

The story of the early Quakers' success as businessmen is well known. Original Friends had come from the middle levels of the

English social order; as Hugh Barbour has written, "few were either outright proletarians or gentry." Yet the earnestness and honesty which characterized Quaker enterprise in both England and America earned them a prosperity which made their testimonies of simplicity and democracy difficult to maintain. English Friends dominated banking, clock making, iron, tin, and brass manufacturing by the end of the eighteenth century. In Philadelphia their success as merchants in the import-export trade, as well as their investment in land and early iron manufacturing, raised them to the level of a local aristocracy before the Revolution. Worldliness and affluence became significant Quaker problems. They played a role, as we have already seen, in the 1827 Separation, but even more significantly they prompted substantial numbers to desert the Society for churches more in tune with the normative values of American life. Even those who retained their fathers' faith constituted a moneyed elite in antebellum Philadelphia. Along with affluent counterparts in other denominations—frequently descendants of early Friends who had become Episcopalians and Presbyterians—these Quakers helped shape the civic and institutional life of the city. Though declining numerically in relative and absolute terms, their influence was still significant in the years before the Civil War.[2]

Because cautious quietists dominated the Society of Friends for several decades before and after the war, Meetings made few attempts to compromise the distinctive testimonies of the original faith. Far from courting the worldly and the affluent, they attacked the commercial temper of the Gilded Age. The size of competing economic units had grown larger than that to which many Quakers were accustomed. Personal integrity and accountability, so readily pinpointed in small enterprises, blurred in the large corporate entities of the late nineteenth century. The economic climate encouraged men to take grave risks with their own wealth and often with that of others entrusted to them. The quick and the clever made sizeable fortunes in brief periods—fortunes which frequently shrank in as brief a span of time. The erratic course of economic development affected all as depressions followed one another with frightening regularity. Older groups of established means longed for the stability of a slower pace of growth.

The Disciplines issued by both Orthodox and Hicksites in the late sixties and early seventies required of Friends complete integrity in their dealings with all men, urged them to keep strict accounts of financial transactions, and inveighed against the evils of speculation. An excess of riches constituted as bad a mark against a man as dire poverty. Monthly Meetings frequently disowned those who failed in business, particularly if they gave preference to some creditors over others. In the event of such a failure, the Meeting appointed a committee to look into the cause of the financial embarassment, gave advice to the merchant, and determined whether or not any rules of financial integrity and fair dealing had been violated. By such inquiries the elders sought to uphold religious principles and Christian honor, but at the same time they were attempting to preserve the image of the Quaker merchant as a man of integrity. The image itself had been muddied in the popular mind; some Americans viewed Quaker frugality and caution as tight-fisted shrewdness, while others regarded their very success as proof of deceitfulness. A sound image might give support to an individual Quaker merchant's best intentions to uphold principle, while it attracted customers. And it was a useful device for marking off a distinctive behavior pattern for a people out of sympathy with the norms of contemporary culture.[3]

Friends viewed debt as an unmitigated evil. Speaking at the Friends' Institute in 1882, Charles Rhoads offered this advice: "From some observation I would advise no young man to borrow money to set up business until he had earned and saved by his daily labor twice the amount borrowed." Indeed, Quakers refrained from beginning construction projects until they had all the funds in hand. Banker Elliston Morris, in persuading commission merchant Joshua Baily to postpone the building of a school, argued that institutions should never be saddled with initial debt. Baily was far from incautious himself. His firm made handsome profits in a recession year, while many of his competitors had been forced to liquidate. Attributing their failures to the practice of making outside investments and speculating in the stock market, Baily offered a formula for success: "Keep your capital in your own business and don't try to do more business than your capital warrants."[4]

Both Yearly Meetings spoke out against the evil of speculation on numerous occasions from the late sixties into the twentieth century. They saw clearly that chronic commercial panics and declines sprang from failure to restrain the orgy of investment. Some worried that Americans had grown so accustomed to depressions and panics that they had come to look upon insolvency as a normal stage of economic development. The Discipline did exercise some restraint upon individuals. A young retail carpet seller whose Filbert Street business was far from prosperous in 1865 was persuaded by his parents not to purchase $500 worth of stock in Vulcan Oil and limited himself to watching the stock price climb in the daily newspapers. Free from any taint of "unlawful gain," he soon gave up his unsuccessful business and lived most of his life on the modest rents he earned on a handful of depreciating Center City properties. But as the barrage of Yearly Meeting pronouncements and editorials against the "snares" of speculation testify, most Friends were doubtless less reticent than the carpet seller's family to invest in growing enterprises.[5]

The more affluent of the two branches of Philadelphia Quakerism issued damning attacks upon the corrupting influence of wealth. They argued that while Scripture did not prohibit "necessary and honest efforts to acquire a competence and the enjoyment of the comforts of life," it did not condone pursuit of wealth for its own sake. As the Meeting for Sufferings viewed it, abundant riches were often built upon a "heedlessness of others' prosperity as well as the defiance of God's commandments." For a quarter-century following the Civil War most Protestant churches eschewed criticism of the wealthy; not until the emergence of the Social Gospel movement in the nineties did some denominations demand curbs on entrepreneurial gain. Orthodox Friends in Philadelphia attacked the pursuit of wealth in the industrial economy not for its iniquitous effects on society as a whole, but for its influence on the individual profit seeker. As *The Friend* put it in 1901: "The snare of those who *will* be rich, is not that they should sometime lose their wealth . . . , but that in the inordinate pursuit of business, they fall into the meshes of peculiarly subtle temptation, into complications of principle beyond retreat, which drown men in destruction and perdition." More extensive criticism of the effects of wealth upon the nation, as well as the souls of men, did not be-

come part of the Quaker attack on the industrial economy until
another decade and a half had passed.[6]

The Hicksites and Orthodox agreed on what they thought were
the responsibilities of wealth. The disastrous depression of the
nineties made all Friends acutely aware that the affluent could no
longer ignore the impoverished, but had duties and obligations to
them. In part an echoing of Andrew Carnegie's pronouncements,
these views were shared by significant elements in American Protestantism. After several years of labor in pursuit of that "competence" which *The Friend* had described as an appropriate goal, the
Quaker businessman would often rechannel his energies into religious or benevolent activities, though this practice put Quaker
merchants at variance with the view of some American businessmen
that those who retired early were in fact "deserters." The jewelry
merchant Samuel Biddle retired from his successful partnership to
devote his later years to the work of the Twelfth Street Meeting.
Germantown manufacturer Philip Garrett retired at the age of
fifty and began a quarter-century of active service in political reform movements, in local and national charities, and on federal
commissions. Other Friends—commission merchant Joshua Baily
is an example—maintained a balance between their financial and
benevolent pursuits throughout their working lives.[7]

Orthodox conservatives grew increasingly distressed by the
handling of trust funds in the Gilded Age. Trustees were admonished never to borrow from such accounts lest they be led inadvertently into deceit and crime. In addressing itself to the subject in
1887, the Yearly Meeting recommended separate bank accounts
as a guard against mixing one's personal funds with those left in
trust by others.

If this precaution is neglected, even honestly disposed persons may
incautiously be drawn into expenses and payments which will partially
or wholly absorb the funds of others under their care; and in the unex-
pected events of life, they may find that they cannot replace that
which has been used and so may appear before the world as defaulters,
to their inexpressible grief.

The warning illustrates the subtle mixing of expediency with high
purpose in Quaker utterances on ethical behavior in the marketplace. Scrupulous honesty in these matters was not only pleasing
to the Lord, but an attraction to those who sought responsible

trustees; self-interest and a careful respect for the interests of others were one and the same.[8]

Friends were not the only ones to raise critical voices against the economic temper of the times. A study of Boston's "first families" in this same period shows how Brahmin patricians spoke of ideals of honor and responsibility in attacking cut-throat competition. These descendants of the antebellum merchant elite had become a defensive upper class in the Gilded Age. To protect themselves and afford some stability in uncertain times, they adopted a conservative economic ethic which they made a test of character, though rooted in concerns over social and economic status rather than religious sanctions. It cannot be denied that some Friends in Philadelphia suffered from anxieties over status encouraged by the shrinkage in their numbers and influence. But strict rules for business conduct had characterized their faith so continuously that this tradition better explains the Quakers' criticism of the norms of the new industrialism. In Philadelphia the harshest critics of change, the Wilburite quietists, lacked the kind of affluence which the Boston Brahmins were attempting to protect. Some had small urban businesses, while others had deserted the city to become working farmers.[9] And in Boston conservative views seem to have inhibited the success of patrician financial institutions. The cautious investment policies of the First National Bank of Massachusetts and the Massachusetts Hospital Life Insurance Company severely limited their ability to form needed capital to give the patricians a stake in the region's development. Quaker conservatism influenced some Philadelphia enterprises founded after the Civil War, but with different results. Conservative investment policies did prevent rapid growth, but they provided a healthy long-range stability. And Quaker ventures were not unsuccessful. Illustrative is the course of the Provident Life and Trust Company.

Founded in 1865 by a group of Orthodox Friends and controlled by an all-Quaker board, the Provident undertook the business of insuring lives, granting annuities, and administering trusts. Beginning frugally in rented quarters and using secondhand furniture, the company progressed in six years to a point where it boasted an insurance income of $503,902 and insurance in force totalling $9 million. That same year, the firm occupied its own building on South Fourth Street, planned by Quaker architect Addison Hutton in classical cast iron design. The stability of this setting was matched by the institution's portfolio. When Jay Cooke's brokerage house closed its doors, bringing panic and depression in 1873, the Provident continued its steady growth, practically undisturbed by the financial shocks on Chestnut Street. In this period, when many insurance firms failed, the Provident admitted a decline in its insurance in force in only a single year. By 1878 that total had risen to nearly $21 million.[10]

In determining whether or not to insure those who applied for policies, the Provident required careful medical examinations. The firm chose agents less for their aggressive selling talents than for their integrity. In the renewed economic confidence of the eighties many companies such as the Equitable and New York Life adopted the "deferred dividend" plan in a race for volume, investing the large accumulations the system produced in the rapidly expanding economy. The Provident's Board of Directors refused to adopt the plan, using its dividends annually instead of accumulating them because its officers believed that too rapid economic growth would undermine security. They also thought annual dividends best served their policyholders. Their probity was affirmed when deferred dividends were outlawed in the wake of the 1905 investigations of the industry in New York. Directed by cautious Friends, the Provident grew substantially, but slowly. Its $316 million insurance in force in 1915 was modest compared to that of the aggressive giants in the mutual insurance field, but it built a foundation in finance which was far less susceptible to the changing moods of the economy.[11]

The partnership of Justus Strawbridge and Isaac Clothier further illustrates the power of the Quaker business ethic. The young Orthodox merchant from Mount Holly, New Jersey, and the Philadelphia-born Hicksite did business for cash only, arguing that they had "no losses from selling on credit to provide for—the paying customer is not therefore *taxed* to *help pay the debt* of a customer who does not pay." The partners kept their percentage of profit low in the interest of rapid turnover. They insisted on "correctness of representation" of all items for sale. An employees' Book of Rules required saleswomen to dress in a regulation somber black in all but the summer months, when white skirts and blouses were permitted. If the business principles they adopted had a long history in Quakerism, their organization of an ever-increasing variety of domestic and imported dry goods under one roof was an innovation. These policies produced an immediate success, and the firm soon expanded west on Market Street.[12]

On the other hand, their very success induced Strawbridge and Clothier to abandon the strict rule against credit purchases. The store added a wide diversity of products other than dry goods and expanded so rapidly as a true department store that its annual income rose to $10 million in 1900. Members of the original Quaker families continued to control the operation, but employees of other faiths rose through the ranks to take positions of responsibility. It was one of these who conceived of an advertising technique which could exploit the positive image of Quaker business integrity. In 1911 the store adopted as its trademark a seal showing William Penn shaking hands with an Indian; it was labelled "Seal of Confidence." Although the management made decisions for new policies and expansion with Quaker deliberateness for a time, by the 1920s it was hard to see much that was distinctively Quaker about Strawbridge and Clothier.[13]

Friends' Meetings took the rules of the business ethic seriously. Those who failed in the counting house even carried their disgrace to the meetinghouse. Resignation from Meeting posts usually followed quickly on the heels of a business failure. One Friend who had served as clerk of the Orthodox Yearly Meeting in 1906 was not even considered for a normal reappointment after his business failed. While it could be argued that bankruptcy compelled such men to devote all their energies to extricating themselves from their financial plight, the disgrace of failure so tarnished the Quaker image that it made continued active Meeting participation unthinkable. The experience of a prominent wool merchant in the Twelfth Street Meeting is illustrative. Prior to 1884, when his business came to grief, this Friend had taken extensive part in the Meeting's affairs. But his financial calamity prompted him to resign from the Property, Library, and Select Schools Committees. He admitted that he and his brother had relied on others undeserving of their trust and had been overconfident about their eventual success. He soon paid off his debts, became an investment broker, and prospered. But the taint of that one financial embarassment prevented him from assuming anything more than a few minor responsibilities in his Meeting for the remainder of his life.[14]

The Hicksites had the same rules relating to financial integrity as the Orthodox, but they expended less effort warning the membership to obey them. At Race Street, Friends were less stigmatized by bankruptcy. One member there, who had "become embarrassed in his circumstances" when he was in his twenties and who tried several different occupations in his lifetime, none of which made him affluent, went on to become a Weighty Friend, serving on several committees and accepting appointment as treasurer and overseer.

Of Friends in the three Meetings studied, only five Orthodox and five Hicksites suffered a business failure. Meetings disowned but two of the ten for economic irregularities. Despite their unwillingness to provide detailed warnings against financial malpractice, Hicksite Friends took the Discipline seriously. Race Street Meeting "testified against" and disowned a carriage builder in 1893 when he made preferences among his creditors. Disownment was not automatic for those in financial trouble as it had been in the eighteenth century. A coal merchant at Arch Street was retained in membership because the general shrinkage in values prompted his failure in 1877. But when further examination eight years later revealed that his firm had incurred liabilities too large for its capital resources, the Meeting disowned him. In an age when economic life in Philadelphia seemed to operate without reference to ethical principles, Friends attempted to maintain older norms of integrity.[15]

Despite these checks to speculative enterprise, some Friends amassed sizeable fortunes. One of the Hicksites—Clement Acton Griscom, a birthright member of the Race Street Meeting and the son of a physician—rose to such prominence in international transport that he fits the old "robber baron" stereotype. Starting as a clerk with the crockery-importing concern of Peter Wright & Sons, he recommended that the firm purchase a sloop. Taking his suggestion, the officers won transport contracts from the oil industry. This speculative venture soon transformed the company into a major shipping firm. Griscom's dealings brought him into contact with Marcus Hanna and John D. Rockefeller, and in 1888, at the age of forty-seven, he became president of the firm. He immediately set about planning the combine which was to become the International Navigation Company. Sent abroad by the Pennsylvania Railroad to study steamship outlets for American goods, Griscom made agreements with King Leopold and Belgian capitalists which led to development of the Red Star Line. For over a decade its ships plied the Atlantic between Philadelphia and Antwerp. In 1902, Griscom helped form the International Mercantile Marine Company, a holding company which combined the once-competitive Red Star, Leyland, Dominion, and White Star lines with Atlantic Transport.

His entrepreneurial genius won Griscom places on the boards of several firms involved in trade. He was a director of three railroads as well as of United States Steel, the United Gas Improvement Company, and four Philadelphia banks. Listed in the Social Register until his death in 1912, Griscom held memberships in the city's most exclusive clubs: the Philadelphia, the Rittenhouse, the Merion Cricket, the Radnor Hunt, and the Corinthian Yacht. His home, "Dolobran," which showed touches of the Shingle Style so popular at Newport, was an eighty-acre estate in Haverford. His sons graduated from the University of Pennsylvania instead of Quaker Swarthmore or nearby Haverford. Griscom left his entire estate of $4.3 million to members of his family. It is not surprising to discover that he was a Nominal Friend; the forces which governed his life were markedly inconsistent with the professions of caution and simplicity which he had heard in the meetinghouse as a young man. While the Race Street Meeting kept him in its records as a member until his death, it appears that he had taken the path from Quakerism to the Episcopal Church sometime before 1912. His funeral took place in the Gothic surroundings of Bryn Mawr's Church of the Redeemer.

Wealth and religious commitment have not necessarily been incompatible in America. Some sociologists have suggested that "church work" has generally been dominated by the favored classes.[16] In the Quaker community of Philadelphia wealth did put limits on the institutional commitment of Meeting members to the faith. Besides Griscom, ten other Quakers in this study were millionaires and another sixty-nine left estates of between $100,000 and $1 million. Considering the antebellum prosperity of the city's

Friends and all the advantages of inherited wealth, this level of affluence at the beginning of the twentieth century is hardly surprising. Three of these very wealthy Friends did resign from their Meetings as adults to join other churches. Yet from the same group, another ten became Weighty Friends. The ten were all from the lower ranks of the affluent, with estates below $500,000. The proportion of the wealthy active in Meeting affairs was lower than that found for some with very modest estates—those who left less than $1,000, for example (Table 18). It was not the truly wealthy, but the comfortable—those with estates between fifty and one hundred thousand dollars—who produced the largest proportion of Weighty and Practicing Friends. Quaker censure of "riches" and speculative enterprise combined with external secular demands on the time and interest of the very affluent to discourage a leading role in the Quaker faith.

The wealthy differed from their less-affluent Quaker peers in a number of ways. An exceedingly high proportion of them were birthright Friends (Table 19). Converts to Quakerism—often attracted by simplicity or pacifism—were not likely to be wealthy; more than two-thirds of those in this study left estates of under $50,000. Besides, inherited wealth and opportunities afforded by Quaker community ties gave birthright members a better chance for wealth than those who joined later. Place of birth also counted for something. All the millionaires were born in cities. The rural-born constituted only a third of the wealthy Friends, while close to half of all other income groups had been born outside of cities (Table 20). Historians have provided ample evidence for the financial difficulties of the foreign-born in urban areas, but they have rarely distinguished between the native Americans born and brought up in the industrial city and those natives who migrated to the urban areas.[17] These modest data suggest that rural life afforded less preparation for the competitive race for wealth. And those who arrived in the city after the age of thirty-five were the least likely to grow rich (Table 21). The route to wealth in Victorian Philadelphia was accessible primarily to those whose roots in the Quaker city ran deep.

Few of the wealthy were members of the Arch Street Meeting (Table 22), whose conservatism was far more sympathetic to those norms which demanded that Friends eschew wealth. These quietists were, however, far from impoverished. Fully half of them left estates between $10,000 and $50,000. Prosperity was greater among the Orthodox at Twelfth Street than among the Hicksites at Race Street. Major changes were taking place, however, in the relative prosperity of Friends in the two branches during the nineteenth century. As Robert Doherty has shown in his examination of the causes of the 1827 Separation, Hicksites in the antebellum period had decidedly fewer financial resources than did the more worldly Orthodox.[18] Seventy-five years erased that difference. Forty-four of the eighty affluent Friends were Hicksites. The rich represented virtually identical proportions of the two branches.

When we distinguish between the two generations in this study, we see that the Hicksites continued to gain (Table 23). The vagaries of economic life after the Civil War seem to have had a levelling influence, and in the new century the followers of Elias Hicks actually outdid their Orthodox cousins in producing wealth. It was in Orthodoxy that the most vigorous attacks were levelled at overabundant wealth at the very time that the 1860s generation of Friends reached their formative years. The preaching of conservative Orthodox leaders may have persuaded them to accept less lofty financial aspirations. These statistics show also that overall Quaker prosperity declined in the new century. In the competitive race of this era of free enterprise, urban Quakers were unable to maintain their previous economic levels.

Not only did the value of Friends' estates register a decline in the 1860s generation, but their influence upon the economy through directorships diminished as well. Forty-four of the Quakers in the membership sample were directors of diverse corporations. But the number fell from twenty-nine in the 1840s generation to only fourteen for those born in the 1860s. Friends who remained in city Meetings after 1900 did not have the economic power that previous generations had had. The forty-four Friends exercised an influence out of all proportion to their numbers. Their economic leverage was concentrated in banking and transportation. These Friends were on the boards of thirty-two banking and trust companies, thirteen major railroads, ten interurban and electric trolley lines, and three shipping companies. The banks were nearly all Philadelphia institutions, some as important as the Philadelphia Savings Fund Society, the Bank of North America, the Philadelphia

National, and the Corn Exchange National.[19] Nathaniel Janney and Charles Richardson were officers and directors of the Land Title and Trust Company. Charles Hinchman was an officer and director of the Quaker City National Bank. Most of the railroads in the group were part of the Pennsylvania system. George Wood and Charles E. Pugh were both influential directors of the parent firm. All five men were born in the 1840s. The forty-four also included directors of fourteen insurance companies, thirty-two manufacturing concerns, four utilities, and three commercial exchanges. Some of these firms were small operations which quickly passed from the scene, but others such as the Penn Mutual Life Insurance Company and the United Gas Improvement Company had considerable weight and endurance in the marketplace.

A wide gap separated the financial standing of individual directors in the group. George R. Meloney sat on the boards of the Rittenhouse Trust Company and the short-lived Dairymen's Supply Company, of which he was president. At his death in 1915 this rural-born Friend left an estate of only $700. At the other extreme was millionaire John T. Morris, who inherited his control of the Port Richmond Iron Works from his entrepreneur father. With important civic, social, and cultural interests, Morris sat on the boards of two of the city's most prestigious financial institutions, the Philadelphia Savings Fund Society and the Philadelphia Contributionship for the Insurance of Houses from Loss by Fire. Founded in 1752 by Benjamin Franklin, the Contributionship had been directed by affluent Friends for over a century. When Morris chaired its board, the firm pursued policies so conservative that it refused to insure theaters and the tall buildings which began to mark the city's skyline at the turn of the century. The soundness of the Contributionship's financial structure was beyond question.[20]

But it is a mistake to view Friends primarily as a business elite. The survey of the three Center City Meetings' membership has uncovered occupational data on 360 Friends. We can speak of their occupational status as "achieved." Another 222 members derived occupational status from their spouses, or in the case of unmarried and unemployed women from their fathers. This is "ascribed" status. An examination first of achieved status reveals that only one-fifth of all employed Friends were executives of large businesses (Table 24). Equal proportions fell into the white collar–

sales category and the small business–skilled craftsmen group. Approximately one-sixth were in the major professions of law, medicine, and higher education, while another sixth were in the lesser professions of architecture, engineering, and school teaching. The tiny proportion in blue collar work gives some indication of the occupational advantage Quakers had over the rest of the population. Statistics on occupations for all males in Philadelphia in 1910 indicate that approximately 44 percent were operatives, service workers, and laborers.[21] The comparable proportion among Friends was a mere 4.2 percent. The increase in the proportion engaged in large and small business when those Quakers with ascribed status are added reflects the occupations of fathers of unemployed women who were merchants in the antebellum years. Clearly the post–Civil War period found Philadelphia Friends moving into more diverse occupations commensurate with the organizational changes taking place in trade and industry.

And the occupational changes continued to take place as the nineteenth century gave way to the twentieth. Examination of the figures for occupational status—with and without the ascribed status group—in the two generations under study shows significant shifts by those born in the 1860s who reached their "working majority" after 1900 (Table 25). The major decline occurred among business executives, confirming the trend already revealed in financial status and directorships. Increasing numbers chose the lesser professions. More modest increases occurred in the major professions and in the white collar–sales group, while a small decrease was registered in the proportion engaged in small business and skilled trades. It may very well be that those in the 1860s generation who went into major business enterprises as executives moved from the city so early as to escape inclusion in this sample. The suburban trend was in full swing and Friends were among the earliest to depart. But many retained their membership in Center City Meetings long after they took residences in Germantown, on the Main Line, or in Delaware county. The move to the suburbs cannot alone account for this flight from major business ventures after 1900. Changes were, of course, taking place in occupational opportunities as commercial life became more specialized and the size of many enterprises grew apace. New patterns of economic organization decreased the kind of independence which Quakers had sought and realized as merchants and manufacturers in the early nineteenth century. As higher education became available for Friends, they turned increasingly to the lesser professions. As engineers and architects they retained some of that independence which fit so well with the business ethic of their faith. And the proportion of school teachers more than doubled from the early to the later generation.

While both branches reflected this move away from major business activity, the trend was more pronounced among the Orthodox (Table 26). The corresponding drop for the Hicksites was more modest. The more determined effort on the part of the Orthodox Yearly Meeting to warn against the snares of contemporary commercial enterprise during the formative years of those born in the 1860s may well have influenced their members to make different occupational choices. The Orthodox registered increases in both the white collar–sales category and in the lesser professions. The conclusion is inescapable: later-generation Quakers in Center City Meetings did not have the elite status of the earlier generation. While over half of the Orthodox born in the forties claimed status in major businesses, medicine, law, and higher education, only 28.6 percent of those born in the sixties did so. Lacking that degree of elite status in the first place, the Hicksites show a much smaller decline. Doubtless the move to the suburbs affected these losses, but the seeming incompatibility of the Quaker business ethic and the enterprise of the day took its toll as well. If the price of adherence to the Discipline was the loss of elite status, some Friends who made occupational choices in the eighties and nineties were willing to pay it. None of the other alterations in occupational status between the generations were as statistically significant as these.

Despite the generalization that the upper classes exercise the leadership in Protestant denominations, studies of particular denominations have shown widespread involvement by both upper- and lower-class parishioners.[22] In Philadelphia Quakerism at the turn of the century there was a wide dispersion of occupational status groupings through all three types of Friends (Table 27). But the two branches did display different patterns of dominance among their Weighty Friends. Orthodox Meetings took direction from an unusually high proportion of those with professional status, including not only law and medicine but engineering, architecture, and teaching. Only those with blue-collar status were missing from the leadership group. Professional leadership was most significant at the Twelfth Street Meeting, which had given strong support to higher education. Hicksite leadership came from somewhat lower on the occupational status scale. Those in the small business–skilled trades group assumed a disproportionate share of the burden of Meeting activity. While many Hicksites had risen considerably in status since 1827, those at the middle levels of the social order were more likely to serve as ministers, elders, and overseers and carry most of the committee work. Higher status seemed to imply a move away from Meeting leadership for the Hicksite, as it did not for the Orthodox, who had known elite status and affluence longer. In both branches major commercial interests were not necessarily inimical to religious involvement, but those interests usually produced the more modest commitment of Practicing Friends.

Opportunities at the top of the occupational scale among the Quakers were no more open to all than they were in the larger society. Research has shown that in the late nineteenth century the sons of the professional and merchant classes filled most of the financial leadership positions in the nation. We have already seen that among Friends, birthright status and urban birth were most frequently prerequisites to affluence. What was true for financial status was also true for occupational status (Tables 28–30). Less than half of those in the small business, white collar, and blue collar groups were urban born; the reverse was true for the higher occupational categories. And higher proportions of business executives and professionals were birthright Friends than one finds in the lower occupational groups. Rarely was a Friend who moved to Philadelphia in middle age likely to make his way in major business and the higher professions; the chances were greater in the other occupational status categories. Most striking is the difference in origin of the business executives. Three-quarters of them were born in cities and 92.7 percent were birthright Quakers. In terms of resources, connections, and opportunities, this was really a closed group into which outsiders found it difficult to gain access. It was apparently easier for the outsiders to make it into the higher and lesser professions than into the merchant elite.[23]

In his study of Philadelphia, E. Digby Baltzell has suggested that
Friends in the city constituted a "parallel upper class," separate
from the fashionable and largely Episcopalian group which dominated the aristocracy. These two groups, in his view, lived side by
side in the nineteenth century, but remained worlds apart in culture and interest. His interpretation focuses upon the affluent community of Friends living in Germantown, which dominated distinctive Quaker business enterprises and had different social and cultural outlets from the Episcopalian upper class.[24] Examination of
the Friends in the Center City Meetings reveals a different picture.
There the allurements of Victorian aristocratic social life caused
a split in the religious community. Affluent Quaker merchants became directors of fashionable Philadelphia banks and corporations.
They and their wives joined the clubs and associations of "Proper
Philadelphia." While they retained their families' religious affiliation, they were drawn increasingly into social patterns which left
them little time for the life of the meetinghouse. They created no
parallel upper-class structure; they became part of the worldly upper class which was taking shape primarily under Episcopalian
auspices. And because they were attempting to straddle two very
different worlds, they contributed to the forces pressuring the Society of Friends to accept the norms of a national culture.

While education, clubs, businesses, associations, and neighborhoods gave structure to the upper class in American cities, it was
the Social Register which defined the membership of what grew
into a national aristocracy. First published in New York in 1887,
it came to Philadelphia after 1890. The directory grew in size as
those first listed determined who in future might be added to the
select list.[25] During the first thirty years of its publication, the
Philadelphia Social Register included the names of nearly 11 percent of the Quakers in this study. Many attributes of these seventy-
six Friends set them apart from the other members of Center City
Meetings. While wealth and high occupational status had never
been deterrents to participation in Meeting affairs, identification
with Philadelphia's upper class was likely to produce a commitment to Quakerism in name only (Table 31). Seven-tenths of those
listed in the Social Register were Nominal Friends; only four of
the ninety-four Weighty Friends were part of the aristocracy. It is

apparent that for aspirants to social prominence the work of the meetinghouse community had become either an annoying intrusion or an outright embarrassment.

What made for the divergence between the norms of religion and aristocratic professions? Quakerism contained, of course, an element of egalitarian ideology. While early English Friends never intended to make a democratic revolution, they did criticize social deference in seventeenth-century English life through the use of plain forms of speech, the testimony of hat honor, and simple dress. None of these prevented prosperous Philadelphia merchants from becoming "grandees" in the late eighteenth century. Quaker Disciplines did argue against membership in certain social organizations which appeared to challenge a belief in equality and the hegemony of the religious community. But those selected for criticism were fraternal organizations such as the Masons. Organizations based on social exclusiveness such as urban clubs and suburban country clubs escaped censure. A class bias appears at work here, but Quaker elders may have viewed secrecy and ritualism as more potent threats to religious faith than social snobbery. Joining the Merion Cricket Club prompted no warnings from conservative Quaker leaders, but it was a significant step in the separation of social life from the orbit of the meetinghouse.

Upper-class interests challenged other Quaker testimonies by partaking of what strict Friends labelled "false notions of reality." Among iron manufacturer John T. Morris's many contributions to the city's cultural life were his membership in the Philadelphia Orchestra Association and his directorship of the Pennsylvania Museum and School of Industrial Arts. Another Twelfth Street Friend, Josephine T. Woolman, was active on a committee to persuade New York's Metropolitan Opera Company and Walter Damrosh to perform in the Quaker City. She was also a founder of the Philadelphia Grand Opera Company. Far from paralleling the structure of the Episcopalian aristocracy, these Friends had been integrated into it. Quietist elders viewed these activities as serious obstacles to the service of Christ. And if they did not criticize aristocratic Friends individually for it, they made their point with more general condemnations of the arts.[26]

Entrance into the upper class was dependent upon occupation and affluence (Tables 32–33). But the inclusion of a few Friends with small business and white collar status and others with estates under $10,000 in the Social Register suggests that wealth and occupation were not the only prerequisites to upper-class status. Lineage was very important; genealogy became popular in these years as aspirant aristocrats attempted to prove their credentials as descendants of colonial men of worth. The high proportion of birthright Friends in this group suggests how important family background was for the aristocracy (Table 34). But the upper class did draw primarily from the active commercial elite. Unlike the Brahmin aristocracy in Boston, Philadelphia's upper class absorbed new wealth. Of the Friends listed in the Social Register more than two-thirds claimed business executive status and nearly three-fifths left estates of more than $100,000.[27]

Many of the Quakers in the upper class were Hicksites whose financial and social position had been considerably lower a generation earlier (Tables 35–37). Equal numbers of aristocrats held memberships in the two largest Center City Meetings, but the group constituted almost a sixth of the total at Twelfth Street and approximately one-twelfth of those at Race Street. Thus, while the upper class recognized the new wealth of the Hicksites, they drew a greater proportion from the old urban wealth of the Orthodox. In social tone, the Twelfth Street Meeting was to Orthodox Quakerism what Saint Mark's on Locust Street was to the Episcopal Church. Only two Friends from the rural ambience of the Arch Street Meeting were listed in the Social Register. Few of the aristocratic Friends had been born in rural communities. At the same time that they rejected the rural-born, Proper Philadelphians began to abandon the city for suburban green at the turn of the century. The upper-class proportion of all Friends declined from the generation born in the 1840s to that born in the 1860's, as Quaker aristocrats transferred to Meetings in Moorestown, Media, and Haverford. The decline also mirrored the decision of Friends in the later generation to seek occupations outside of the city's major business activity. But in the 1890s the typical Social Register Friend was a Philadelphia-born Orthodox merchant whose estate approximated $100,000 and who, despite his birthright status in the faith, played no part in the corporate work of the Twelfth Street Meeting of which he was a member.

It is also likely that this typical upper-class Friend lived in a townhouse on the elegant tree-shaded streets around Rittenhouse Square. For it was behind the brownstone and brick facades of

Spruce, Locust, and Delancey Streets that Philadelphia's self-conscious Victorian aristocracy resided between 1880 and 1910. Market Street, the prime east-west thoroughfare in Center City, marked the northern boundary for "Proper Philadelphia" residences. As the snobbish put it, "Nobody lives north of Market Street." The aristocrats never felt compelled to define the southern boundary of this section; south of Pine Street lived blacks and an increasing diversity of European immigrants. In the nineties the major proportion of Social Register Friends living in the city had residences in the Seventh and Eighth wards south of Market (Table 38). The second largest group lived in Germantown. Residence in both facilitated participation in the social engagements which knit Proper Philadelphians together. In Center City, south of Market Street the more established Orthodox Friends outnumbered their Hicksite cousins three to two in the 1890s (Table 39). More than half of the total living in this section were Twelfth Street Friends.[28]

The elite neighborhood in the 9th and 10th wards north of Market Street harbored Friends of a very different sort. Here around Logan Square the Orthodox predominated just as they did to the south. But the environment north of Market Street nurtured a serious Quakerism which the aristocratic tone of Rittenhouse Square inhibited. In the substantial but simpler row homes on Arch and Race Streets lived active Friends who gave clear evidence of their religious commitment. In the 1890s this section had the highest proportion of Weighty Friends of all the regional residential areas and it contained one of the smallest groups of Nominal Friends in the city (Table 40). The Rittenhouse Square area, on the other hand, housed a proportion of inactive Quakers nearly twice as large. In the nineties several Twelfth Street Friends of the business and professional elite lived in homes on Arch Street. Lawyer George Vaux Jr. resided at 1715; insurance executive Charles Roberts lived across the street at 1716. Both left estates of more than $100,000 and were active in civic affairs. Two physicians lived on Arch Street as well: Mary Branson at 1719 and S. Mason McCollin at 1823. All four were Weighty Friends. In the Society of Friends in the 1890s it could well have been said, "Nobody lives *south* of Market Street!"

Yet by the nineties the Quaker presence in the neighborhood was already in decline. One fifth of the Friends in our sample who lived in the city lived in Center City north of Market in the 1880s. But the percentage fell from 20 to 14 at the turn of the century and to 7.5 after 1910. The Quaker elite moved either south of Market or to the suburbs by 1919, when Christopher Morley was shocked to discover signs reading "Apartments," "Vacancy," and "Furnished Rooms" in the 1600 block of Race Street just above Friends' Select. The exodus of earnest Friends reveals their vulnerability to worldly fashion in residential taste, but other factors also cut short the section's vitality as an elite neighborhood. When the Pennsylvania Railroad decided to build the Broad Street Station opposite the new City Hall it had to construct a wide masonry viaduct to carry its tracks west from the new terminal to connections across the Schuylkill River. Completed in the early eighties, this "Chinese Wall" occupied a major portion of the land between Filbert and Market Streets. Despite its tunnels the viaduct isolated the Logan Square neighborhood from the rest of Center City. The *coup de grace* came from the city itself, which built a broad boulevard from City Hall to Fairmount, the site of a planned Art Museum. Open to vehicular traffic in 1918, the Benjamin Franklin Parkway cut across the grid pattern of streets diagonally, levelling hundreds of homes in its path. The Baroque planning of the Parkway, the construction on redesigned Logan Circle of public buildings patterned after the Place de la Concorde in Paris, and the eventual completion of the Art Museum gave Philadelphia some of the finest vistas of any American city, but the residential neighborhood had been sacrificed in the process.[29]

The kind of residential concentration evident on some blocks of Arch Street was rare for Friends in turn-of-the-century Philadelphia. Despite injunctions to avoid contact with "strangers," Quakers integrated with the rest of the population through housing. Even in its heyday, the Logan Square section was never an enclave of Quaker exclusiveness. As in the urban neighborhoods of most American cities, a mixture of ethnic groups and native Americans lived in close proximity in many parts of Philadelphia. The pattern of modest row homes on narrow streets and alleys behind larger homes on wider thoroughfares assured a regular mix of humble wage earners with the prosperous. While convenience and sociability prompted like-minded Weighty Friends to cluster on Arch Street or on some streets in the Powelton section of West

Philadelphia, the city's extensive electric trolley lines obviated this necessity by the nineties. Family visiting, the core of Quaker social practice, went on in spite of the wide scattering of Friends in so many parts of the city. For Americans, regardless of status, as Maurice Stein has suggested, "spatial neighborhoods" are less significant than "true communal congeniality . . . between people scattered throughout a city."[30]

Only a handful of Friends remained in working-class sections along the Delaware River. Russian Jews settled in the eastern end of Center City and in parts of South Philadelphia which had concentrations of Italians. In Kensington and Richmond to the north recently arrived Poles, Germans, and English immigrants gained employment alongside native Americans. Quakers of modest estate chose the working- and middle-class districts west of Germantown Avenue in North Philadelphia. So many Hicksites had settled in the area of the 29th Ward that Race Street established a Preparative Meeting at Girard Avenue and 17th Street in 1871. By the eighties Friends north of Lehigh Avenue were numerous enough to warrant opening small Hicksite and Orthodox meetinghouses there. Three-fifths of the North Philadelphia Quakers fell into the occupational status categories of white collar and small business (Table 41). Most inhabited the monotonous and undistinguished row housing constructed after the Civil War. Business and professional people lived in larger homes on 16th Street, Girard Avenue, or on Green Street just north of Center City, which boasted plain but ample residences one architectural historian has dubbed "houses Quaker in excelsis." To the northwest lay Germantown, which had been incorporated into the city in 1854. It attracted Friends from the professional and business elite lured by the ease of railroad commuting. These Friends took little interest in the affairs of their Meetings in Center City. A conservative Quaker characterized them as "rich and cultivated" people who demanded learning and urbanity in their religious leaders. Germantown more than doubled its residential proportion of the Quaker total between 1880 and 1920 (Table 42). Many Friends left North Philadelphia addresses after the turn of the century, but generally their status dictated a move to places other than Germantown.[31]

Across the Schuylkill River lay an inner city suburb which provided more ample housing than that available in North Philadelphia. A cluster of villages at mid-century, West Philadelphia attracted prosperous Quakers to Italianate villas in the Powelton section and Victorian mansions south of Market Street. Active Friends chose Powelton, while aristocratic Quakers preferred the "Drexel Colony." Horse car and trolley lines to Center City encouraged the growth of middle-class row housing west of these neighborhoods. Completion of the Market Street Elevated to 63rd Street in 1907 assured rapid growth of the entire section. The Hicksites had built a meetinghouse at 35th Street and Lancaster Avenue as early as 1851. Quaker population increases necessitated its enlargement in 1902. Another Preparative Meeting—an Orthodox one—housed at 42nd and Powelton opened in 1878. Of the Friends in our sample 118 lived in this section in the first decade of the new century. By the 1910s it was the urban residential region with the largest proportion of Quakers. West Philadelphia grew more rapidly than the rest of the city and it attracted fewer immigrants.[32] An unusually small proportion of the West Philadelphians were Nominal Friends (Table 43). Most were in the lesser professions, white collar, and small business classes.

Americans moved about a great deal in the nineteenth century, as examination of the urban and rural population has begun to show. Quaker tradition counseled otherwise. An 1873 Discipline argued that "the dissolving of old, and the forming of new connections" necessitated by residential changes were frequently "attended with effects prejudicial to a growth in the Truth and service thereof." This social control, which might have worked well to preserve stable farm communities, was ill suited to the vagaries of urban life. Only a sixth of the Quakers studied remained at a single address throughout their adult lives. But diaries suggest that a residential change remained a serious question which some Friends weighed with unusual solemnity. Not surprisingly, Weighty Friends showed less residential mobility than others (Table 44–45); Nominal Friends moved most frequently. Statistics for the Quakers confirm findings by others that greater prosperity induced less movement in the nineteenth century.[33]

Residential movement led ultimately to the suburbs for most Quakers. As early as the 1880s more than a seventh of Center City Meeting members lived in the five-county area outside Philadelphia (Table 42). By 1915 the proportion had risen to more than a third.

Attracted by its green rolling hills, most Friends moved to the region west of the city, settling in communities along the Pennsylvania Railroad's main line to Paoli and on its commuter route to Media. Quakers preferred the towns of Haverford, Lansdowne, Moylan, and Swarthmore, but as in the city they scattered to various locations. Interurban electric lines which connected with the Market Street Elevated also provided quick access to the city from these western suburban communities beginning in the new century. Towns north of the city served by the Reading Railroad developed more slowly and drew fewer Quakers. Some lived across the Delaware River in Camden, New Jersey, but more settled in surrounding towns such as Moorestown, Haddonfield, and Riverton. Railroads and interurban lines tied these points to ferry crossings on the Delaware in Camden.[34] Those who moved to these diverse suburban locations sustained a deep interest in the affairs of the city Meetings, which they continued to attend (Table 43). Among suburban dwellers after 1910 there was a greater proportion of active Friends than in the combined sections of Philadelphia itself. Distance never seemed to discourage participation in institutional Quakerism, and many of the suburbanites wanted Meetings at the historic site of the faith to remain vital. The occupational distribution of suburban Friends differed hardly at all from that of their urban counterparts (Table 46). Along with the lawyers and brokers who bought homes on the Main Line, Friends in clerical work and small business relocated in Media and Lansdowne. Suburbanization among Friends was more than an elite phenomenon. It reflected a deep-seated antipathy toward life in the industrial city which cut across status lines.

CHAPTER 4 | # Response to the City

Between 1871 and 1901, at the juncture of Broad and Market Streets, the city of Philadelphia erected a massive Victorian monument which soared 547 feet to dominate the skyline of the Quaker City. Almost as an afterthought the city asked Alexander Calder to design a thirty-seven-foot statue of Philadelphia's founder to place atop this new City Hall. Calder's rendering of William Penn, which sat for many years in the hall's courtyard before final placement, provided a striking contrast to the French Renaissance flamboyance of the building. The juxtaposition reflected the changes wrought by two centuries of development. From beginnings of Quaker simplicity and the moral imperatives of a holy commonwealth, Philadelphia had been transformed into an industrial city plagued by crime and local unrest and directed by political professionals who ignored moderation and traditional moral standards.

Surveying the commercial and industrial metropolis which had grown up around them, Quakers in Philadelphia found much that was troubling. The concentration of people—two-thirds of a million by 1870—provided ready hands for the expansion of diverse factory production, but it brought in its wake a multitude of social and economic problems which demanded remedy. Frenzied pursuit of profit produced new wealth for some and economic catastrophe for others. Shorn of the restraints of older values, the economic system alternated between boom and bust. Workingmen organized and went out on strike, producing near-riotous conditions and disturbing the already shaky economy. J. Donald Cameron, James McManes, Matthew Quay, and Israel Durham gave representation to a diverse working-class population whose ties to the Republican organization had been built on the ward and precinct level. By the thousands, natives poured into Philadelphia from the rural farms of Pennsylvania and New Jersey, while immigrants from Europe crowded into the wards along the Delaware River. This very social diversity seemed to hasten the decline of older standards. The sick and needy, now larger in numbers, taxed the capacity of existing philanthropy. Political corruption became the order of the day. Worldliness and iniquity seemed everywhere. Even the quietists could not ignore what the industrial growth of the Gilded Age was doing to the social environment.

Although Lincoln Steffens claimed that Philadelphians were "contented" with corrupt "boss rule," a modest band of genteel reformers mounted campaigns to restore integrity to municipal government in the last decades of the nineteenth century.[1] Conspicuous among these reformers, who were derisively labelled "Mugwumps," were members of the Society of Friends. There was little ground for understanding between the Quaker ethos and City Hall. But the effort by some Friends—particularly the affluent merchant elite—to destroy the hold of the bosses on the reigns of power would have borne more fruit had it not been for two significant inhibiting factors grounded in Quaker experience. The first of these was the Friends' tradition of avoiding active participation in politics; the second was their attachment to the Republican party.

The rule "on Civil Government" in the books of Discipline issued by both the Orthodox and Hicksite branches advised "all in profession with us, to decline the acceptance of any office or station in civil government, the duties of which are inconsistent with our religious principles; or in the exercise of which they may be under the necessity of exacting of their brethren any compliances against which we are conscientiously scrupulous." First penned after the French and Indian War, this rule aimed at preventing the kind of confrontation between conscience and military necessity which had induced many Quaker legislators to withdraw from the Pennsylvania assembly in 1756. Supported by a threat of disownment from the Society, it served to warn Friends against the contaminating influence of an active political life. Obeying the Discipline to the letter, quietist leaders in both branches gave little heed to political questions in their official pronouncements. In 1875, in a rare acknowledgment of the political world, *The Friend* attributed the causes of political corruption to the Civil War, which substituted a workable pragmatism for the moral basis of human judgment, but it had no remedies to recommend to its readers. Even the Hicksite *Intelligencer* lauded the prohibition of political activity, claiming that the Quaker "attitude of observation, caution, of readiness to object or oppose, has been vastly more helpful to the general welfare than if [Friends] had involved themselves in the ordinary conflicts and struggles of political place seeking." One exceptional Quaker did hold a brief tenure as Philadelphia's mayor in the 1850s, but only two Friends served as city councilmen in the late nineteenth and early twentieth centuries. Quakers elected to the federal legislature were equally rare, and Philadelphia produced none of them.[2]

But in the late eighties liberals began to argue for an end to the prohibition. Speaking in 1887 at the Race Street meetinghouse, Thomas Speakman condemned the city's political system for its tendency to "ostracize and exclude the best qualified and most worthy men from public places." He urged his Hicksite listeners to pattern their behavior on that of Quaker political leaders in early Pennsylvania and to "interfere to restore governmental affairs if possible to something like their original purity." On the Orthodox side, Rufus Jones and Isaac Sharpless, who epitomized the progressive spirit based in the Twelfth Street Meeting and Haverford College, urged Friends to abandon their political hesitancy. As editor of *The American Friend* after 1894, Jones gave considerable attention to local as well as national politics in articles and editorials. Haverford's President Sharpless argued that, in spite of the dangers and temptations, Friends had a Christian responsibility to take an active part in politics. He himself served for many years as a Republican committeeman. Like many late-nineteenth-century liberal reformers, Jones and Speakman were inclined to encourage independency as the route to governmental purity; for them, the demands of party seemed to prevent men from voting and acting according to the light of individual conscience.[3]

Most Friends were burdened not only by a traditional hesitancy about political activity but by the thorny question of party loyalty. The political organization of their preference was the Republican party. When the party had first made its appearance in the city in 1856 with a relatively undiluted stand against slavery, Friends had flocked to support it. Rufus Jones estimated that nearly every Friend who had the suffrage voted for Abraham Lincoln. Admitting that he had been a Republican from the time of the party's origin, Swarthmore President Magill characterized the G.O.P. as a "party of reform."[4] Concern for the Negro and Indian minorities had done much to build the image of the Republican party in Friends' minds as an organization of principle.

More practical matters also promoted Republican loyalty among the Friends. As merchant-philanthropist Joshua Baily put it, the party's principles "crystallized into law have done so much for the salvation and regeneration of the country and the promotion of her material welfare." One policy which affected that welfare was the protective tariff. After 1861 the federal government afforded increased protection for several Philadelphia industries—iron, steel, glass, and wool—in which Friends had a financial stake. For many Quaker business executives the tariff was a cardinal element in their Republican faith. Mugwump Charles Richardson and Hicksite wool merchant Theodore Justice were both high-protectionists. Yet others remained loyal to the G.O.P. in spite of free trade sentiments. Francis R. Cope, a Quaker shipping merchant, saw tariff protection at the root of political corruption; he was bound to the Republican party instead by its moral principles.[5]

Mugwump reform groups in the three largest Northeastern cities responded in different ways to the problem of corruption. In New York, where the "ring" was controlled by Democrats, reformers fell naturally into the Republican party, where fulminations against Tweed and Tammany were echoed by the party faithful in search of office. Boston reformers, facing a powerful statewide Republican organization interested only in political jobs and the tariff, bolted to the Democrats in 1884.[6] But in Philadelphia the Mugwumps' aversion to both parties drove them into short-lived independent political organizations, where internal dissensions and frequent unwillingness to support reform Democrats diluted the force of their challenge. While Friends in the movement were not the only ones held back by political caution and distrust of organization, they must share responsibility for the failure to achieve only two municipal electoral victories in the four decades after 1870.

The first evidence of restiveness with City Hall corruption appeared in Philadelphia in 1870, when the publisher Henry Charles Lea helped form the Citizens' Municipal Reform Association. Lea, whom the *Philadelphia Bulletin* later dubbed "the original mugwump," was the product of a Quaker-Catholic marriage, although he himself turned to Unitarianism. He induced many Friends to join the association during its seven-year battle with "the Gas Ring." The city's Gas Trust, under the direction of the wily James McManes, controlled thousands of jobs in the city administration and had numerous contracts to dispense, and from this power base McManes was systematically mulcting the city of funds while the utility he directed provided totally inadequate service. Lea and his colleagues conducted investigations which proved the Trust's delinquency but did nothing to disturb its power. The Reform Club, an offshoot of the Municipal Reform Association, was established in 1872 to provide a genteel social setting in which independency might flower. Clement Biddle and T. Wistar Brown were among its numerous Quaker members. These modest beginnings provided the nucleus for the Committee of 100, which was to achieve the only Mugwump victory of the nineteenth century.[7]

The adverse publicity given McManes' Gas Ring paved the way for the election and re-election as city controller of a relatively unknown Democrat, Robert E. Pattison, who used his office to pry into the relationship between the city government and the utility. Publication by the *New York Herald* of Pattison's disclosures brought the city's social and financial elite to her defense. Over one hundred merchants, banker, lawyers, and professional men—all Republicans—organized a committee to promote the cause of reform. Chaired by retired Quaker merchant Philip C. Garrett, the group met in December 1880 to endorse a ticket for the municipal election of the following February. While the Quaker proportion of the city's population was less than 1 percent, nearly one-fifth of the Committee's members were prominent Friends. Garrett and Oliver Evans, who was distinguished by his plain Quaker garb, were among those who favored the re-election of Republican Mayor William Stokley. But when, under party pressure, the incumbent refused to agree to the Committee's reform principles, the endorsement was withdrawn—a victory for Friend Joshua Baily. The group finally backed Democrat Samuel G. King for mayor and reform Republican John Hunter for receiver of taxes, The Democrats united in common cause with the Committee's slate.[8]

The victory of the King-Hunter ticket in February 1881 was seen by Quaker Jacob Elfreth as a lesson to "the Ring men that the people still have some voice." But even before the Committee had nominated King, Richard Vaux had realized that the election of an honest executive was pointless by itself. Exposure and eradication of the Ring's power over the city councilmen, he wrote Lea, was a necessary prerequisite to real reform. The Ring's eventual destruction was, however, the result not of Mugwump efforts but of state G.O.P. leader J. Donald Cameron's decision to dump McManes. And while Mayor King was publicly investigating the corruption, Matthew Stanley Quay was quietly substituting his own influence for McManes'. When King ran for re-election in February 1884, with the Committee of 100's endorsement, the reorganized Republicans were strong enough to ensure his defeat. The Quaker Mugwumps and their colleagues on the Committee had failed to build upon the successful beginnings of 1881. Unwilling to strengthen their ties with the Democrats and uncertain where political activism would lead them, they neglected to seek the ward and precinct support they needed to launch a continuing challenge to the organization.[9]

Quaker influence on the Committee had extended even to matters of procedure. The group entertained free discussion and rarely took a vote on important questions, reaching conclusions "by a consensus of judgment which was thought safe to act upon"—a secular "sense of the Meeting." Stung by their defeat, the members decided to disband. While some saw usefulness in keeping an eye on City Hall to detect and publicize fraud, the "sense of the Meeting" dictated an abandonment of political action. The decision eased Quaker consciences torn between reform hopes and the demands of political reality. Although the committee held annual reunions as late as 1893, these were more social than political in character, expressions of the Philadelphia preference for nostalgia.[10]

The reform movement that had the greatest attraction for the Mugwumps was the drive to replace the spoils system with a nonpartisan civil service based on intellectual merit. For Friends concerned about possible compromises with their principles, it was a natural outlet, more a moral question than a political one. Usually silent on governmental questions, Quaker weeklies spoke out forthrightly in support of President Grant's civil service bill in 1872 and the Pendleton Act of 1883. Hicksite lawyer Joseph Parrish, a former member of the Committee of 100, castigated the "ungodly doings" of the spoils system as incompatible with Christianity. Samuel Morris, writing President Hayes in 1877, saw in the extension of the civil service system one way of attaining that righteousness "which truly exalteth a nation" and of destroying the corruption which lowers "the standards of business morality throughout the community." Quaker merchants with extensive dealings at the Customs House were particularly anxious to get high standards in the public service.[11]

Friends were conspicuous in their support of the Civil Service Reform Association of Pennsylvania, and many were on its executive committee. In 1891 the membership included four Copes, two Woods, two Bailys, two Garretts, two Justices, and practically all the officers of the Quaker-run Provident Life and Trust Company. One of its members was Charles Richardson, an Orthodox Friend, who was for many years on the executive committee of the National Civil Service Reform League and gave major addresses to the league's conventions in 1902 and 1903. He served for a time on the city's Civil Service Board of Examiners; as a testimonial to the standards he demanded there, Quay-lieutenant Mayor Samuel Ashbridge dropped him in 1899. Joshua Baily was still contributing to the work of the National Civil Service Reform League in 1913.[12]

The first indication of renewed efforts by the genteel reformers against the Quay organization came in 1887. The Citizens' Municipal Association which came into being that year set for itself three primary tasks:

(1) to sustain the constituted authorities in faithful administration of public service; (2) to secure a strict fulfillment by public officers, employees, and contributors, of all their obligations to the City, and to the citizen; (3) to promote such legislation as shall be most conducive to the public welfare.

The guiding spirit behind the Association was a retired Quaker dry-goods merchant, Joel J. Baily, who served as chairman of its executive committee until his death in 1903. His cousin Joshua headed the Association's Committee on Abuses and Complaints, which made itself thoroughly unpopular at City Hall by denouncing the standards used in granting transportation franchises. The fact that the group served only as a watch-dog committee and eschewed endorsement of candidates for office attracted Friends who had remained aloof from other reform organizations. Hicksites such as machine manufacturer J. Sellers Bancroft and department store executive Morris L. Clothier joined the association. Among Orthodox supporters were real estate dealer Dillwyn Wistar and Germantown trust officer Elliston P. Morris.[13]

Some Friends lent support to a more politically active reform group, the city's Municipal League, which was founded in 1891. It lobbied for extension of civil service to all departments in the municipal government and sought "the conduct of the city's affairs by enlightened methods and upon business principles." On the state level it worked for the adoption of the Australian ballot and for a system of personal registration. By 1896 the league had units in twenty-five of Philadelphia's forty wards and could claim 5,000 supporters. When its endorsement of several Democratic candidates for city offices in the nineties gave pause to some Republican reformers, the league stated its purpose was to secure "the practical separation of municipal affairs from state and national politics." After remaining aloof from the organization for several years, Philip Garrett decided in 1898 to give it wholehearted support, but he found it necessary to assert that he remained a Republican nationally.[14]

The league's vice-president was Charles Richardson, the most active of the Mugwump reformers in the Society of Friends. He played a prominent role in the founding of the National Municipal League and in 1897 was one of those chosen to formulate a theory of municipal administration under its auspices. More politically acute than his fellow Quaker reformers, he sought a wider base of support than "the ultra respectable few" on which he could regularly depend and used what he regarded as expedient means in appealing for support from the party rank and file in the fight for ballot reform in Harrisburg. Richardson sensed also that a multiplicity of reform organizations vitiated the effectiveness of the cause. As he wrote Henry Charles Lea in 1899, "It is only on rare occasions that it seems to be possible to get independents to forget their independence so far as to unite in a common effort."[15]

More direct in confronting the Republican organization were two Friends who won election to the municipal legislature. Charles Roberts, a member of the Twelfth Street Meeting, stood for the Common Council as representative of the Ninth Ward in 1886 and was re-elected continuously until his death in 1902. From the outset of his term, by continually raising objections and calling for investigations, he made clear that despite his Republican affiliation he would be no willing tool of the organization. In the fall and winter term of the 1890–91 session Roberts voted in a minority of two or one on nine separate occasions, and during the 1894–95 sessions he stood alone in his opposition to measures before the Council on ten different occasions and voted with minorities of two to five on twenty-two other bills. This record of persistent dissent was stoical in character; there was something rather affecting about its hopelessness. Yet it was clearly in tune with the spirit of genteel reform. The fact that Roberts remained a perfect gentleman in his disagreements with the majority, never showing any antagonism or impugning its motives, gave his performance the proper touch of good breeding. Named to head an investigation of the United Gas Improvement Company, he attempted to disqualify himself because he owned stock in the firm, but when other councilmen prevailed upon him to head the investigation anyway, his criticism of the gas company outdid that of all the committee members. His death removed one of the strongest examples of probity and integrity from the city's legislature.[16]

Five years after Roberts' death, another Friend did battle with the U.G.I. William G. Huey, who had been elected to the Common Council representing the Fifteenth Ward, served at Mayor Weaver's request as chairman of a commission reinvestigating the city's lease with the utility. Huey's opposition to the leasing arrangements dated from 1897, when he had offered a resolution in Council to look into offers of U.G.I. stock to councilmen voting for the lease. But unlike Roberts, this Race Street Friend maintained a more consistent Republican party loyalty which prevented him from voting with the Mugwumps on most local issues, and his membership in the Union Republican Club in 1904 suggests that he had closer ties with the G.O.P. organization than most Friends.[17]

To induce independent Republicans to vote for Democratic reform candidates in state elections in the nineties, temporary organizations were established to make desertion of the G.O.P. more palatable. When Democrat Pattison made a successful bid for the governorship in 1890, the reformers created the Lincoln Independent Republican Committee to support him. All but the diehard protectionist Republicans among Friends joined the committee. In 1898 the short-lived Honest Government party drew nearly as much Quaker support in the abortive attempt to elect Methodist clergyman Silas Swallow—a marvelously ill-named prohibitionist—to the governor's chair. Charles Richardson and others were well aware of the weakness of mixing the temperance and political reform causes, but they saw it as the only practical means by which to challenge Senator Quay. The limits of Quaker Mugwump effectiveness were made apparent by James Rhoads' assertion in 1891 that the primary goal of the reformers was the purification of the Republican party.[18]

When Philadelphia's Municipal League disbanded in 1904, the Quaker reformers shifted their support to the newly formed Committee of Seventy, whose president was Quaker publisher John C. Winston. The Committee's membership came to include many older Friends, some of them elders of the cause of municipal reform: Joshua Baily, William H. Jenks, Charles Richardson, Walter Wood, J. Gibson McIlvain, and Asa S. Wing. Younger Quakers made their appearance in the lists for the first time: Frederick H. Strawbridge, J. Henry Scattergood, and Charles F. Jenkins. An attempt by Quay-lieutenant Israel Durham to secure extension of U.G.I.'s lease on the city's gas works had given the group a real opportunity to press for reform at the polls in 1905. Internal squabbles within the Republican organization and the mounting demand for a veto of the gas-lease "steal" pushed Mayor John Weaver into the arms of the reformers. An independent organization, the City party, came into being and received the blessing of the Committee of Seventy, which urged voters to shun the G.O.P. The City party ran candidates against the Republican organization for lesser city posts in the November election. At the same time a statewide independent group united with the Democrats and ran Chester Mayor William Berry for state treasurer. The reform excitement spread to many parts of the city and engaged the support of diverse religious leaders who helped establish prayer meetings on behalf of cleaner government.[19]

So intense was the fervor that it shattered precedents in the Quaker community. Speaking at the twenty-fifth anniversary of the Friends' Institute, Francis R. Cope Jr. gave vocal support to the City party's insurgency and praised the work of the Committee of Seventy. A public letter lauding "the movement" was sent to President Sharpless to read to the student body at Haverford. In this mood of excitement the Hicksite Representative Committee even wrote Mayor Weaver, encouraging him "to be faithful as an instrument of divine providence for the maintenance of good order, and the suppression of every influence that has a tendency to corrupt the morals of mankind." Rufus Jones used the pages of *The American Friend* to rip into the shoddy construction work and financial fraud of the Roosevelt Boulevard contractors. Quaker Committee of Seventy members, particularly Charles Jenkins and J. Henry Scattergood, spoke on behalf of the City party ticket. On election day the reformers were victorious. One enthusiastic analyst said it marked the end of "the oligarchy" in Philadelphia. Isaac Sharpless called it "the most significant municipal revolution in the history of America."[20]

In their optimism both commentators betrayed the naiveté of the Mugwump view of politics. Mayor Weaver was soon wooed back into the Republican organization, and contrary to Charles Jenkins' hopes, the City party was dissolved soon after Boies Penrose bested it in the gubernatorial race of 1906. Years of experience told the Mugwumps that the same fate awaited their Committee of Seventy if changes were not effected in its program. Under John Winston's leadership it retreated from the political activism of endorsing candidates and supporting parties to become a watchdog organization devoted to uncovering election frauds and improving the machinery of democracy. If survival is the proper test, their decision was a wise one. This agency of good government is still performing those functions in the 1970s.[21]

While the committee worked for reforms which could be characterized as "progressive," its very aloofness from party gave it more the appearance of a Mugwump survival. In 1905, Baily, Richardson, Jenks, and McIlvain were all over sixty. Nor can it be said that the reform administration finally elected in 1911 reflected youthful vigor; Rudolph Blankenburg was over seventy when he won the mayoralty on the Democratic and Keystone tickets. A few Friends campaigned against the Republican organization that year, but while they applauded the Blankenburg program they did not play a significant role in carrying it out. The only Quaker to serve in the administration was the Hicksite Frank L. Neall, who briefly headed the street cleaning department. Years of battle against Quay and his successors had not really altered the Friends' view of politics.[22]

Indeed, when their support of moral principles relegated them to a minority position the Quaker reformers seemed to find it comfortable. After the defeat of one reformer in 1891, Joshua Baily wrote: "We must be content with what Edwin Arnold says, 'The truth is with the remnant.'" The previous year architect Walter Cope, in urging the breakup of the Lincoln Independent Republican Committee, expressed the belief that what really counted in the battle with the Quay organization was the silent force of independence. Lawyer Joseph Parrish had asserted, concerning "We 'Independents and Republicans,'" that "any words of soberness and truth which we may see fit to speak . . . perhaps have a greater force by reason of our very helplessness as a political power in this locality." The Quaker roots of these sentiments are clear. Like their fellow Mugwumps in New York, these Philadelphians saw themselves as the "moral stewards" of the community.[23]

Because the Disciplines of both branches urged Quakers not to involve themselves in politics, one might expect to find only the worldly and nominal members of city Meetings among the Mugwump reformers. This, however, was not the case. It is true that Charles Richardson and Joseph Parrish were both Nominal Friends. But Walter Wood and William Jenks at Twelfth Street and J. Gibson McIlvain at Race Street were Practicing Friends, and Mugwumps Charles Roberts and Nathaniel Janney were both Weighty Friends. While no clear correlation can be found between Quaker institutional involvement and political reform, it does appear that Mugwumps were products of Friends' schools. Janney, Jenks, Richardson, and Wood all attended Westtown, while McIlvain, Parrish, and Roberts attended other Quaker institutions in the city. The guarded education instilled in its students high standards of morality which were at variance with the worldly behavior at City Hall. Only the conservative quietists at Arch Street viewed the Discipline prohibition of political involvement as such a serious matter that they remained aloof from the reform efforts of these years.

None of those who took part in the late nineteenth-century reform movements came from the middle or lower levels of the occupational hierarchy. Nor were they professionals and intellectuals like the most celebrated of the Boston Mugwumps; Quaker educational leaders like Isaac Sharpless and Edward Magill were really on the periphery of the movement. The leaders of the Philadelphia reform effort were prosperous merchants and bankers. Charles Richardson began his career in real estate and became first president of the Land Title and Trust Company. Charles Roberts was a partner in a glass manufacturing firm and president of the Spring Garden Insurance Company. John C. Winston built the firm that bore his name from a modest printer of Bibles into a major publishing house with diverse publications. William Jenks traded in cotton and J. Gibson McIlvain in lumber, while Walter Wood manufactured iron. Nathaniel Janney was in real estate and banking. The only attorney among them was Joseph Parrish. Most of them had been born into prosperous merchant families, although Richardson's father had been a bookseller and Parrish's a druggist. Thus, in occupational background the Quaker reformers were more like the Mugwumps of New York or the later Progressives of Pittsburgh than the good government crusaders of Boston.

Quaker Mugwumps were truly affluent. Wood and McIlvain were both millionaires. Roberts' bequest of fifty thousand dollars to Haverford College affords one measure of his wealth. Several were listed in the Social Register. Although none belonged to the most prestigious clubs of the Philadelphia aristocracy, they were active in lesser ones and in the most significant cultural associations. Richardson summered in Maine at Bar Harbor, while Wood sojourned at nearby Northeast Harbor, both of them "watering places" of the city's social elite. Though the Mugwumps declared their goal to be the restoration of government to "the people," their emphasis upon qualifications for office and their support of civil service reform reveals that their true aim was to return their own socioeconomic class to power. Few of them came from the generation of Friends born in the 1860s. The Quakers in that generation rejected positions in business for white collar and professional posts, and after the turn of the century, when these later-generation Friends reached adulthood, the Quaker component in urban political reform declined. The occupational shift helps explain the meager support Friends gave the progressive campaign which brought Rudolph Blankenburg to City Hall in 1911. If one of the key elements in helping Friends overcome scruples about political activity had been their position in the city's socioeconomic elite, which was thrown on the defensive in the Gilded Age, the situation in the Progressive Era was very different.

Several historians have explained the municipal reform impulse of the late nineteenth century in terms of a status revolution. They have claimed that the Boston Mugwumps "nursed a sense of missed chances" and that others suffered from feelings of alienation brought on by industrial transformation. Yet the very generation of Friends in Philadelphia which gave overt support to political reform remained in a secure position economically and socially. Nor did they suffer from that other urban malaise, a loss of identity. All were birthright Friends who were sustained by the traditions and community of Quakers. All but Jenks, Janney, and Winston were Philadelphia-born. While these men were witnessing the loss in numbers and influence of the Society of Friends, they certainly did not feel economically or socially impotent themselves. We may rightfully question the sincerity of the Mugwumps' democratic rhetoric in the light of their demands, but we should not discount the significance of their moral arguments.[24]

The Quaker merchants of late-nineteenth-century Philadelphia were drawn to the reform movement by a sense of civic and moral responsibility. As businessmen they sought the application of sound mercantile principles of efficiency and frugality to municipal government. As Friends they sought to restore the moral health of the community in tune with religious standards which harked back to Penn's holy commonwealth. As members of the upper middle class they sought to defend Philadelphia's civic reputation. They thought not so much in terms of democracy as propriety. But their unwillingness to build a permanent organization outside the Republican party gave them little chance to undermine the "machine" in the wards and precincts. And they were doubly encumbered by the Quaker political dilemma. As they deserted both the Friends' tradition of political aloofness and the party of their natural allegiance, they were haunted by doubts. So burdened, their movement was a predictable failure.

Although they were personally secure, the Quaker reformers witnessed enough unwanted economic and political change to prompt them to join the chorus of Victorian antiurbanism. Quaker rhetoric took on a rural coloration. Desirous of taking advantage of its economic opportunities, Friends had chosen to live in Philadelphia, but they made no effort to conceal their distaste for what urban life had become after the Civil War. The Orthodox Discipline of 1880 reminded young Friends that their morals and distinctive principles took precedence over economic advantages in reaching a decision as to what trade to pursue, "particularly before deciding to come from the country into a populous city, where snares and temptations abound, of which they may yet be wholly ignorant, but which if they are exposed to them, may lay waste their moral standing, and even jeopardize the salvation of the soul." In 1903 an Orthodox group opened a special residence hall on Summer Street for young Friends moving to the city for the first time.[25]

Friends penned glowing tributes to the rural countryside. Hicksite leaders enjoined the membership to avoid fashionable resorts during the summer months so as to seek communion with nature, which was thought to offer special insights. As one Orthodox Friend put it in 1872: "How omnipresent is our God! not less in the city than in the country, but in the latter *everything* is His, and it is no effort to recognize His mighty hand." These were more than mere echoes of antiurban Transcendentalism. The arguments partook of a Quaker practicality, and health was a frequent theme. Friends extolled the pure air, more nutritious food, and outdoor exercise of a rural existence. Westtown School took every opportunity to encourage camping, hiking, bicycling, and canoeing by students and teachers as weekend activity. Issues of economic and social well-being entered the argument in 1898, when *The Friend* reprinted the rather dubious assertion that "a better living, more comfort . . . , better health and more respectability and independence, with brighter prospects of substantial gains, are possible in the country."[26]

Quaker praise for farming knew no bounds. Friends saw agriculture as a natural way to avoid the dual evils of poverty and riches. The fortunate farmer could escape the "harassing anxieties, the plausible temptations attending unscrupulous competition, and the corroding fears of disastrous speculation" which burdened urban businessmen. Acknowledging the need to strengthen rural schools, a 1915 report of the Hicksite Education Committee concluded that "at the head of all sciences and arts, at the head of civilization and progress, stands—not militarism, the science that kills, not commerce, the art that accumulates wealth—but agriculture, the mother of all industry and the maintainer of human life." In 1918, thanks to a $400,000 bequest from a birthright Philadelphia Friend, Helen R. Bacon, Westtown established an agriculture department, which offered courses in animal husbandry, horticulture, forestry, and gardening. From its founding in 1877, the monthly periodical *The Farm Journal* was edited and published by Philadelphia Hicksites. Even millionaire Friends proved the adage, "Scratch the Quaker and find the farmer." Transportation executives Clement Griscom and George Wood both engaged in the dairy business as a sideline to their mercantile pursuits.[27]

Literary flights involving descriptions of arcadian purity appealed to many Quakers who found the problems of urban life too depressing or too difficult of solution. But others demanded more realism on the subject. Haverford professor Rufus Jones tried to persuade Friends that a rural environment was no "Garden of Eden." But though he warned that rural religious life was "lower" than most people supposed, Jones had to admit that Quakerism was better adapted to rural communities than large urban centers. While the 1904 editors of *The Friends' Intelligencer* viewed rural life and farming as ideals, they argued, like Jones, that Quakers had been satisfied to condemn the city instead of trying to save it. Because most people lived in cities out of necessity, the editors believed it better to improve housing and sanitary conditions instead of trying to move people out to vacant land. Their demand for more serious study of urban economic and social conditions reflected the influence of the Progressive forces at work in the social settlements.[28]

We have already seen how the commercial temper of the modern city challenged the tenets of the Quaker business ethic. But the dangers Friends saw in industrial Philadelphia were not confined to the banks and brokerage houses of Center City. The great mass of the laboring classes which populated the rapidly growing area north of Spring Garden Street as well as the mean row house districts of South Philadelphia posed further worries for those who hankered after a smaller, more socially homogeneous city. The old deference of workingmen to their employers in a simpler era gave way to harsh confrontations between organized laborers and management. The critical spirit which Friends had developed toward postwar commercial leaders did not predispose them to take the side of workingmen in clashes over wages and working conditions. They were truly devoted to the Gospel of Work, believing it to be the fountain of all human intelligence without which men would easily be demoralized. When labor union leaders began to talk about an eight-hour day, Friends worried over the appearance of this demand of "an underlying assumption that labor is an undesirable thing." Friends may have opposed economic expansion which was too rapid, but their commitment to the concept of production itself was strong enough to prompt them to view any strike as an immoral interference with man's basic economic function. They deplored work stoppages because they deprived laborers in related industries from gaining a livelihood. They fretted too over capital denied the opportunity to earn a profit in strike periods.[29]

Friends' love of pacific relations strengthened their antilabor predisposition. As workers rioted against railroad wage cuts by destroying property and battling with police, what sympathy there was for their cause in Quaker circles evaporated. Some in Philadelphia began to think of workers as an anarchic bomb bent on pillage and destruction; they even favored brute force and weaponry as the only way to check the violence. And their anger led some to urge the death penalty for convicted rioters. Yet Philadelphia in these years experienced only the mildest sorts of labor strife as "law and order" forces in the city government employed large numbers of police to confront strikers. More in line with pacific Quaker ideals was the suggestion that arbitration be used to settle labor disputes. Rufus Jones urged this solution during the railroad strike of 1894, although he viewed the workers' tactics as "ill advised and radically wrong." A decade and a half later, when a transit strike against the Philadelphia Transportation Company crippled the city, Jones served on a special panel of religious leaders which recommended settlement by arbitration. With such procedures older Orthodox Friends had no sympathy. The aging Joshua Baily believed that the P.T.C. could employ anyone it wished and discharge workers whenever it thought necessary. He declared that the employees of Joshua L. Baily & Company were not permitted to dictate how he ran his business; if they tried, he would quickly replace them.[30]

While considerable agreement with such conservative views could be found in most Protestant churches in the late nineteenth century, a small minority of churchmen grew more sympathetic to labor in the wake of the force used against strikers. It prompted even some to question the capitalist system. Within Philadelphia Quakerism hardly anyone doubted the efficacy of that system until the twentieth century. Yet some concern for workingmen appeared among the Hicksites in the 1880s. Reports about the exploitation of children gave them a less sanguine view of management, although they remained optimistic about working conditions and enforcement of the child labor law. By the time of the anthracite strike against the Reading Railroad in 1902, *The Friends' Intelligencer* reflected prolabor sympathies. Its editor urged the mine operators to use their "initiative powers" to create better conditions and demanded that they act with candor and justice toward the unions. After the strike settlement, the editor concluded: "We have been carried a long step forward in our understanding of the powers and limitations of organized capital." Not all his Hicksite readers—some of them affluent capitalists—could have agreed. From the Orthodox the only hint of sympathy for workers appeared in Charles Rhoads' classic exposition of the Quaker business ethic, when the author admitted that employers often kept wages at levels which were far too low. Though he urged management to be generous, Rhoads found justification for wage cutting in times of depression and insisted that employees always remain dutiful. With the earliest nineteenth-century concern about labor exploitation which eventually evolved into the Social Gospel, only a few Friends had any sympathy.[31]

If support was wanting for union efforts to improve the material conditions of the laboring classes, one might expect to find a deep concern for their spiritual health. That concern may have been present, but it was given modest expression. Other Protestant churches—notably Episcopalians and Congregationalists—awoke to the fact that vast hordes of unchurched working people had settled in their cities. The "institutional churches" they developed in their underused downtown edifices attempted to reach this urban proletariat with social programs. In Philadelphia, besides the Wanamaker-supported Bethany Presbyterian Church, the most celebrated of these attempts developed out of Grace Baptist Church, from which Russell Conwell spawned diverse socially useful institutions. Following quietist doctrines against proselytizing, Quaker Meetings made little effort to save the souls of the unchurched. Where evangelistic efforts appeared, they came from individual initiative. The rare street meetings were attempts to foster Christian behavior, not to make converts to Quakerism. Joshua Bailey's sponsorship of a revival meeting which featured evangelist Dwight L. Moody and packed Wanamaker's Depot in 1875 was very atypical of Friends. Restive under quietist domination in the Yearly Meeting, he and his fellow Gurneyites feared that the Society was more exclusive than inclusive. As the *Friends' Review* asked in 1872, "'Must not something be wanting in the Society as it is now . . . that it makes so few converts, while other denominations number, annually, their hundreds and thousands?"[32]

Friends could well have used conversions to recoup membership losses. English Quakers in these same years ran First-day schools, catering primarily to working-class adults, which produced a fair number of converts to the faith and helped build a 24.5 percent increase in London Yearly Meeting's membership between 1871 and 1901. Some Philadelphia Hicksites opened similar schools in the early sixties, although the classes primarily attracted young Friends. After the Yearly Meeting took them over in 1886, the schools expanded in number, increasing their enrollment among those outside the faith, and put more emphasis on adult education. But while there were 72 of them in 1902, tutoring nearly 2,500 non-Friends a year, they produced disappointing results. Twelfth Street did not try this method of evangelism until 1914. While "strangers" attended meetings for worship in Philadelphia frequently, they were sometimes met with rudeness from older, tradition-bound quietists. Late in the nineteenth century, both Twelfth Street and Race Street appointed committees to welcome visitors and help them understand Quaker practices. Yet it was not until 1901 that Race Street put up a sign outside the meetinghouse informing the public of the hours of worship. When Twelfth Street Meeting consented to put notices of its hours of worship in the *Public Ledger* and in the city's hotels in 1902, it was a daring innovation. Evening social events featuring talks on a wide variety of topics attracted outsiders to Twelfth Street in increasing numbers in the nineties. Courses offered next door at the Friends' Institute had a similar effect, but this rather intellectual evangelism was hardly the kind that spoke to the needs of the urban poor.[33]

Friends did accept into the faith those who had discovered Quakerism on their own initiative and could satisfy Meetings as to the sincerity of their intentions. Nearly 14 percent of the Friends studied were convinced adults (see Tables 51–53). By generally avoiding organized efforts to convert others. Meetings may have attracted a more stable, faithful membership; the converts, not surprisingly, were much more likely to become religiously active. Among those born in the 1840s, the proportion of women was higher; quietism and aloofness from worldly problems may have made the faith unattractive to men in the late nineteenth century. As more diverse groups were drawn to the Society of Friends by First-day schools and evening social meetings, the number of converts rose. But these convincements produced Friends whose participation indicated a more fragile commitment. Convinced adults in the earlier generation came to Quakerism in response to their own spiritual promptings. A greater proportion of them became Weighty and Practicing Friends than was true for those in the later generation, some of whom may have been attracted by the social efforts to welcome "strangers" in turn-of-the-century Meetings. In other words, the quietists had been right.

Friends' failure to take their distinctive message to the unchurched masses was the result of more than Quietist conviction. Reports from the Midwest indicated that converts there were having an influence on Meetings which the Philadelphians viewed as pernicious. The introduction of a paid ministry, formal services, and hymn singing into Ohio and Indiana Meetings was clearly attributable to evangelistic zeal and a desire to accommodate recent converts. All but a tiny minority of Philadelphia Quakers wanted to avoid such changes. Even as recipients of charity, the large number of native and immigrant working people in late nine-teenth-century Philadelphia interested them far less than smaller groups suffering racial and religious discrimination. And giving charity for those in need was one thing; converting the poor to the Quaker faith was quite another. The exclusiveness which worried the *Friends' Review* in 1872 came about at least in part because some of the affluent were not above a smug condescension. When English First-day schools brought working-class converts into their Meetings, it produced a social rift which weakened the fabric of the corporate community.[34] Perhaps the Philadelphians had learned of the problems in English Quakerism for they did little to change their aloofness.

Usually unwilling to impose their own religious standards on others, Friends did try to curb certain abuses which they believed lowered the moral climate of Philadelphia. In the case of theatrical productions, their opposition differed from other Protestant oppo-sition in that it sprang from their criticism of the unnatural and imaginative nature of the drama, pandering to "the grossest pro-pensities of our nature." The Orthodox leadership viewed theaters as breeding grounds of crime. Confirming the strength of its oppo-sition, the Arch Street Meeting in 1887 disowned a Friend who attended plays regularly and commended theatrical performances in a published book. Even the Hicksite Yearly Meeting became the scene of a bitter controversy when in 1915 it was learned that plays were being performed at the George School. The advent of motion pictures brought attacks on the new medium from both Yearly Meetings, the Orthodox lending their voices to those call-ing for film censorship by state authorities. When spectator sports won popularity in Philadelphia in the eighties, Friends objected strongly to the violence displayed in some of these contests, and they helped win a temporary ban on prize fighting in the city in 1885. The Orthodox denounced intercollegiate football as de-moralizing, though, when few other churches agreed, they con-tented themselves with admonitions to Friends to avoid the sport. They believed that these contests led to gambling and "pool sell-ing," practices which had also won their censure. They lobbied successfully with others in Harrisburg and Trenton to prevent re-peal of the ban on horse racing in both Pennsylvania and New Jersey. Their sabbatarianism, of course, was hardly unique. In

1876 the Orthodox Meeting for Sufferings distributed 50,000 copies of an appeal urging continued enforcement of the Sunday closing ordinances. Demands for their abandonment had come in the wake of the Centennial celebration in Fairmount Park. As late as 1919 an Orthodox Committee on Public Morality lobbied to prevent changes in the rule against Sunday amusements in New Jersey cities.[35]

The prevalence of organized vice in cities produced drives for "social purity" by many church groups. Friends had not become involved officially in the attempts to end prostitution in the nineteenth century, although some individuals supported such work outside of Meeting channels. But Philadelphia's worst "tenderloin" district was located in the old Quaker preserve of the Northern Liberties, where some Friends still lived. One crusading minister estimated that between Sixth, Arch, Broad, and Green Streets there were at least 300 houses of prostitution in 1896; certain blocks of streets long identified as Quaker residential areas, such as Arch and Race, contained dozens of these establishments. The national publicity given these revelations may have influenced the Hicksites' decision to join the drive against vice. The Philanthropic Labor Committee formed a special department devoted to "purity," whose members distributed literature among students in Philadelphia and secured "White Cross Pledges" from some of them. When a grand jury advocated "the licensing and regulation of vice by Civil Authorities" in 1902, Friends were quick to express their opposition. The Hicksites provided financial aid for the American Purity Alliance and the National Vigilance Committee in supporting the Mann Bill in 1910 which outlawed interstate traffic in women for immoral purposes.[36]

The most significant of the efforts to deal with urban evils was the temperance movement. Many Protestant churches—especially the evangelical ones—came to regard alcoholic beverages as the key to social ills in the nation's burgeoning cities. Friends in Philadelphia divided over how far they would support the organized temperance crusade, but most felt sure that if the liquor question could be solved, American cities would be better places in which to live. As early as 1878 the Hicksite *Friends' Intelligencer* claimed that more than any other factor, intemperance had encouraged the growth of crime, pauperism, political corruption, and "a dangerous class in all our large cities." Twenty years later, Rufus Jones went even further: "We honestly believe that the liquor problem is beyond all question the greatest problem now before the nation, and the greatest moral problem in the world." As the spokesman for the progressive spirit in Philadelphia Quakerism, his views reflected the urban, middle-class side of the temperence effort and drew support from the evangelical wing of the Orthodox body, which had taken up the cause in the 1880s. In the Hicksite Yearly Meeting, on the other hand, the impetus for temperance work came from rural Friends who were fearful of the changes at work in the industrial city. Though diverse elements supported the cause, in Quakerism the rural spirit was dominant. The country dweller's fear of changes in the distant city and the urban middle-class attempt to improve city life were both essentially rooted in rural Protestantism.[37]

As an unnatural stimulus which barred a person from a clear view of reality, the drinking of "spirituous liquors" had been a disownable offense among Friends since the middle of the eighteenth century. Committees of the Monthly Meetings inquired each year as to the number of Friends guilty of this transgression. Those admitting consumption increased through the late nineteenth century. In the Twelfth Street Meeting the number of men classified as intemperate rose from an average of twelve or below in the late sixties to over sixty by the turn of the century. An 1882 decision to interpret the Discipline's injunction to include wine or anything which could intoxicate accounted in part for the large increase. The 1882 change culminated an eight-year effort by rural Burlington Quarterly Meeting and its allies in the city to get a more stringent interpretation, but even rural Friends had mixed feelings, as the Orthodox Yearly Meeting debates on the intoxicating capabilities of sweet as opposed to hard cider show. Responding to rural pressures, the Hicksites made signing tavern licenses a disownable offense in 1879 and eight years later added a strong prohibition to renting property to the manufacturers and sellers of intoxicants. These were significant moves for the Hicksites, who were liberalizing many provisions in the Rule of Discipline in these same years.[38]

Friends began extending their temperance concern to those beyond their own faith in the seventies. In the early years of the Women's Christian Temperance Union, many Quakers of different persuasions supported this organized attempt to convert slum dwellers and laboring men into sober, dutiful citizens. The W.C.T.U.'s tactics of mild persuasion attracted Friends to its work. But when under Frances Willard's leadership the organization involved itself with other reform causes, some of its Quaker supporters were disenchanted; they viewed the original W.C.T.U. as a "moral instrumentality." Branding attempts to increase the number of its supporters through such alliances as "mere expediency," these Friends warned that joining forces with the Prohibition party was a descent into "the miry pool of political partisanship." If men like Joshua Baily found ties with the Prohibition party offensive in 1888, they understandedly balked at allying with the Populists in the nineties. Like many other Protestant denominations in the East, the Quakers abandoned the W.C.T.U. when it chose to stake its lot with those desirous of making major changes in the American social order.[39]

Friends also launched local efforts of their own to combat the evils of intoxicants. Joshua Baily put his own funds to work for the cause in Philadelphia. City saloons were in the habit of offering customers free lunch, but the fare was so highly spiced that large quantities of liquid refreshment were required to go with it. Those frequenting the saloons returned to factory and office ill-prepared for the afternoon's work. To offer workingmen an alternative, Baily opened a coffeehouse at 15th and Market Streets in 1874. Five cents could purchased a pint mug of coffee and two ounces of wheat bread. Other fare was available at reasonable prices. "The Central Coffee House" did such a thriving business that Baily opened another on South Fourth Street. While he made no profit on the ventures, he continued the operations until 1899. As a friend of Neal Dow and temperance advocates of other faiths, Baily was the most active individual Quaker leader in the cause. His membership in the National Temperance Society even brought him into cooperative efforts with the Catholic Total Abstinence Union and Bishop John Ireland of St. Paul, who spearheaded the liberal Catholic drive for this reform.[40]

Orthodox Friends through their Meeting for Sufferings penned occasional memorials against the evils of drink in the state. Struck by a $78 million annual expenditure for liquor by Pennsylvanians in 1879, the Meeting demanded repeal of all laws permitting the sale of intoxicating drinks in the entire commonwealth. Plans to allow sale of drinks in Fairmount Park prompted the Meeting to make several pleas to the legislature. To some Friends, these memorials seemed ineffectual. They formed a Temperance Association in 1880 which was independent of the Yearly Meeting. The group opened coffee stands and a lodging house in West Philadelphia. Members distributed temperance tracts at the city's railroad stations and supplied their literature to others working in the cause. In the nineties, as the W.C.T.U. lost support, sentiment in favor of coercive prohibition legislation grew. Rufus Jones urged Quaker backing for the Anti-Saloon League when that organization was only in the planning stage. The Temperance Association grew closer to the work of the league in Pennsylvania. After 1900 the annual meetings of the association featured discussions of the issue from diverse aspects; Friends spoke in 1911 on the liquor industry as big business and the attitude of the medical profession toward alcohol. By that time nearly all Gurneyite Friends agreed on the necessity for total abstinence and many were anxious to see strict prohibition laws enacted.[41]

The Hicksites showed no reticence to involve their Yearly Meeting in the attempt to fight the evil in Philadelphia. Their Temperance Committee viewed the danger from alcohol as so pressing that it authorized for use in Friends' schools books which contained religious sentiments not in keeping with Quakerism. After acquiring pamphlets employing medical and scientific evidence from the National Temperance Society for their own schools, they began an effort directed at the public school system. First trying to convince teachers and administrators of the value of educational programs on the evils of drink, they switched in 1885 to an appeal to several state legislatures for mandatory hygiene instruction on the subject. None too sanguine about the success of their anti-liquor propaganda among the laboring classes, the committee expressed the hope that at the very least their work had prevented Friends from becoming addicted to the practice. Not all Hicksites supported the committee's efforts; in denying sanction to the demand that all Friends be urged to vote as a bloc in the 1889 liquor referendum, the Yearly Meeting upheld the tradition of conscious diversity which had marked nearly all its activities. But the drive to obtain abstinence for the entire city made increasing claims on the time of a significant segment of the Hicksite body in the last decade of the nineteenth century.[42]

Traditional independence at first restrained the Hicksites from uniting with others to mount an organized effort to attain that goal nationally. While they sent observers to a Temperance Congress in Saratoga Springs in 1898, they authorized no more than an exchange of views with the regular delegates. At the Washington convention of the Anti-Saloon League in 1901, however, Hicksite delegates attended from Philadelphia and one of their number was elected to the league's Board of Managers. Forsaking the older W.C.T.U., the Hicksites soon committed themselves to the more vigorous league in its effort to gain coercive legislation from Congress. Within Pennsylvania a discouraging series of reverses prevented the Temperance Committee and like organizations of other churches from gaining the local option and prohibitive legislation they sought in Harrisburg. Only in attempting to guard Friends from the influence of the saloon did the group have any success. Thanks to its efforts, Philadelphia authorities refused licenses to taverns which sought to open on 15th Street near the meetinghouse and the Friends' Central School. The Orthodox never gave support to the Anti-Saloon League, but the Yearly Meeting evidenced its concern for the cause by penning a memorial to Congress in 1914 favoring national prohibition. Like many Protestant groups which looked back fondly to a simpler, rural America, untroubled by industrial growth and immigration, Friends celebrated ratification of the Eighteenth Amendment as a major victory in the crusade to cleanse urban America of crime and poverty.[43]

The antiurban rhetoric gave comfort to those who had migrated to the city and were alienated by their new surroundings. Nearly half the Friends in the Center City Meetings had been born in places with fewer than 2,500 inhabitants. The homogeneous composition of the rural communities which they had left behind ill-prepared them for the heterogeneity of their urban neighbors. How could the host of social organizations or the blocks of anonymous row homes afford any sense of community or individual identity for the newcomers? If they could not, the faith of Friends could and did. Surrounded by shade trees and green grass, meetinghouses offered a rare contrast to the cobblestoned streets and concrete which dominated the city. High brick walls often served as barriers between the harsh noises of commercial traffic and the silence of their worship. And the Meeting as a corporate body offered the newcomers identity and significance. As the bearer of social and cultural values, it tied them to their own rural past. In worship and community they found continuity for themselves and their families in a time of rapid change.

It is not surprising that so many of the rural-born Friends made the Quaker community the focus of their lives. Among the Weighty Friends fully five-eighths of those whose birthplaces we know came from rural areas (Tables 47–48). Friends born in cities constituted a slight majority of the urban membership, but they accounted for smaller proportions of the Weighty and Practicing Friends. This was true for all Quakers in the sample, but it was more pronounced among those born in the 1840s than for those born in the 1860s. This helps explain the tardiness of their response to growing urban problems. The Arch Street Meeting, which clung most tenaciously to the Rule of Discipline and opposed accommodation with contemporary culture, had the smallest proportion of members who were born in the city (Tables 49–50).

In the early twentieth century, when Friends born in the sixties reached their most active years, the rural bias among Friends was far less pronounced, and the Meetings began to deal with the social ills around them in a more serious way. But at Arch Street rural dominance was actually greater than it had been before. As the area around the meetinghouse became more and more commercial and the Quaker population in the neighborhood declined, rural-born Friends transferred their memberships there to sustain this bastion of conservative Quakerism as a Monthly Meeting, even though they themselves lived in the growing suburbs or in more distant rural towns. As a last preserve of quietism, this oldest of the city Meetings retained a rusticity and rural flavor up to the time of the First World War, a constant reminder of the difficulties of adjustment which the modern city had imposed on earnest Friends.

| Benevolence
Near and Far

The demands of Philadelphia's industrial growth brought on a massive influx of immigrant labor in the decades following the Civil War. These newcomers crowded into river-front wards, creating major problems in health and housing. But Friends seemed not even to see the new arrivals and their social problems. Turning away from the immigrant masses assembling on their own doorsteps, they remained locked into established avenues of philanthropy or directed their energies toward Indians in Kansas and Nebraska and toward Russian religious sectarians—the Doukhobors—settling in the western provinces of Canada. In all their philanthropies, Friends took on the role of guardians of Protestant culture. Ignoring their own beginnings as sectarian critics of the social order and their continued estrangement from many American norms, they attempted to assimilate their charges into the dominant middle-class ethic.

Historians disagree as to why comfortable Protestant groups involved themselves in the problems of the poor through various forms of urban philanthropy. Carroll Smith-Rosenberg has explained the development of city missions and the Association for Improving the Condition of the Poor in New York in terms of the evangelical fervor of the antebellum period. In her view, the desire to convert the destitute and fallen only gradually evolved into a more pragmatic and materialistic social meliorism. In his study of Boston's later charity organization, Nathan Huggins has deemphasized religious motives and stressed the desire to maintain social stability in the face of community disintegration. He asserts that the charity reform movement was "protective of class and property interests and, despite its Christian rhetoric, left Christ pretty much out of its judgements."[1] Friends went about their philanthropic business in Philadelphia with a moral pietism, but their evangelism was of a very reserved sort. Only a few of their urban agencies came into being during the period in which Joseph John Gurney's evangelical ideas had their impact in Philadelphia Meetings. Clearly they were not trying to make converts to their faith as the New York mission workers had earlier in the century. Friends' response to the Society for Organizing Charity—like their efforts to deal with liquor, gambling, and prostitution—suggests that their goal was to control the urban populace. They did fear disorder, and they did have something to protect. They clearly sought to instill in the city's poor the values of diligent labor and responsibility which were so much a part of their own religious tradition. There is no necessary dichotomy between their social and religious motives; they were products of the same dynamics.

For the city's poor and destitute, Friends supported an array of benevolent institutions, some of which could trace their origins to the eighteenth century. Consistent with quietist professions, Friends sustained these institutions by personal, rather than corporate, benevolence. Like much of Victorian philanthropy, their charity organizations offered opportunities for supporters to give public expression to Christian responsibility for the less fortunate. In many cases greater importance attached to the salvation of the donor than the effect upon the recipients. Those who deliberated at board meetings and wrote generous checks to charities were sustaining Quaker traditions in philanthropy and helping to maintain the Quaker reputation for "doing good." Image building and self-congratulation were no doubt among the motives which prompted the Orthodox in 1897 to publish a little book which listed all the charities they sponsored in Philadelphia. Yet these philanthropies quite often gave expression to vital religious conviction frequently fostered by "refreshing seasons" of corporate worship in the meetinghouse. Benevolence of Friends, as Sydney James has suggested, offered a way of making a civic contribution without becoming ensnared in a worldliness which compromised Quaker testimonies. If the benevolence betrayed a concern for reputation, it also did offer tangible help to some of the needy in industrial Philadelphia.[2]

The last three decades of the nineteenth century were relatively barren times in the innovative development of Friends' philanthropies. The prevalence of quietism kept new institutions for the needy to a minimum. Of the fifty-four Quaker-sponsored charities whose founding dates were listed in a city-wide compilation in 1903, only fourteen had made their appearance after 1870. Quite a few had been in operation since the eighteenth century. As might have been expected, these philanthropies clung to earlier notions of benevolence long after urban realities demanded altered programs. Typical were those run for indigent women, which provided employment in sewing for the poor. The garments prepared in this labor were often sold at half-price to the very women who had been paid a modest wage to make them. The Orthodox supported three such institutions: the Female Society for the Relief and Employment of the Poor (1795) on North Seventh Street, the Western District Dorcas Society (1821) at the Twelfth Street meetinghouse, and the Catharine Street House of Industry (1847) in Southwark. The last of these had many prominent Friends on its board, but was not an exclusively Quaker agency. Besides offering poor women employment, it provided baths and lodgings for eighty people on Catharine Street and sponsored a medical visitor for the neighborhood. A Hicksite House of Industry, run by the Northern Association of the City and County of Philadelphia (1844), provided similar services for the area around Seventh and Green Streets in the Northern Liberties. And from 1868 to 1888 the Penn Sewing School offered free training to women seeking proficiency in the trade; it met in the Race Street meetinghouse. So narrow and limited were these operations that twentieth-century social investigators declared some of them to be deficient both as charities and as employment.[3]

While they did not take part in organized efforts to stamp out vice in the city through publicity and lobbying as the Hicksites did, the Orthodox gave support to institutions designed to rehabilitate fallen women. Prominent Friends dominated the board of the Magdalen Society (1800), which had its headquarters in the Quaker neighborhood around Logan Square. The society offered prostitutes a chance to rise through a common school education, the inevitable instruction in sewing, and assistance in gaining respectable employment. An association of women Friends headed by Rebecca Branson ran the Howard Institution (1853) on Poplar Street in North Philadelphia, which offered shelter to discharged female prisoners and any homeless woman in need of care. In the two-year residence available there, women could receive training in laundry work, sewing, and domestic service. Both institutions could accommodate but a small number of clients at a time and they excluded blacks from their services. Friends were also on the board of the Indigent Widows' and Single Women's Society (1817), which ran a hundred-bed home for the aged on Chestnut Street in West Philadelphia. And they supported the Western Soup Society (1837), a very small organization offering temporary shelter to women and children in the area of South Street west of Broad. Other smaller endowments directed by Quakers in the city dispensed funds to those applying for aid.[4]

Orthodox interest in indigent children found expression in the Aimwell School (1796), which offered instruction for poor girls preparatory to high school. The school attracted fifty-five students to its Northern Liberties location at the turn of the century. Considering the availability of free public education, Friends might have used the funds for more pressing social needs had they been more innovative. The Hicksites displayed greater awareness of social realities when they launched two agencies in the 1880s to deal with the needs of the city's young. The Friends' Home for Children (1881) offered temporary shelter for youngsters between two and twelve years of age. Located in West Philadelphia, the home took in 389 children in the first seventeen years of its operation and placed approximately one-third of them in permanent homes. The Beach Street Mission (1880) provided a Sunday school and other programs for children in an effort to keep them off the streets in an area near the Delaware River docks in the Northern Liberties. The mission taught sewing to girls and developed a modest recreation progam for boys. Later it displayed considerable adaptability in evolving into a full-fledged social settlement in the Progressive Era.[5]

Medicine and science have always made strong claims upon Quakers, who were attracted by their practicality. Twenty-five of the 710 Friends in our sample became practicing physicians. The health care facilities of the city received sustenance from Friends in other occupations who served on hospital boards. Quakers dominated, although they did not control, Philadelphia's oldest health care institution, the Pennsylvania Hospital (1751). Its board president at the turn of the century was Benjamin H. Shoe-maker, its treasurer was Henry Haines, and a Weighty Twelfth Street Friend, Daniel Test, was for many years the hospital's superintendent. The Friends' Asylum for the Insane had pioneered in the care of the mentally disturbed from 1813, when it first opened its doors in then-rural Frankford. It was governed by an all-Quaker board of managers, but accepted patients from other faiths. Prominent Orthodox financial leaders dominated the board of the Germantown Dispensary and Hospital (1864). And a Practicing Friend from Arch Street, Dr. Anna Sharpless, was the founder and president of the West Philadelphia Hospital for Women (1889), although Friends were less conspicuous on its board.[6]

A few Friends' charities dealt with other problems. The Friends' Charity Fuel Association, founded by the Hicksites in 1835, fur-nished 248 tons of coal a year at half price to the needy and free to the very poor. An older philanthrophy, the Pennsylvania Prison Society (1787), which aided discharged prisoners, attracted strong Quaker support. Personal visits with inmates by individual Friends was a tradition of some standing. Quaker interest in the aged received expression in active support of the Old Man's Home (1864) in West Philadelphia.

The pattern of Quaker involvement in urban philanthropy re-veals a tendency to adhere to the familiar. Their preference for aiding women and children reflected a hesitancy to do anything which might encourage needy men to think that they could receive assistance without working. Like most other Protestant philanthro-pists of the age, they give little thought to the effects of the busi-ness cycle upon the urban proletariat. Although they attacked the orgies of financial speculation which made nineteenth-century de-pressions so severe, Friends seemed unprepared to acknowledge that poor working men could not control their occupational destinies. When compared to the institutions of private philan-thropy which had been aiding the poor in New York City even before the middle of the century, Quaker agencies in Philadelphia appear inadequate and unrealistic.[7]

But even the existing institutions suffered from uncertain financial backing in these years. Income for some was so meager as to put in question their survival. In analyzing the problem in 1909, Isaac Sharpless concluded that general philanthropy was deficient among Friends. He acknowledged that their schools were well supported, but he claimed that "In the matter of intelligent, well-directed charitable and missionary labor there has been no such general liberality. While such movements have been sustained, it has been rather by generous gifts of a few than by the spontaneous outpouring of the many." The Sharpless assessment is confirmed by an examination of the bequests of Quakers in the membership sample. Some Friends left ample funding for hospitals and social agencies, but they represented a small minority of those studied. Of the 388 Quakers whose wills were found, more than five-sixths left nothing to charity (Tables 54–55). Of the sixty who made charitable bequests, a third left funds to Quaker philanthropies only, but this kind of provincialism marked most nineteenth-century giving. The proportion of the Orthodox leaving charitable bequests was somewhat greater than that found among the Hicksites, whose humble origins early in the century gave them less experience in this sort of beneficence. Generational differences in giving were modest. This measure of philanthropy does not take into account giving during the lifetime of the donors, a practice lauded by *The Friends' Review* in 1873 because it offered a greater chance to direct or modify the benevolence. If widely employed as a preferable alternative to bequests in wills, this practice may explain the paucity of benevolence found in the membership sample.[8]

Friends' social and economic conservatism prevented them from breaking out of traditional forms of philanthropy in this period of rapid urban change. And the centripetal forces of quietism and internal division sustained the tendency for Quakers to look within their own society for those in need. Yet individual Friends participated in the major reform of social welfare which developed in Philadelphia before the turn of the century. Prominent citizens of many faiths met in 1878 to consider reorganization of the city's charitable efforts. Hicksites Henry M. Laing and William W. Justice and the Orthodox philanthropist Philip Garret were among the active participants. What emerged from these meetings at the Board of Trade was the Philadelphia Society for Organizing Charitable Relief and Repressing Mendicancy. Modelled on an English association of the same name, and similar to contemporary organizations in several Eastern cities, the S.O.C. sought to coordinate and make more efficient the diverse efforts to aid the urban needy. Ward associations were charged with the responsibility of investigating the specific needs in their districts. This produced a clearer picture of overall welfare needs in the city; it also meant more severe tests could be imposed before charity would be offered. It was cautious reform at best.[9]

The Quaker response to its founding suggests that most interest centered on that aspect of the work which would prevent exploitation of existing charities by the indolent. The *Friends' Intelligencer* attributed the creation of the S.O.C. in part to "a feeling of self-protection." Orthodox Friends lauded the efforts of the S.O.C. in sustaining the work ethic. They believed that if the masses were permitted to think that charity would care for them whether or not they found work, "an army of tramps, paupers, and communists would overrun the country." Philadelphia's S.O.C. remained more decentralized than those in other cities and, therefore, it failed to gain truly efficient control over the city's diverse relief agencies. But its investigative procedures illuminated the health and housing problems with which the next generation dealt by more professional and imaginative means. Friends held superintendencies in several ward associations, worked as house-to-house visitors, handled special investigative projects, and served as vice presidents of the organization. In so doing, they contributed to the conservative spirit of this reform. One of the active participants, Cornelia Hancock, who had worked for years in Quaker-sponsored Negro schools in the South before assuming direction of S.O.C. operations in the Sixth Ward along the Delaware River, believed that the best investigator of need was "the wood pile." Philip Garrett, an S.O.C. vice president, chaired a city-wide committee to promote "Provident Habits."[10]

Through the end of the nineteenth century the Friends' view of the poor reflected considerable class bias. Their distrust of the city and its influence prompted them to work for the imposition of measures of social control over urban behavior, but most of the prohibitive measures they urged were those which attracted support from other Protestant denominations. Friends' reputation for "doing good" had been made nearly a century before; many of the institutions they created at the time of the nation's birth found it difficult to adapt to the changing needs of the urban populace. Their alienation from the city—from its economic norms, its corruption, its changing moral standards, its very diversity in bigness—prompted them to criticize change, but to abstain from dealing with it. They embraced old ways and old standards. And instead of looking within the city of Philadelphia itself for their primary field of benevolence, they sought out traditional recipients of their aid even when this philanthropy took them far from the Quaker city.

As veteran critics of the treatment meted out to Indians by Americans as they moved westward, Friends maintained a justifiable pride in their own tradition of just treaties and respect for Indian rights. Reduced in numbers nationally to less than a third of a million, the original Americans had been driven to the plains and mountains of the West through attrition and broken promises. The Indian wars at the conclusion of the Civil War brought this problem into sharper focus. They prompted Friends in Philadelphia to shed some of their quietism and speak out in defense of the Indians. The Hicksite Representative Committee, impelled by the fear of wholesale war against the Western tribes, asserted in 1867 that Friends would not be "accountable if we remain supine and lend no helping hand for the amelioration of these afflicted children of the forest." Philadelphia delegates joined representatives of five other Hicksite Yearly Meetings in a conference at Baltimore which produced concrete recommendations for the consideration of Congress. Indians, the group believed, should be assigned good "tracts of well-watered country, to be secured to them in perpetuity" and be given cattle and agricultural implements. Agents should be chosen for their high moral character. The stated purpose of this policy was to "enlighten the Indians, in order that they may relinquish their nomadic habits, adopt the customs of civilized life, and accept the benign principles of Christianity." In January 1869 representatives of seven Orthodox Yearly Meetings met to discuss how they could best help their Indian friends. True to their Wilburite tenets, the Philadelphians did not participate. But their Meeting for Sufferings penned a memorial demanding justice for the impoverished and oppressed tribes. The group suggested that a policy of kindness and honesty would be far less costly to the nation than the maintenance of war against the Indians.[11]

Pressured by Friends and other religious groups to reject a military solution, Ulysses S. Grant decided to embark upon an experiment in the administration of tribal reservations. Impressed by the sincerity of the Quaker recommendations submitted to him in the early months of 1869, the new President placed the burden on Friends to put their sentiments into action. By entrusting the administration of large sections of Western lands occupied by the Indians to the Quakers, Grant hoped to put an end to the mistreatment of the tribes. Asked to nominate sixteen of their own members as agents in the Northern and Central Superintendencies, the Quakers took responsibility for close to 25,000 reservation Indians in Nebraska and Kansas. As one Philadelphian put it, the Society was "arraigned on trial" before the world to give concrete support to its testimonies. While the President continued to make military appointments to some agency posts, he was sufficiently persuaded of the merits of the Quaker approach to ask eleven other denominations to assume similar responsibilities for several of the other Western tribes in 1870.[12]

Mindful of the corruption and exploitation which had marked the Indian administration before 1869, Friends went to great lengths to guarantee a just regime. Agents and other employees were screened carefully before appointment, and some were eliminated for the mere hint of fiscal malfeasance or associations with the liquor interests. The Indian Committee of the Hicksite Yearly Meeting in Philadelphia took on the staffing and direction of two Nebraska agencies. Thomas Lightfoot, a member of the Upper Dublin Meeting, went to the Great Nehama Agency, where the Iowa and Sac and Fox tribes were living. The other agency—the Otoe—was assigned to Albert L. Green. Besides collecting clothing and supplies for the two western outposts, the six Hicksite Yearly Meetings spent nearly $60,000 to assist the Indians in Nebraska in the ten-year period between 1869 and 1879; over a third of the total was donated by Philadelphians. Among the Orthodox, an Associated Executive Committee on Indian Affairs was organized in Damascus, Ohio, in 1869. When Philadelphia Yearly Meeting refused to participate, a local Indian Aid Association was created to channel the interest of those who wanted to contribute to the Executive Committee's work in Kansas. Because the Orthodox effort was more centralized, Philadelphia contributors did not develop a direct personal involvement. Their financial contributions were also less than those of the Hicksites; expenditures of the Aid Association averaged between $2,500 and $3,000 a year.[13]

A belief in the nobility of Indian character attracted some Philadelphians to the cause. Others supported the agents' efforts because of the long-standing tradition of friendship between Quakers and Indians. The letters which the agents and their wives penned to Philadelphia describing the conditions of the tribes under their care prompted others to take a new interest in the Indians. After reading Mary Lightfoot's dispatches from the Great Nehama Agency, the affluent Mary Jeanes became a tireless worker and frequent contributor to the relief and educational programs of that Nebraska agency. Deborah Wharton not only was among the most active gathering clothing for distribution among the Friends' western charges, but even paid a visit to the Lightfoots in 1873 to observe the agency at first hand. Other Philadelphians took a special interest in individual Indian children and began sending clothing for their personal use. When the educational endeavor enabled the youngsters to write letters of thanks, the Eastern donors received especially gratifying evidence of the success of their philanthropy.[14]

If the initial impetus for Friendly philanthropy came from sentiments of love and sympathy, the continuation of Quaker support resulted from the growing conviction that the Indians must be educated. When the Otoes failed to occupy houses constructed for some of them, Philadelphians who had given the supplies and paid the craftsmen grew anxious. When he learned that the Otoes preferred not to remain rooted in one place and had plans for migrating to the Indian Territory (Oklahoma), John Saunders expressed singular discouragement and instructed Agent Green to impress upon the Otoes "how unsettled" Eastern Friends had become over this situation. The Orthodox group acknowledged how strong the nomadic trait was among the tribes and considered appointing an agent who would travel with them in their migrations, but the difficulty of finding a Friend suitable for such an assignment dissuaded them. By "education" the Quakers meant the inculcation of the dominant white culture's values. Nomadic habits and common property were not among them. In urging the end of tribal loyalties, the Friends sought to convert their charges into small, land-holding farmers who worked hard, saved their earnings, and respected private property.[15]

The Indians did not even show respect for personal items such as clothing, which they threw away as soon as it was soiled or torn. Samuel Jeanes believed Friends would withdraw the hand of philanthropy if the Indians did not learn the arts of repair and laundering, which he regarded as important steps in the direction of civilization. Thomas Lightfoot reported a more serious unconcern for property; his charges readily gave away their ponies and other goods and displayed far more interest in the custom of "pipe dancing." To enforce a proper respect for property he found it necessary to depose those tribal chiefs who were discontented with these values of white culture. Often Lightfoot appointed younger men in their place to win acceptance of the "new ways." Convinced of the correctness of their own norms, Friends could not see the degrading effects these moves had upon social relations within the Indian community. But in pressing the standards of individual initiative upon the tribes, the Quakers saw that common action and community responsibility might be sacrificed. They did urge the agents to try to strike a balance between these conflicting values; some suggested an occasional compromise with Indian ways to ease the transition.[16]

There was always the danger that too much charitable relief might imperil the development of industry and simplicity. As William Canby Biddle put it.

> Of course we all understand that our object is to improve the Indians and in helping them to avoid everything that would tend to prevent them from aiding themselves. . . . We must be careful to avoid pauperizing them, which would result if we aided those who were voluntarily idle, so as to make them as comfortable as those who are industrious.

The Hicksite Yearly Meeting noted in 1872 that the Otoes were supporting a teacher, a blacksmith, and mill shops, all with their own funds. They lacked money to pay a farmer; the Meeting considered supplying it, but Friends may have thought this would endanger Otoe initiative, for they decided merely to request the agent to encourage the pursuit of agriculture. Deborah Wharton insisted that only necessary articles be sent to the Indians, fearing that "artificials" might discourage proper training in what was valuable. Two years after she had begun teaching, Mary Lightfoot claimed that "not a vestige of Indians costumes [such] as blankets, leggings, shrouds, or paint ever enter our school room."[17]

Hicksite "practical righteousness" placed such items as soap and water before the preaching of Christian doctrine. Thomas Lightfoot was proud that his charges began washing themselves and their clothing for the first time in the seventies. Orthodox agents induced the Kiowas, Comanches, and Apaches to sign pledges of total abstinence from tobacco and liquor. They impressed them also with their parental and filial duties. Disturbed to hear that Indian women were ill-treated, Friends urged a division of labor between the sexes more in tune with standards of genteel Philadelphia homes. Mary Jeanes sought to change tribal attitudes by sending men's clothing which required sewing to the agencies: "If the men value clothing it will give the women and girls [who received instruction in sewing] a higher value, showing place and labor better suited to the sex than outdoor work." Thomas Lightfoot tried to impress upon his charges the idea that it was disgraceful for a man to strike his wife. To secure obedience on this score, he attempted to instill a sense of shame in those who mistreated women. In their concern for assimilation, however, those financing the benevolence stopped short of racial amalgamation. One wrote Mary Lightfoot that she should try to prevent intermarriage between whites and Indians, citing the strange results of race mixing she had observed when on a charitable mission in South Philadelphia.[18]

A few years into their work in Kansas and Nebraska, Friends began to realize that their idealization of the Indians had not prepared them for some of the harsh realities of frontier life. They hoped both to subdue Indian contentiousness with love and to gain respect by fair dealing, but some tribesmen had been whipped into a fighting spirit which was beyond taming by gentle Quaker agents. Thomas Lightfoot and the Orthodox agent Lawrie Tatum both had to take decisive action against "contumacious" Indians, whom they turned over to the Army for punishment. This dependence on the military for enforcement of the agents' orders was unsatisfactory from all points of view: it violated the Quaker testimony of pacifism and weakened authority on the reservations by dividing it. At last pressure from western settlers and the Army, both demanding a tougher policy, and from the two political parties hungry for patronage induced President Hayes to phase out the Grant experiment after 1877. Although some Quakers remained working with the Indians for a few years, Orthodox and Hicksite involvement in Kansas and Nebraska through agents of their faith and choosing had ended by 1885.[19]

Though outdone by the Philadelphia Hicksites in supporting the Grant experiment, the Orthodox Yearly Meeting had sustained an active Indian Committee throughout the nineteenth century. But the sole recipient of this committee's benevolence was a small farm and school at Tunessasa, in Cattaraugus County, New York, which the Philadelphians had founded in 1804 adjoining the Alleghany Reservation. While the Orthodox elders refused to involve the Yearly Meeting in the Grant experiment of 1869, they spent around $2,500 that same year to support but twenty-five students at Tunessasa. In its earliest days the school's mission had attracted the direct involvement of several Philadelphians who had felt called to work among the none-too-prosperous Senecas and descendants of Cornplanter on the Alleghany. But in the forty years after 1870 nearly all the Friends who foresook home and comfort for positions at Tunessasa were Ohio and Iowa Quakers. The ritualization of this Philadelphia benevolence into annual appropriations and reports was broken only by religious visits to the school by Quaker ministers such as Rebecca Masters and Joseph S. Elkinton. It was the religiously conservative and respected Elkinton family which had initiated the Tunessasa project and which helped sustain it so long. By 1913, with stronger public schools drawing an increasing number of older Indian children, Tunessasa was reduced to a primary institution. Critics voiced the belief that funds being spent there—over $13,000 in 1913—were needed in less narrow missionary endeavors. But this philanthropy had become so much a part of the Yearly Meeting tradition that it survived even the process of self-examination and reassessment in the Progressive Era.[20]

Friends continued to lead the attack on federal Indian policy in the years after the Grant experiment. Fearing that all the educational and agricultural improvements of the Grant era would be undone by the demoralizing influence of military governance, the Orthodox Meeting for Sufferings attacked plans for shifting the Indian Bureau from the Interior to the War Department in 1879. In the wake of a growing national concern with the subject, the same meeting prepared in 1891 a lengthy history of white atrocities against the tribes, 10,000 copies of which were distributed to the Y.M.C.A., colleges, newspapers, and magazines. Still hopeful that the benefits of individual ownership on Indian initiative would be salutary, the authors protested the new policy of alloting lands to the Indians to hold "in severalty" and the public sale of the rest of the reservation land. A handful of Philadelphians participated in the Indian Conferences sponsored by New York Friend Albert K. Smiley in the eighties and nineties which succeeded in blocking legislation providing inadequate compensation to the Indans for sale of their land.

Orthodox philanthropist Philip Garrett served on the Board of Indian Commissioners which Congress had established in 1869 to provide nonpartisan oversight of the tribes; George Vaux Jr., the lawyer, served twenty years as its chairman. Greater numbers of Friends worked through the nonsectarian Indian Rights Association, which lobbied to reform Indian policy. The Hicksite Yearly Meeting Indian Committee sponsored various modest teaching enterprises in the West and supplied some tribes with clothing and goods even in the first decade of the new century. Support was also forthcoming when Richard Henry Pratt, a Presbyterian, founded his Carlisle Indian School in 1879. Susan Longstreth, Wistar Morris, and Bryn Mawr's president James Rhoads served on the Carlisle board of trustees. Appearing before the Hicksite Indian Committee in 1896, Pratt recommended that Friends open a school in eastern Pennsylvania which would offer opportunities for Indians to escape the reservations. The Committee disagreed: "as the Indian is in the west his salvation must be mainly worked out there, and . . . it is a mistaken idea that he can in any great measure return to live in the east." That Friends held such views in the light of the successful assimilation work of boarding schools like

Carlisle shows that they felt more comfortable when the objects of their philanthropy remained at a distance from Philadelphia.[21]

Friends deserve credit for pressing the government for a fresh approach to the Indian situation at the conclusion of the Civil War. While Philadelphia Quakers were not among the most vocal national critics of federal Indian policy, they were not wanting when it came to appointing agents and financing educational enterprises. The Hicksites, less hampered by internal splits than the Orthodox were, involved themselves directly and enthusiastically in the operations of the Nebraska agencies. By introducing Friendly principles of business integrity, Quakers of both branches improved the efficiency of the Indian administration and redirected efforts so that the tribes were better served. Desirous of protecting their charges from more aggressive entrepreneurs, they advised the Indians fairly on how they should preserve their lands in the face of lucrative offers from whites. Indians on the Alleghany Reservation made it a habit to turn to Philadelphia Friends for advice on all their dealings with governments, business, and outside individuals. The schools they founded and supported offered instruction in fundamental skills. Some few Indians commenced work as settled farmers as a result of Quaker efforts. Nor can the Friends be faulted for the kind of proselytizing in which other denominations engaged. While Friends sought to encourage the Indians to accept Christianity, as usual they gave priority to more practical matters. This kept Friends out of most—but not all—competitive squabbles which diverted the energies of proselytizing denominations from more important work in their agencies.[22]

But even if their record compares favorably with that of the other churches, the Quakers displayed a marked insensitivity to most of the Indian patterns of behavior. The assimilation of the Indians into the dominant white culture may well have been the most humane way to prevent the destruction of the tribal remnants in the seventies. Yet Friends saw assimilation in these years not as an expedient to preserve the Indian peoples, but as a necessary step in their "civilization." Despite their own quarrels with the dominant patterns of American life, they would not accept cultural pluralism as an ideal for American democracy. Friends saw the norms of the Protestant ethic as constituting a higher order of civilization. Their very distance from the reservations had insulated them from the realities of Indian existence. On the one hand, it encouraged their paternalism and sense of civilizing mission; on the other, it persuaded them that love and kindness could solve all problems on the reservations. Perhaps Friends cannot be faulted for failing to embrace cultural pluralism; very few Americans did so in the seventies. But it was a measure of how far they had travelled from their own beginnings as critics of the dominant culture that Quakers in that decade were pushing for a kind of uniformity which they would have found intolerable two centuries before.

In another benevolent enterprise established on the prairies of western Canada twenty years later, Friends proved that their views of cultural deviance had changed little. The objects of this philanthropy were the Doukhobors, a Russian sectarian group which had been persecuted by Tsar Nicholas II. In 1895 Tsarist authorities had begun driving men, women, and children from their homes in the Caucasian mountains into the malarial regions around Batum as a punishment for the Doukhobor refusal to serve in the military. When the religious minority dramatically burned all their weapons, idealistic reformers took note. When Tolstoy and other Russians publicized their plight, English Friends were among the most active groups attempting to relieve the Doukhobors and arrange for their emigration. The Quakers persuaded the British government to accept around 1,100 migrants on the island of Cyprus in the summer of 1898 and guaranteed £11,000 to finance the settlement. Earlier that spring other British and Russian reformers opened negotiations with the Canadian government, then anxious to find immigrants to develop its newly opened western prairies; promises of exemption from military service sealed the bargain. It was at this point that Orthodox Friends in Philadelphia first heard of Doukhobor suffering and decided to raise funds to help them get started in the new world. By the time the first shipload of Doukhobors arrived in Nova Scotia, the Philadelphians had raised $5,575 to aid them.[23]

The ease with which pockets opened for this cause surprised those Quakers who had been laboring with little success to find financial support for needy minorities in the United States. Two years of effort netted more than $30,000 for the settlers in western Canada, and more was found in the years that followed. What explains such philanthropic enthusiasm? Besides being pacifists, the Doukhobors—the name translates as "Spirit Wrestlers"—held several religious beliefs closely akin to those of the Friends. They followed no liturgical form in their worship, nor did they have church buildings, priests, or sacraments. Central to their faith was the belief that the immanence of God was present in each man's spirit. These similarities do not adequately explain the Quaker interest, for it was known at the time that some Doukhobor practices differed markedly from those of Friends. The Doukhobor religious meeting, or sobranie, involved a great deal of emotional singing and spontaneous chanting. More significantly, they accepted the absolute rule of a leader, Peter Verigen, who received his power by inheritance. Why then did the Quakers extend the hand of benevolence so eagerly? The explanation lies in part in the early interest British Friends had shown in the Doukhobors. Correspondence between the Yearly Meetings in London and Philadelphia had been renewed in 1897 after forty-one years without communication. The Philadelphia enthusiasm for the project was in part a gesture of friendship and solidarity with English Friends who had exhausted considerable sums in financing the short-lived settlement on Cyprus. The powerful Elkinton family, which had always opposed organized philanthropy, showed considerable interest in these Russian pacifists; its stamp of approval opened the way for support even from the Wilburites in the Yearly Meeting. Joseph Elkinton himself boarded the *Lake Huron* in Halifax harbor in January 1899 and joined 1,000 of the first Doukhobor arrivals in prayer.[24]

Elkinton and his son Joseph made several visits to the Doukhobor colonies in Saskatchewan. Upon her death in 1903, Clementine Cope left $15,000 for the promotion of education among the Russian immigrants. The bequest was used to open a school at Petrofka in the fall of 1906 which was maintained by the Meeting for Sufferings for six years. The Doukhobors had shown such facility in taming the prairie wilderness that rather quickly Friends shifted the emphasis in their philanthropy from food, clothing, and implements to education. A part of the motive was to provide religious instruction which might correct what the Quakers regarded as "chimerical notions of religion" among the new settlers. But these religious differences were mild compared to the gulf that separated the Doukhobors from their Philadelphia benefactors on economic, political, and social questions.[25]

Friends had made initial donations of food, clothing, seed, and tools to the Doukhobor community as a unit, and they recognized that a communal effort was necessary for survival in the first months. But as time passed and the Doukhobors prospered, their Philadelphia benefactors urged them to shift to individual landholding, which Friends described as being "agreeable to Divine law." The Canadian government refused to register land grants save on the basis of individual ownership. Despite these pressures, about 80 percent of the immigrants under Verigen's leadership maintained a communistic economic organization. Friends soon decided to limit their benevolence to the Prince Albert Colony, where the more affluent arrivals had settled and where the shift to individual holdings had taken place; it was among them that the Quaker-financed school was established. When he visited Saskatchewan in the summer of 1902, the younger Elkinton tried to shed his "Anglo-Saxon preconceptions" and view the land question from the Doukhobor standpoint. While he decided that the Canadian authorities should not force an abandonment of communal land holdings, he concluded that the Doukhobors' "inherited tendencies and limitations sadly limit their mental outlook." Friends also argued that the newcomers should abandon their scruples about registering births and marriages with the government, explaining the necessity of surrendering some distinctive practices for the common good.[26]

Friends were distressed when a zealous group in the Doukhobor community, regarding all God's creatures as brothers, refused to use animals for work or hides for shoes and clothing. But distress turned into acute embarrassment in 1903 when the most anarchistic Doukhobors—a tiny minority called "the Sons of Freedom" —began a series of nude marches across the prairies to protest the demands of the Canadian government. The combination of the land-holding squabble and the nude demonstrations weakened Friendly concern about the Doukhobors at the very time that it was most needed. Responding to increasing hostility toward the Doukhobors among British settlers in Saskatchewan, Ottawa took a harder line in dealing with them. The Quakers offered no protest when the authorities demanded an oath of allegiance. When the

Russian immigrants refused to comply, they lost over half the lands originally granted them. This forced Peter Verigen to lead most of the community across the Rockies into British Columbia, where he hoped that his communistic experiment on purchased land could succeed unmolested. It was not until the Doukhobors' promised exemption from military service was put in jeopardy during World War I that Friends assumed the role of advocate in urging Ottawa to respect the pacifism of the settlers.[27]

The Friends provided no educational assistance for those Doukhobors who rejected American individualism because their offers were spurned by Verigen. They were probably correct in attributing his opposition to education to a desire to keep his followers ignorant and dependent upon his leadership. But that was not the whole story. The fear that the Quakers would use schools to dissuade young Doukhobors from following their faith prompted Verigen to reject their offer. Friends had occasionally left a decidedly unfavorable impression upon the objects of their benevolence. The younger Joseph Elkinton made clear that he thought of the Doukhobors as "reliable servants." He even asked some young girls in one settlement if they would be interested in returning to Philadelphia with him to become domestics. The Russian reformer Bonch-Bruevich accused the Friends of "arrogant benevolence." Instead of turning to philanthropic enterprises at home, the Philadelphians persisted in their efforts to provide an education for those who had migrated to British Columbia. Frustrated by Verigen, they whined about "the dwarfing influence of the crafty Doukhobor leader." Canadian educational officials finally persuaded them to drop their plans for a school at Thrums in the Kootenay Valley.[28]

As with the Indians, Friends had placed the emphasis in their philanthropic efforts upon assimilation. Perhaps the pacifism they shared with the Russian sectarians led the Philadelphians to expect a ready acceptance of all their values. While their unhappiness with the settlers' land-holding arrangements is understandable, the Quakers' lack of sympathy for Doukhobor desires to maintain their community free from alien interference is decidedly less so. Tsarist oppression had forged the Doukhobor community in Russia just as Anglican and royal persecution had welded together a Quaker community in England two centuries earlier. But forgetful of much of their own past—of early Friends who had gone naked as a sign into English cities in the 1650s, of refusals to swear allegiance to Stuart kings and the Anglican Church—Friends ignored these similarities.

While the Quakers had been marketing the values of the Protestant middle class among minorities on the distant plains, a more significant challenge to the hegemony of those norms was developing within their own city. The influx of Irish, German, and British immigrants during the middle of the nineteenth century had accounted for a major share of Philadelphia's growth, adding significantly to the labor force upon which its industrialization was predicated. The large Irish contingent in the city's foreign-born population which had prompted nativist violence in the 1840s maintained its dominance throughout the century; even in 1900 the Irish constituted a third of the foreign born in Philadelphia. The Irish presence had assured the rapid growth of the Roman Catholic Church; new patterns in immigration, which were first made manifest in the nineties, promised to vastly increase the Catholic population. Italians, Poles, Austrians, and Hungarians in increasing numbers chose to settle in Philadelphia in the new century. The religious census of 1916 revealed nearly a half million Catholics in the city. By 1910, the presence of 76,900 Russians—most of them Jews—in the waterfront wards along the Delaware added to the complexity of the alien elements in the Quaker city. To some Protestants these developments threatened the survival of American civilization. Attacks upon the nation's immigration policy rose sharply as nativist organizations such as the American Protective Association and the Immigration Restriction League were founded in the Midwest and New England. A few Philadelphia voices were raised to join this chorus.[29]

Fears about the consequences of unrestricted immigration were reflected by editorial writers of some of the city's newspapers in the nineties. But no consistent response to the immigrant question emerges from Philadelphia Quakerism in the late nineteenth and early twentieth centuries. In some instances, Friends defended groups of the foreign born from their detractors, while on other occasions they expressed doubts about the nation's ability to absorb so many newcomers. Many upper-class Philadelphians felt that impoverished immigrants were taking over parts of the city which had familiar associations in their youth and therefore were rightfully theirs. This sentiment received classic statement when authoress Elizabeth Robins Pennell visited the Fifth Ward, where she had grown up. In a gilt-edged memoir of the glories of a now lost genteel urban civilization, she wrote:

It is the Russian Jew who, with an army of aliens at his back—thousands upon thousands of Italians, Slavs, Lithuanians, a fresh emigration of negroes from the South, and statistics alone can say how many other varieties—is pushing and pushing Philadelphians out of the town.

Mrs. Pennell's outrage no doubt struck a responsive chord in some of her Quaker readers.[30] Those who had the widest interest and experience beyond the boundaries of the Quaker community were most susceptible to the growing nativism. But just as Friends had shown reluctance to join other political movements, they eschewed organized nativism of the Immigration Restriction League variety as too political. Other allegiances restrained them as well. The city's commercial and industrial enterprises' continued demand for a cheap labor supply had long held in check arguments for closing the door to foreign workers.[31] Traditions of benevolence for Negroes and Indians inclined the Quakers to a reserved spirit of sympathy for these new minorities when attacks were levelled against them. And Friends did not articulate demands for the assimilation of immigrants as clearly as they had done in their dealings with the Indians and Doukhobors.

In the late sixties Orthodox Friends expressed concern about possible corrupting effects on the "original population" of the increasing numbers of Chinese entering the United States with "their demon-worshipping paganism." Yet eleven years later, when Congress considered excluding the Chinese, these same Friends rose to their defense. *The Friend* lauded the Oriental contribution to the prosperity of the Pacific states and characterized the newcomers as "docile and intelligent, and proverbially industrious." In commending President Rutherford B. Hayes for his veto of the 1879 measure, the Quakers characterized the exclusion of Chinese immigrants as contrary to Christian principles and the ideals enunciated in the Declaration of Independence. In indignant editorials Orthodox periodicals provided detailed reports of atrocities against Chinese laborers in the Western states. Gurneyite support of the

Chinese is quite understandable; their growing interest in foreign missionary activity prompted a concern over the reaction to exclusion in China. But the quick reversal in attitude toward the Chinese by conservative Friends who opposed foreign missions is less explicable. The violence meted out to Orientals in mining and railroad construction camps probably contributed.[32]

The strong anti-Catholic strain in American nativism had grown less significant in Eastern cities by the last three decades of the nineteenth century. Friends had displayed little sympathy for Roman Catholics in Philadelphia during the urban riots of the tumultuous forties and they continued to view Romanism in the seventies as a "clogging, deadening influence." But while some Quakers could still use phrases such as "priest-ridden" to describe Catholic communities even in the first decade of the new century, criticism of Rome diminished significantly in the eighties and nineties. Friends in the temperance movement had found allies in St. Paul Bishop John Ireland and the Catholic Total Abstinence Union. Fears of a Catholic quest for temporal power abated as the Papacy lost sovereignty over much Italian territory. And as Friends saw increasing numbers of Catholic children attending the public schools, they abandoned their previous concern about the Americanization of Catholic immigrants. The Baltimore celebration of the Catholic Centennial in 1889 produced favorable comment, and the Church and Pope Leo XIII won plaudits for their growing liberalism. By 1893 the *Friends' Review* was favorably quoting Philadelphia Archbishop Patrick Ryan's public encouragement of Christian unity for philanthropic endeavor.[33]

Nativist appeals to Anglo-Saxon racial superiority won few converts among the Quakers. A handful of the more affluent Friends found models for their life style in the English country gentry, but these celebrations of Anglo-Saxon distinctiveness included no invidious comparisons to the less pure races as Boston Brahmin pronuncements did. *The Friend* warned that unity of Anglo-Saxon peoples could promote racial antagonism and rivalries which would inevitably lead to war. In 1901, in denouncing allegations of a "yellow peril" from Japan, it concluded that "we are not indebted to our whiteness for our civilization, but to Christianity for all that is good in it." Rufus Jones had ridiculed the idea of America's taking up the "white man's burden" in the Philippines and the

Caribbean two years earlier, pointing to white atrocities against Georgia Negroes as proof against the claim of Anglo-Saxon superiority. As pacifist anti-imperialists and advocates of Philippine independence, Friends rejected the notion that Anglo-Saxon peoples should take responsibility for the guidance of so-called "lesser breeds" on other continents. A few voices could be heard within the Quaker community which echoed the popular racial distinctions. Philip Garrett, president of the Philadelphia Society for Organizing Charity, made the often-used distinction between "old" and "new" when he compared the influence of morally superior British, Scandinavian, and German immigrants on American society to that of Italian "banditti" and fruit vendors; yet Garrett was quick to admit that all Italians were not alike. Haverford College instructor William Draper Lewis, who offered innovative courses in politics and sociology in the early nineties, proclaimed the superiority of the Aryan race. In spite of Lewis's popularity with many Haverford alumni, he was unable to win acceptance of these racial views among the leaders of the Society of Friends. Yet when racial matters ceased to be abstract, Quaker colorblindness on this issue nearly buckled under the strain. Late in 1890, a recently converted Japanese Quaker and the daughter of a prominent Arch Street Friend sought the approval of that Meeting to marry. The Meeting gave its approval only after two applications and a lengthy examination of the couple. Arch Street's decision to ignore her parents' opposition, which in this case came from its most active and influential minister, measured the Quaker reluctance to give credence to the popular views of racial distinctiveness.[34]

The immigration policy which won early Quaker support was that of selectivity. Because he believed that the flow of immigrants was "conducive to industrial well-being," Philip Garrett thought it necessary "to keep the current healthy." Alarmed by the increasing numbers of newcomers depending on the charitable resources of American cities, he told the National Conference on Charities and Correction in 1888 that stricter laws were needed to bar contract labor. He advocated an increase in the head tax, more stringent administration by Treasury officials, and clear exclusion of criminals and anarchists. A decade earlier the editor Wilmer Atkinson had urged the establishment of "a quarantine at every seaport for testing the moral health of every immigrant and require him to show wherein he is worthy . . . to become a fit subject of our hospitality." While Atkinson did not specify the diseases he hoped to bar, he and his fellow Hicksites in the temperance movement were sure that the decline in sobriety was tied to the increase in the foreign population. Friends also expressed fears that immigrants were unprepared for the responsibilities of citizenship and that they would be unable to distinguish between despotism and freedom. Like other Mugwump reformers, Friends saw the immigrant populace as the political base for urban bossism.[35] But through the end of the nineteenth century, most Quakers clung to the view that immigration in itself was a positive economic good. The distinctions they made between good and bad immigrants had less to do with religion, racial background, or country of origin than with social behavior and ideology.

The possibility of threats to the established order prompted increased attention to immigrants after the Haymarket Riot in Chicago. The *Friends' Review* commented that the anarchists executed for having caused police deaths in that fray "well deserved the extremest punishment of the law." When the Pullman strike crippled the nation's railroads in 1894, Rufus Jones placed the responsibility on the foreign born:

During the early years of the nation's History the people of the Old World were welcomed to our shores, and many of our best citizens came from countries where their rights and liberties were interfered with. . . . But the strikes and court records have been showing that we are receiving hordes of the worst type of human beings from the shores of the Old World. Our cities are being populated with material which cannot be assimilated to our free institutions, and it is now becoming evident that in many cases we have opened our doors to receive paupers, criminals, and red-handed anarchists.

He admitted that foreigners could not be blamed for all the nation's difficulties, but he thought "the number of men engaged in recent riots who bore foreign and unpronounceable names is cause for solicitude in this direction." Like many of the scholars and religious leaders of the Social Gospel movement with whom he was in contact, Jones looked upon immigrants as a threat to the political, social, and economic order.[36]

Despite these outbursts of nativist sentiment, Friends in Philadelphia never addressed themselves formally to the problem of immigrant assimilation in the city. They spoke of the subject only in abstract terms, as in 1909 when the Hicksite Yearly Meeting listed assimilation as one of several issues of national concern. Individual Friends such as Charles Pugh worked through the Y.M.C.A. to develop Americanization classes and other assistance for the newcomers, but he did so as a labor-relations expert and vice president of the Pennsylvania Railroad, which employed so many recent immigrants. Not only did Friends fail to create social institutions specifically for the foreign born, they even moved existing agencies out of neighborhoods suddenly dominated by immigrants. The Twelfth Street Meeting had run a school for Negro children at 718 Catharine Street since 1884, but the influx of Italians and Jews after 1900 transformed the neighborhood. Blacks walking to the school were pelted with stones by immigrant waifs. In 1918, Friends moved the school to a location nearer its Negro constituency. Most Quakers agreed with an article which the *Friends' Intelligencer* reprinted in 1915 asserting that compared to immigrants, blacks were under greater disabilities because of slavery and therefore more deserving of Quaker benevolence.[37]

When confronted with the daily needs and problems of Indians and Doukhobors—and Negroes as well—the Quakers became eager assimilationists. They urged the adoption of middle-class norms as a positive and dispassionate civilizing act, not as a defense of American culture against the polluting influence of inferior ways. The foreign born arriving in Philadelphia did not attract any particular attention in Friendly circles. There was no special persecution or mistreatment of these immigrants to alert Friends to their needs. The Quakers saw them not as a threat, but merely as an addition to that "class" of Philadelphia's population which performed the less attractive tasks underlying the city's industrial and commercial development. Most Friends accepted the need for the continued influx of European laborers as a prerequisite to the city's prosperity—a prosperity in which they had a direct interest. When this influx threatened their own concerns, Friends naturally began to doubt the workability of unrestricted immigration. When the needs of the foreign born taxed existing charitable institutions, some Quakers urged a greater selectivity at American ports of entry. Yet the Friends never moved to create social agencies to deal with the wants of immigrant communities. The threat of industrial violence produced a search for scapegoats; the foreign born received the brunt of the blame for strikes and riots in American cities particularly in the nineties. But the violence which had struck in Chicago and Pittsburgh did not spread to Philadelphia. This relative calm and the return of national prosperity after 1896 restored confidence and kept the Quakers from joining the restrictionist crusade.

CHAPTER 6 | Tutoring the Freedmen

Among all the disadvantaged groups in America, it was the black minority which elicited the strongest and most consistent benevolence on the part of the Quakers in Philadelphia. Quaker interest in blacks had a long history. The earliest protest against slavery in North America had emanated from the group of Quaker artisans in Germantown in 1688. Attacks upon "the peculiar institution" begun by John Woolman in the mid-eighteenth century had eventually led Philadelphia Yearly Meeting to threaten disownment of members who continued to hold slaves. Friends had also taken the lead in early abolitionist activities. But as the voice of abolitionism became more shrill and the responses to it more violent, conservative Friends had drawn back. Some had continued to agitate for emancipation through the Pennsylvania Abolition Society, but the Orthodox Yearly Meeting warned in 1837 that their vocal enthusiasm would lead to violence and a compromise of Quaker distinctiveness. Many Philadelphia Friends were frightened by a mob's burning of Pennsylvania Hall in 1838. A growing fear that political agitation would lead to war severely limited Quaker anti-slavery activity in the forties and fifties. Nonetheless, some evangelical Friends at Twelfth Street boycotted the products of slave labor through the Free Produce movement, while their rural counterparts converted their homes into stations on the "underground railway."[1]

Even before the Civil War Friendly concern for the black minority in their own city had received concrete institutional expression. Orthodox Friends had founded the Association for the Care of Colored Orphans in 1822, when feeling against Negroes was so great that the group had to wrap its efforts in secrecy. Its orphanage, "The Shelter," had an annual budget of approximately $10,-000 in the Civil War decade and housed seventy children in its commodious quarters in West Philadelphia. Its charges—between eighteen months and eight years in age—were schooled within the institution and eventually indentured out to homes in Philadelphia. Operating without state aid, The Shelter derived income from invested funds. It operated in the city until 1914, when the directors decided to move it to a rural location in Delaware county. A similar institution had been founded in 1855 by the Hicksites to end the practice of selling the labor of black children taken from the Almshouse. The Home for Destitute Colored Children was established in a residence on the Darby Road outside the city where approximately forty youngsters lived under the direction of a Quaker couple. Two other Orthodox agencies, the Home for the Moral Reform of Destitute Colored Children and the Emlen Institution for the Benefit of Children of African and Indian Descent, were at work in the middle of the nineteenth century. By 1903 neither remained open; their funds were made available to needy black children through other institutions in the city.[2]

Quaker relief for blacks did not always flow through formal agencies. Lucretia Mott reported that members of the Race Street Meeting prepared gift packages of clothing, toys, and candy for poor black families in the city each Christmas; some at that season gave turkeys to homes for the aged and orphanages. In one of these, Friends had a significant interest. Opened in the last year of the Civil War, the Home for Aged and Infirm Colored Persons was designed to relieve "that worthy class of colored persons who have endeavored through life to maintain themselves, but from various causes are finally dependent on the charity of others." The home's board was nondenominational, but Orthodox and Hicksite Friends played a major role in its direction. The moving spirit behind the institution was a successful black lumber merchant, Stephen Smith, who provided most of the funds for the new quarters adjacent to Fairmount Park into which the home moved in the early seventies. By 1892 it housed 107 old people and had an annual budget of nearly $25,000. The Hicksites also sponsored infant schools—an early example of the modern-day care center—to assist Negro working mothers. And an Orthodox group ran the Bethany Mission for Colored People (1856) in the eastern section of the 15th

Ward.[3] For the 22,000 blacks in Philadelphia in the sixties Friends had built a structure of benevolence which did much to meet their special needs.

The relief proferred to blacks was primarily available on a segregated basis. In 1868 the Arch Street Meeting was administering a trust fund created three decades earlier for the education of poor white children. When the Friends' Home for Children was founded by a group of Hicksites in 1881, it too had a "whites only" policy. The Penn Sewing School opened its classes in the Race Street meetinghouse to Negro girls in the late sixties; this produced an exodus by four offended white students who insisted they had learned in their churches that if exposed to blacks "they would be burnt up." Quaker eagerness to attract needy whites to their agencies prevented the ready abandonment of the tradition of segregation. But Friends were earnest advocates of desegregation in public transportation. Quakers levelled attacks against the city's streetcar lines and the Philadelphia and West Chester Railroad for their Jim Crow policies. After attempts by prominent citizens to convince the streetcar owners and the courts to tackle the issue proved fruitless, the Hicksite Representative Committee, in a departure from its usual silence on public issues, petitioned the state legislature to terminate the practice in 1867. Favorable action in Harrisburg later that same year ended the policy of restricting the Negroes to certain streetcars.[4]

The Friends' philanthropic project for blacks which produced the greatest enthusiasm in the sixties was far from the Quaker city. As slaves in the Southern states came under the supervision of the Union Army during the early years of the war, news of their wants produced a ready response among Northern abolitionists. Boston was the first to send supplies and teachers to the sea islands of South Carolina, which came under Union control in 1861. A Philadelphia Committee raised funds to support this relief work at Port Royal and later constituted itself as the Pennsylvania Freedman's Aid Society. Several Friends participated in its funding and served on the board, but distinctive Quaker activity did not begin until the spring of 1862, when women's aid committees were established by both the Orthodox and Hicksites. The two Quaker groups independently collected nearly 10,000 garments and sent them along with approximately $7,000 for other supplies to several locations throughout the South in the first year of their work. Encouraged by the Emancipation Proclamation and the changing climate of opinion toward blacks in the North, young Quakers in the Philadelphia area were prompted by conscience to join the effort. Reuben Tomlinson foresook a clerkship in a Philadelphia bank to take part in the experiment on St. Helena Island in South Carolina. Cornelia Hancock left her home in southern New Jersey to serve as a nurse in a freedmen's hospital in Washington, D.C.[5]

It was not until late 1863 that men from the Philadelphia Meetings organized to support the cause. Prior investigation of needs and the securing of reliable agents had always been Quaker prerequisites to commitment. But establishing such contacts in the midst of the confusion of the freedmen's camps was no easy task. Six prominent Orthodox Friends visited the South well before organizational steps were taken. Marmaduke Cope toured the Peninsula area of Virginia and reported that Negroes living near Yorktown needed instruction in the rudiments of domestic economy and lacked the most basic of farm implements. Other Friends reported the universal want of proper clothing and medical aid in the freedmen's camps. But more than evidence of need and the search for reliable contacts had slowed the move to organization. Quietist power had prevented the Yearly Meetings from creating their own committees to funnel aid to the South. Even older Friends in the evangelical Twelfth Street Meeting remained cautious. When a structure was finally created to deal with the problem, the impetus came from younger Friends. Among the founders were twenty-seven-year-old John B. Garrett and his brother Philip, two years older, Joel Cadbury Jr., twenty-five, and Edward Bettle Jr., twenty-two.[6]

They created what eventually came to be known as the Friends' Freedmen Association. In the first few months the group raised $53,800, which went to supply the needs of freedmen at Hampton, Yorktown, and Norfolk, Virginia, and New Bern, North Carolina. Seeds, agricultural implements, hospital supplies, slates and school books, as well as bundles of clothing were collected and shipped by packet to the Chesapeake for delivery to an agent at Yorktown, where 7,500 of the "contrabands" were living. The Hicksites created a similar agency—the Association for the Aid and Elevation of the Freedmen—in January 1864. They concentrated their efforts around Washington, but some of their aid went to communities on the Peninsula and in South Carolina. The work of preparing clothing and goods involved more and more Friends directly. Volunteers staffed the Friends' Freedmen Association headquarters near the Arch Street meetinghouse, where systematized division of labor speeded the preparation of garments. Sewing groups gathered in meetinghouses throughout the city. Lucretia Mott rejoiced in the alteration of public sentiment: "We are really beginning *to do something!*" It amused her to see "the Biddles, Parishes, Whartons, and such like alive to the subject" which she had agitated in near-isolation for decades. One Race Street Friend knit over two hundred pairs of stockings for the freedmen. Others made lengthy visits to Negro soldiers in local hospitals several times a week.[7] Expression of the deep Quaker concern for black people which had been dammed up for over two decades by fears of war and violence came flooding forth as hostilities came to an end in 1864 and 1865.

As they dealt with the freedmen's needs, Friends confronted social and economic realities in the South which involved them in other Reconstruction efforts. The Orthodox women's group investigated poorhouses in the Richmond area crowded with rural blacks who wandered to the city in the aimless mobility of that first summer of freedom. To relieve pressure on these institutions the group opened an orphanage on the outskirts of the city; in a year's time this new facility was so overcrowded that 150 children were brought north to Philadelphia and "placed out" in receptive homes. Andrew Johnson's amnesty program of 1865 undercut hopes for Negro landownership by ousting the freedmen from land they had begun to farm and returning to private ownership many school buildings which Friends had staffed in the wake of their relief efforts. When Northern protests failed to gain support, groups in Boston and New York made private purchases. Philadelphia Friends made a modest move in this direction when they bought an eighty-acre plot on the Peninsula and a smaller one of thirty-four acres at Greensboro, North Carolina. The Friends' Freedmen Association granted ten-year mortgages to aid black purchasers. By 1890 a section of Greensboro called Warnersville, to honor the Quaker teacher Dudley Warner, was a prosperous black community of more than five hundred persons.[8]

Appalled by high prices being charged by contractors authorized by the Army to sell to blacks on the Virginia Peninsula, Orthodox Friends decided to provide an alternative. Establishing stores at Hampton and Yorktown, the Quakers sold goods at close to cost to the freedmen in the region. The response was so overwhelming and the turnover of goods so great that a net surplus of $3,000 remained when they closed in 1866. Most of the sales, which totalled nearly $217,000 in two years, were modest furnishings for the small cabins into which blacks had moved. Friends sought to shield the Negroes from the unscrupulous; they hoped in the process to set an example of integrity in economic relationships for the freedmen. From the very first the Friends' Freedmen Association sought to develop in blacks habits of thrift and industry which had made the Quakers themselves so prosperous. Friends had idealized the freed slaves, and it shocked them to hear that some Negroes equated freedom with idleness. When the news first reached Philadelphia that some blacks were unwilling to enter into labor contracts, Friends placed the blame on Southern planters. Only gradually did reports from reliable agents persuade Quakers of the necessity for the Freedmen's Bureau compulsory contracts. These reports reinforced the conviction that an educational effort was needed which would inculcate proper attitudes toward work, thrift, and property. As long as they were supplying material aid, Friends were haunted by fears that too generous charity would maintain laziness among the freedmen.[9]

Philadelphia Friends approached this benevolent enterprise with a deep sense of obligation. They thought in terms of a debt owed black Americans for the years of oppression they had endured in bondage. And in their eminently practical way the Quakers regarded relief and educational assistance modest down payments on an obligation too great to be cleared from the ledgers of conscience overnight. Slavery had been a sin not only for those who perpetuated it in the South but for Northerners whose acquiescence had assured its survival. Quaker silence in the last quarter-century of anti-slavery agitation contributed to guilt feelings in the sixties. Acts of repentance were needed to assuage that guilt. As an 1863 plea for funds put it: "we need for our own souls' sake as well as for their perishing bodies to keep the fountains of mercy and compassion in full flow."[10]

Since the Philadelphians regarded slavery as "a state bordering on barbarism," they saw education of the former bondsmen as a matter of considerable importance. Reports from agents such as Reuben Tomlinson and teachers like Yardley Warner confirmed Quaker suspicions about Negro vice and immorality. But most Friends agreed with Warner's view of these frailties as justification for love and charity. Joseph Parrish urged Quakers to acknowledge the freedman as a man with moral responsibility: "He is an entire man—rude it is true, dwarfed in intellectual vigor it may be; and yet his entire manhood is undoubted." Once acknowledged, this imposed clear duties on Friends to lead the freedmen "to holy Christian living." Daily Bible readings were instituted in all the schools they created for blacks in the South, and teachers were well supplied with religious tracts. Yet Friends were never guilty of the proselytizing which turned Baptist and Methodist missionaries into zealous competitors for black additions to their membership rolls.[11]

Schooling and the advice of Friendly teachers had social and political purposes as well. Parrish had urged Quakers to encourage and support those institutions in the Negro community which would afford social stability. He recommended particularly the teaching of conjugal and parental duties to strengthen the family. A circular letter read to the South Carolina freedmen in 1867 adjured them to have legal marriages performed so that they might attain "that station in religious and civil society which you should occupy." An Orthodox report seven years later expressed gratification at the number of unions formed under slavery which had been solemnized in churches since the war. Friends had voiced some hesitancy about granting suffrage to the freedmen, but when Radical Reconstruction assured blacks the right to vote, it gave Quaker schools an urgent task to prepare their charges. Teachers were directed by the Friends' Freedmen Association Instruction Committee to inform the freedmen of their duties as "citizen rulers of a great republic; let them understand that when they send men to represent them in National or state councils they should be full advocates of free schools for all, freedom of worship, equality before the law, and whatever goes to emancipate men from vice and to make a great people powerful for good and not for evil." The absence of distinctive Quaker views in this injunction reflected the Friends' unwillingness to impose more than general Protestant principles upon their untutored charges. The curricular diet included large servings of the gospel of hard work, thrift, and respect for property. Ultimately its aim was to offer blacks a chance to gain independence and the means for advancement in a competitive world.[12]

In the first flush of enthusiasm Friends opened elementary schools as rapidly as they could staff them. The Hicksites supported operations in northern Virginia around Washington and on the coast of South Carolina. In 1869 their association was maintaining ten schools with a student enrollment of 632. The Orthodox program reflected the greater affluence of its members. The same year, some 3,700 black students received instruction in thirty-seven schools in southern Virginia and North Carolina under the aegis of the Friends' Freedmen Association of Philadelphia. Overall expenditures by the two associations that year totalled nearly $25,000. The Orthodox group alone poured more than a quarter of a million dollars into relief and instruction between 1863 and 1871. When compared to the efforts of other denominations, these expenditures reveal a significant concern. The Northern Presbyterians, for example, spent a total of $56,000 for their educational effort in 1872, but that was raised in more than a thousand churches in several states. Quaker financial commitment was supplemented by individual devotion. Several of the F.F.A.'s thirty-seven institutions owed their development to visits by Yardley Warner of Germantown to black communities in Virginia and North Carolina; in 1869 he established schools in Tennessee which were later conducted by Indiana Quakers. Martha Schofield and Cornelia Hancock labored for decades in the Hicksite schools of South Carolina, where they contended with increasing hostility from Southern whites.[13]

Perhaps the most interesting of these Friends was Reuben Tomlinson, whose work in South Carolina earned him the distinction of being the only Quaker "carpetbagger" from Philadelphia. As a teacher and later superintendent on St. Helena and Ladies Islands, he showed diplomatic talents in the handling of problems of race relations. In 1865 he joined General Rufus Saxton's staff, which settled 40,000 freedmen on the coastal lands around Port Royal, and for five years he served as state superintendent of education, working with the Freedmen's Bureau to establish new schools for blacks. He maintained his membership in the Race Street Meeting but abandoned Quaker scruples to become active politically in South Carolina, representing Charleston county in the notorious 1868–69 session of the state House of Representatives, which legislated so many Radical measures. An active campaigner for the Radicals, he made an unsuccessful bid for the governorship when a split developed in their ranks in 1872. While characterized by the New York *Nation* as "sagacious and honorable," he was board treasurer of the Greenville and Columbia Railroad in 1870 when stock fraud netted the participants $2,000,000. When Wade Hampton's Redeemers took power in 1877, Tomlinson returned to the North, where he publicly chastised the federal government for failing to protect the rights of Southern blacks, who he predicted would soon be exploited and oppressed.[14]

Yet Friends had been anxious to withdraw from their role as educational entrepreneurs long before the removal of federal troops signalled the end of Reconstruction. The Orthodox association did not consider itself a permanent body, but one founded to meet an emergency situation. As early as 1868 it had laid plans to turn over its schools to the individual states. But the failures of some state legislatures to finance adequately an educational system and Quaker fears of diminished public efforts combined to postpone such action into the seventies. The 1873 depression struck a severe blow to the work of all Northern churches. The Friends' Freedmen Association turned down opportunities to hire teachers for new schools in 1873, but the panic did not force a cutback in programs as drastic as in other denominations. The Methodist Freedmen's Aid Society lost 70 percent of its budget from 1873 to 1874, while the Congregationalist American Missionary Association was nearly destroyed by the depression. Voluntary contributions to the F.F.A. fell off 17 percent from 1872 to 1873, but they remained unchanged for the three years that followed. Sustaining donor interest was more difficult once the emergency material needs of the freedmen had been met. The enthusiasm of the mid-sixties had burned itself out. Hicksites in Philadelphia were quicker to abandon the cause than other Friends. Their association received only $1,119 in contributions in 1872; thereafter ten-dollar donations were so rare that they warranted special thanks in the pages of the

Intelligencer. Henry M. Laing, the organization's treasurer, personally helped sustain most of the association's work until 1879, when he announced that its funds were completely exhausted.[15]

Having taken part in the reconstruction of the South, Philadelphia Quakers viewed with alarm reports they received at the time the Redeemer regimes came to power. One of its teachers wrote the F.F.A. from Raleigh in 1877: "The colored people ask me what has come to the people of the North, that [the freedmen] have been given over as they have been in this election, and I know not what to tell them." Reports of black fears and white atrocities crowded the pages of *The Friend* in March and April of 1877. Orthodox Friends sought some way to express their continued concern for the freedmen. Contributions to the F.F.A. rose nearly 50 percent in 1877. As late as 1880 the Orthodox group continued to sustain eighteen schools and was spending $10,000 a year to maintain them. Disappointments over the freedmen's pace of improvement had led some Northerners to question black abilities and potential. Yet Orthodox Friends in 1880 were still willing to excuse the tardy progress of blacks in the light of "their uncivilized origin, and two and a half centuries of enslavement." They decided to reassess their activities each year thereafter, but for the time being they reaffirmed their desire to wipe out the debt owed the Negro people.[16]

The growing willingness to sacrifice the freedmen to national reunion was more than a political phenomenon. Northerners who had been sympathetic to the abolitionist and Radical causes were exhausted by continued appeals for aid. While Friends may have been tardy in joining the ranks of Northern philanthropy to support the black cause, they remained more persistent in the endeavor than did others. As businessmen some of whom were dedicated pacifists, the board members of the Freedmen Association could appreciate the value of reducing tensions between the North and the South. Free-flowing trade and national unity were positive goals. But their traditional sense of apartness from the wider culture reinforced their desire to care for minorities. Friends sought no agitation of the Negro question. They determined merely to continue offering education as an open door of opportunity for the Southern freedmen. As a vehicle of Quaker concern it was so very appropriate, involving no demonstrative confrontation or use of public power. And by 1880 educational benevolence for blacks was a tradition of more than a century's duration.

In the Quaker city itself the Orthodox had been providing instruction for free blacks since 1770. That year Philadelphia Monthly Meeting, prodded from Anthony Benezet and others, had founded "The School for Black People and their Descendents." The elementary instruction it offered in the rudiments of reading, spelling, grammar, arithmetic, and geography was of some importance for blacks who were denied admission to the public schools until 1819. A substantial number attended the Raspberry Street School, as Friends called it, in the antebellum period, but increasing employment opportunities for young blacks led to diminished attendance in the sixties; by 1873 something over a hundred boys and girls were enrolled, although the school occupied a Center City building capable of handling far greater numbers. Sharing quarters around the corner on Locust Street the Joseph Sturge Mission School and the Beehive School, both founded in 1865, sought to administer to particular needs of the black community. The former offered Sunday Bible classes to blacks of all ages, while the latter taught standard elementary subjects and practical arts such as knitting and sewing to younger children. The Beehive School had 110 students under two teachers in 1881.[17] At a third Center City location the Philadelphia Association for the Instruction of Poor Children offered schooling for black girls and infants of both sexes in the Adelphi School. This Orthodox group had organized to offer instruction as early as 1807. At the end of the century it was tutoring fifty youngsters. Whites—most of them Friends—did the teaching in all these elementary institutions.

The Quakers had been aware of the need for education among adult blacks for some time. A group of young Friends had organized the Association for the Free Instruction of Adult Colored Persons in 1789. Its work had an intermittent life until 1845, but thereafter it offered rudimentary studies, "suited to the unlettered condition of the class for which they were designed." This evening instruction attracted a sizeable number of adults, particularly at the end of the Civil War, when blacks began to migrate to the city from the South. At its height the program was training 200 men and 300 women, about one-third of them freedmen. So great was the demand that the association opened a branch across the Delaware River in Camden, which it later turned over to that city's black community to run for themselves.[18]

By far the most significant educational institution created for blacks by the Orthodox Friends was the Institute for Colored Youth, the only private school offering courses for Negroes on the secondary level in Philadelphia. Chartered in 1842 as a school to prepare Negro teachers in either "school learning or in the mechanic arts and agriculture," the Institute had an enrollment of nearly 200 at the end of the Civil War. Its academic department included Latin and Greek and it improved the training in chemistry by securing a graduate of the Yale Scientific School in 1876. Friends kept in touch with those colleges which admitted blacks so as to find the most talented to serve on the faculty. Before he received appointment from the Grant administration as minister to Haiti, Ebenezer Bassett, a graduate of the Connecticut State Normal School, served for fourteen years as the institute's principal. Octavius V. Catto, his successor, was only thirty-one when he was killed in the riots which broke out in Philadelphia when blacks attempted to exercise their new Fifteenth Amendment right to vote in the election of 1871. The first two black women to receive bachelor's degrees in the United States—both at Oberlin—joined the faculty in the mid-sixties. One of them, Fanny M. Jackson, remained at the Institute for thirty-six years. As principal for twenty-seven of them, she had an important influence on Negro education in the area. The demand for black teachers in schools throughout the Philadelphia area was greater than the institute could provide. By 1888 it was estimated that three-quarters of the Negroes teaching in the area were institute graduates. The 1879 enrollment at the institute was over 300.[19]

Through the end of the 1870s Friends had established a record of providing educational opportunities for the black minority which was more consistent than that of other Northern churches with philanthropic interests. While the elementary institutions under Quaker care served largely as outlets for Friends with a calling for individual service as teachers, the Institute for Colored Youth reserved its teaching positions for black professionals who provided responsible adult models for their students. Few white Protestants had offered blacks these chances. Yet beneath the surface of

Friends' generosity lay habits of condescension, views of black inferiority, and fears of the Negro presence which undermined the possibilities for the true friendship of equals expounded in Quaker rhetoric. In the decades after 1880, pressures from the larger culture which sanctioned views of the Negro "as beast," increased legal discrimination, and wholesale lynching put a real strain on the Quaker defense of the black minority and the continuation of programs of education.

One basic defect in the Friends' dealings with Negroes was their insensitivity to black norms and traditions. Accepting prevailing views of African barbarism, Friends believed that there was little in black culture worthy of respect. In the roles of teacher and guide, they used the opportunity to bear witness to some Quaker testimonies and imposed those norms on blacks even when it hindered interracial communication or lost them pupils. Quaker abhorrence of "unnatural" emotional expression was bound to conflict with Negro behavior patterns which were an amalgam of African tradition and adaptation to slavery. In participating in a religious meeting with blacks in 1879, one Quaker minister gave unusually foreful direction to the proceedings out of fear that the blacks might give vent to their emotions or break into song. Music became an issue of considerable disagreement. When the public schools began to offer instrumental music and Friends refused to follow suit, the Raspberry Street School suffered a loss in enrollment. In 1878 Fanny Jackson requested that the subject be offered at the Institute for Colored Youth, after school hours and at student expense, but the board refused to permit it. Drawing, though banned in most schools Quakers ran for their own children, was permitted at the institute in 1867 when offered free of cost to the school. But when pressed to make it part of the regular course of study five years later, the board refused. In the eyes of many Friends the corrupting influence of these arts was sufficient to warrant their omission from the curriculum despite urgings for inclusion by teachers, pupils, and parents.[20]

Four years after Negroes had won the ballot in Pennsylvania, Quakers criticized their political aspirations, which had "led to an undue inclination for legal and forensic acquirements." Warning of the corruptions of politics, they urged blacks to pursue more solid studies. The Friends' testimony against political activity had more weight in determining this advice than assessments of the needs of the Negro community. But the advice also reflected the belief that blacks should not aim too high in preparing for occupations and presaged the later enthusiasm for industrial training. Friends displayed a singular lack of trust in the Negro professionals in their employ. So seriously did the businessmen who served as board members of the Institute for Colored Youth take their stewardship responsibilities that they passed on every book placed in the school library or chosen for classroom use, prepared examinations in consultation with the principal, and handled all discipline cases themselves. Each new course proposed by the principal was carefully scrutinized before gaining approval; many did not pass the test. Fanny Jackson, who in 1881 married Levi J. Coppin, a bishop in the African Methodist Episcopal Church, made numerous attempts to expand and diversify the institute's offerings. As an early advocate of industrial training, Mrs. Coppin may have been instrumental in persuading the board to add an industrial department in the mid-eighties. Many of her proposals were turned down for lack of funds. But the managers' caution cramped black professional initiative unduly. In the eyes of the managers, black educators were as much in need of guidance as the young who came to the Quaker schools for instruction.[21]

Many Northern churches which continued to sponsor schools and colleges for blacks in the South were confronted with a "black power" movement beginning in the nineties. At issue was the continued practice of maintaining whites in faculty, administrative, and trustee positions. Philadelphia Friends had blacks teaching in their schools rather early in their development. Seven of the seventeen teachers supported by the Hicksite association in 1871 were black; the Orthodox had twelve salaried blacks—six "teachers in charge" and six assistants—out of a teaching staff of thirty-six on the F.F.A. payroll by 1875. Yet Quaker readiness to hire black teachers can be explained more in terms of practicality than social understanding. Friends had a difficult time finding white teachers to work for the modest salaries they offered. The F.F.A. encouraged the best black students to take "Normal training" at the Danville, Virginia, school and then placed them in elementary school posts vacated by whites. By 1879 the Orthodox group expressed satisfaction with their work and asserted, "The saving in transportation alone for northern teachers is considerable and we are thankful to say the efficiency of the schools remains the same." The Christiansburg Institute in Virginia, which became the sole recipient of aid from the F.F.A. in the nineties, had an all-black faculty in 1887. Evidence suggests that Christiansburg had a black principal in the eighties as well. But positions as managers or trustees of these schools—both in the South and in Philadelphia —were entrusted only to Friends. Grassroots committees of blacks in North Carolina communities pressured the Quaker schools and often effected changes in the educational program. In one location the local committee opposed the appointment of a Negro teacher and begged a departing white to remain because it believed students would not take direction from "one of their own." Yet in another the white teacher clung tenaciously to her post, despite opposition of "the colored committee," because she believed a local Negro teacher suggested as a replacement did not come up to standard.[22]

Diminished financial support forced the Friends' Freedmen Association to abandon all its Southern elementary schools in the last two decades of the century and focus on teacher preparation at Christiansburg. A sharp reversal of attitudes had taken place in Philadelphia. In an 1884 editorial the *Friends' Intelligencer* spoke of blacks as an "emotional race" whose condition and behavior were "debased." The realistic appraisals of Southern race relations which had appeared in *The Friend* in the seventies gave way to sugar-coated testimonials from hard-working former slaves who uttered praises of the Protestant gospel of success. Celebrations of Quaker concern for slaves in more optimistic times helped assuage the guilt feelings that persisted over Northern abandonment of blacks in the South. Disappointed with the Negroes' rate of progress, many began a reappraisal of Radical Reconstruction. As Friends and other Northern reformers fought municipal corruption in their own cities, they grew increasingly critical of the waste and corruption of the Radical Southern legislatures. Francis R. Cope had been a strong supporter of schools for blacks in the South, but by the late seventies he could condone the withdrawal of Northern protection in part because of "the discredit [brought] on the whole system" by Reconstruction politics. Like many of his colleagues on the board of the Friends' Freedmen Association,

Cope was a businessman who was anxious to remove impediments to sectional harmony in the interest of trade.[23]

In the wake of the withdrawal of Northern protectors, Southern blacks became attracted by rumors of better opportunities in the West. A mass exodus from the coastal states took thousands of Negroes to Arkansas and Kansas. Friends in Philadelphia responded generously to pleas for aid for the refugees, who were taxing the resources of communities like Topeka, which was receiving 600 new migrants a week in early 1880. But as they met to coordinate their relief efforts, none saw anything salutary about such geographical shifts. One Friend suggested that they promote land schemes on the Greensboro model to assure blacks of economic independence. Another urged the Freedmen Association to send agents South to persuade blacks to remain there. The F.F.A. declared that Negroes would be better off in the South "than in untried lands." While the association did not want to limit the blacks' freedom to select their own homes, it saw a general exodus as "fraught with incalculable evil." A stable Southern labor system was naturally advantageous to national recovery from the depression of the seventies. And the exodus had raised the specter of thousands of blacks flooding into Philadelphia itself. W. E. B. DuBois estimated that close to 15,000 did drift into the Quaker city between 1875 and 1895. Most of these were destitute, and while some found employment, more burdened the charitable organizations of the city, many of which looked to Friends for support. A vast increase in Philadelphia's poor black population was something practically all Quakers wanted to prevent.[24]

Such views strongly influenced the policies of the F.F.A. in developing the Christiansburg Institute through the second decade of the twentieth century. Beginning in 1898, land purchases made possible an agricultural program at the school, and further expansion of the property advanced the F.F.A. goal of attempting to make Negroes self-supporting Southern farmers. In 1904 board member Henry S. Williams asserted that the urban environment of the North was inimical to blacks, creating converts to crime and alcoholism. The Freedmen Association termed migration from the South "a menace to society," while the black principal at Christiansburg urged Negroes to remain in the environment and occupation to which they were suited by nature. A special appropriation to improve farm equipment and employ an Agriculture Department farm demonstrator in 1914 had as its avowed purpose to stem the tide of increasing black migration. Their anti-urban bias also prompted Friends to move the Institute for Colored Youth to a farm site in Delaware county in 1903 at the very time it was serving the growing black population of Philadelphia. While the changes in both these Quaker-run schools were dictated by a reasoned policy to which the managers were converted, they reflect a marked hostility to the black presence in the Quaker city itself. If Friends expected to check the rise of the Negro population, they must have been sadly disappointed. Blacks numbered 84,459 in 1910—nearly four times the figure for 1870.[25]

The educational philosophy to which the Quakers subscribed in the nineties was that of Booker T. Washington, the black accommodationist whose Tuskegee Institute set the pattern for Negro schooling for decades. Friends had moved to provide industrial training at the Institute for Colored Youth before Washington won national prominence in 1895. Mrs. Coppin, the principal, who strongly favored this program because of the want of technical training for blacks in Philadelphia, secured a modest contribution to the program from the Negro community, which responded enthusiastically to the courses in carpentry, bricklaying, printing, cooking, and dressmaking begun in 1889. An evening session taught trades to adults. By the end of the century enrollment figures suggest a declining interest in the academic department; the managers decided to emphasize manual training and cut back on academic subjects. Christiansburg came under the influence of Washington directly in 1896, when he visited the school and recommended changes in its program. He criticized "the want of cleanliness, thrift, and order," suggested conversion to an industrial school with "simple" classroom work, and nominated a Tuskegee graduate for the principalship. Friends quickly adopted his proposals and in 1887 enunciated a school policy of "thoroughness in the rudiments and the eschewing of ultra advanced subjects." Changing its name to the Christiansburg Normal and Industrial School in 1901, the institution became a part of Washington's educational empire and henceforth drew its staff exclusively from Tuskegee and Hampton. Two years later the Freedmen Association designated the school's clientele to be "the untalented nine-tenths" of the black population.[26]

Like the industrial training offered at Tuskegee, the trades taught at Christiansburg and the Institute for Colored Youth did not keep pace with technological change. Mrs. Coppin remembered in 1913 that financial stringency had prevented the installation of machinery for industrial courses at the institute in the nineties: "The managers always refused to take any money from the State, altho [sic] it was frequently offered." Friends preferred to manage their institutions independent of outside authority, but the paucity of support from their own community compelled them to seek appropriations from Harrisburg in 1910. By then the institute had been moved to Cheyney in Delaware county. Mrs. Coppin's successor, Hugh Browne, believed that adequate integrated opportunities in the public schools made the continuation of this segregated secondary institution unnecessary. He had persuaded the board to establish a teacher training institute open only to high school graduates. Combining instruction in agriculture and academic subjects in a two-year course, the school opened with fourteen students in the fall of 1904. The following summer, the first of a series of summer school programs recommended by Washington attracted Negro teachers to the campus from the Southern states. Within a decade the number of students in the regular program had risen to 93, while 122 participated in the summer session. Attempts to secure assistance from Carnegie and the Slater Fund proved abortive, and Orthodox Friends found it increasingly difficult to finance the growing operation at Cheyney on their own. They accepted state aid and contemplated widening representation on the board to Hicksites and even non-Friends. While the Cheyney venture was designed to increase professional opportunities for blacks, it was slow to achieve this. Even in 1918 Pennsylvania did not recognize its graduates as qualified to teach in the public schools because their instruction had been vocational.[27]

Friends naturally turned to their own members to fill the schools' professional and commercial needs. The Freedmen Association refused Principal Charles Marshall's suggestion that they give the contract for building a barn to people in Christiansburg who would work with the students. Friends chose instead a more familiar builder from Bucks county, Pennsylvania. They also awarded him a contract to construct a dormitory the following year. Yet carpentry was one of the very trades they were teaching at the school. At Cheyney the managers rejected a recommendation from a local Quaker physician in 1905 that medical responsibilities at the school be entrusted to a Negro doctor living in the area. The Quaker physician received the appointment himself and consented to offer his services without charge. Financial stringency often worked against hiring a black whose position was too shaky to offer free or cut-rate services. Black professional educators, however, had gained sufficient stature that they could bargain with Friends for power over curriculum and teacher recruitment. Both Browne and his successor, Leslie P. Hill, established limits on trustee interference before accepting the principalship of Cheyney.[28]

When the institute moved to Cheyney it closed down the evening trade school which had been run in conjunction with the industrial department. Friends had hoped to move it to another location more convenient to the city's black population, but the cost of the new venture at Cheyney forced them to abandon these plans. They finally arranged to transfer the students to the Berean Training School of the Presbyterian Church. The Association for the Education of Adult Colored Persons had terminated its evening school offerings in 1890. Though the organization pointed out that five public night schools offered a similar program, it admitted that the prime reason for its decision to fold was the decline in income from its subscribers. To meet expenses in 1889, the directors had had to use some of its modest invested principal. Declining interest on the part of supporters also closed the Beehive School in 1888. The elementary institutions faced real competition from the public schools. The one at Twelfth and Pine was far better equipped than the nearby Raspberry Street School. As a result, enrollment at the latter dropped to a mere forty-seven in 1893. The committee charged with its direction recommended that the school be closed in 1900 and its endowment used for manual training of black youth. But so tradition-bound was the Arch Street Meeting that it rejected the suggestion. The school continued to exist as an outlet for women Friends called to the service of blacks for another eighteen years.[29]

A far more successful school was founded at the very time that it appeared Friends were forsaking their historic concern for blacks. Using funds bequeathed by two of its members, the Twelfth Street Meeting founded an elementary school for blacks in the Southwark section in 1884. Holding classes in the rooms of the House of Industry on Catharine Street, the Western District Colored School attracted over a hundred students a year in the formative stage of its development. The staff made periodic visits to the students' homes, where they tried to fill needs they discovered. In the wake of the 1893 depression unemployment left many black families there destitute. The managers consulted with "experts in philanthropy" and made curricular revisions at their bidding. They sent the teachers to observe methods in the public schools and kept salaries competitive with levels there. When "industrial instruction" became popular, they instituted courses in shoemaking, shoe repairing, and later carpentry for boys and instructed girls in cooking. Yet when some of these skills appeared to offer few opportunities for students, the managers readily abandoned the courses. To maintain standards in academic subjects, they invited public school teachers to prepare examinations for their students. By 1901 they had introduced calisthenics and physical education. The institution had considerable success in dealing with students who had been expelled from the public schools. Though lacking Quaker distinctiveness, the school's freshness and adaptability were in marked contrast to the moribund institution on Raspberry Street. But its ultimate success was compromised by demographic changes. The blacks who lived in Southwark in 1884 had been supplanted by Italians and Jews in the new century. Attendance began to decline after 1910.[30]

Friends generally won applause from the black community for their philanthropic and educational efforts. Richard Wright Jr., a bishop of the A.M.E. Church, excused the Quaker tradition of maintaining segregated institutions for Negroes. He believed Friends' desire was "to encourage independent action" and foster "self-confidence and opportunity." Those black institutions entirely separate from white direction have had salutary effects in promoting pride and independence. But such results could not have come from the Quaker-sponsored schools in which paternal condescension stifled black initiative and limited self-respect. Like most white Americans in the nineteenth and early twentieth centuries, Friends regarded Negroes as a class apart. It never occurred to them to integrate black youth into the schools they provided for their own children. There is no record of any Negroes enrolled in the Quaker day and boarding institutions in these years. The segregation pattern applied even to Friends' school employees. When the Westtown School erected a building in 1919 to house the unmarried men who worked on the campus, it partitioned the black quarters off from the white. Haverford and Swarthmore kept their doors closed to Negroes throughout the period. In 1905 Swarthmore admitted a black on the basis of his record but with no knowledge of his race; he was politely sent home when he arrived at the campus in September. One Quaker professor there believed that the only education suited to blacks was that which taught "the dignity of labor, the religion of common honesty, cleanliness and chastity." Yet a controversial philosophy professor, Jesse Holmes, had ultra-liberal views on interracial marriage.[31]

In judging Quaker treatment of American blacks after the seventies, it is important to consider the tenacity with which some Philadelphians held to their original concept of "the just debt" owed the Negro people. Some more affluent Friends employed that idea rather literally in writing generous checks. Orthodox merchant Joshua Baily was personally vigorous in raising funds for the Kansas refugees of the 1879 exodus. Most of the land purchases and construction of new buildings at Christiansburg were completed because of his contributions and his ability to persuade others to join him. A First-day school class of Baily's had raised funds for and corresponded with a young mulatto in Virginia in the late sixties. Baily kept in touch with him and personally financed his education through the Hampton Institute and Oberlin College. The Hicksite Anna T. Jeanes had an even greater impact on black education. While she gave the Yearly Meeting $20,000 for use in "freedmen's schools" and other humanitarian work, she channelled even more through Washington's educational empire. Her gift of $200,000 to the Southern Education Board in 1905 went to promote free schooling for both white and black. The bulk of her estate of $1,000,000 was placed in a trust which became the Rural School Fund. Income from the estate financed the work of young black women who worked as county supervisors in the attempt to upgrade schools throughout the rural South. Such individual witness on the part of Northern philanthropists was rare at the turn of the century. The personal generosity of Anna Jeanes and Joshua Baily was as much a part of the Quaker relationship with blacks as the rigid condescension displayed by others.[32]

In the work of relief and education in the sixties, Philadelphia Friends were but a part of a major melioristic effort made by Northern churches. But the Quaker contribution was out of all proportion to their numbers. Unlike other denominations, Friends did not seek converts to their own faith among the freedmen. As they were to do among the Indians of the West and the Doukhobors in Canada, they sought to inculcate general Protestant principles conducive to the stability of the social order and the improvement of the minority population. They saw this education as a mass of black self-improvement, but they did not envision it as leading to equal competition between the races. Quaker control of school policies and distrust of black professionals through the end of the century offers ample testimony to the significance of this condescension.

Because Friends were gradually disassembling the walls of exclusivity which had hedged in their faith, they became increasingly susceptible to contemporary attitudes on race and Reconstruction. Still under quietist influence, the Yearly Meetings did not conceive of organized philanthropic efforts as expressions of Quaker distinctiveness. Such benevolence would have been required to maintain major educational efforts for the freedmen. As they became part of the educational empire of Booker T. Washington, Friends remained insensitive to black cultural needs, urged Negroes to remain on Southern farms, and settled and markedly reduced aspirations for the objects of their philanthropy. The schools they supported in the South and in Philadelphia were filling important black needs, and in some cases their efforts exceeded those of other denominations. But it was only as Friends began to reassess their own principles and commitments after 1910 that they reaffirmed their traditional concern for the former slaves with a greater sensitivity. By then they were dealing with the effects of a massive black migration to Northern cities like Philadelphia.

CHAPTER 7 | Quaker Women
and Social Feminism

Because from its earliest years the Society of Friends offered opportunities for women in the ministry and because some of the leaders of the women's rights movement have been Quakers, historians have attributed to Friends a role in social feminism far in advance of their contemporaries. An examination of Quaker attitudes on the proper role for women and the activities of women Friends in Philadelphia in the late nineteenth and early twentieth centuries reveals, however, a less progressive climate than we have been led to expect. Seventeenth-century English Friends had opened opportunities for women in the ministry because they believed that the Spirit made no sexual distinctions in choosing human agents through whom to speak. They had never intended to bring about a revolution in the social status of women. Though some women preachers had given vent to an emotionalism which made them quite unpopular with men dedicated to plainness and simplicity, most gave no such offense. In fact, they had a positive impact on the growth and development of Quakerism in England and America, and their claim to a right in the ministry remained secure. From the very beginnings of Quakerism in Philadelphia separate Monthly and Yearly Meetings were established for women. There they were assured an opportunity to speak and to conduct their own religious affairs unhindered. But their dependence on the coordinate men's Meeting for approval of their undertakings and substantial funding of their operations left them largely impotent as an independent force.[1]

These arrangements were hardly questioned until the second third of the nineteenth century. The leadership given the cause of

148

women's rights by Hicksite Lucretia Mott clearly raised questions in the minds of many about the inequality of women in the Meeting structure. Yet the Hicksites maintained this structural double standard through the Civil War years. Women were forced to seek male sanction for their own Monthly Meeting's decisions on membership and violations of the Discipline, while they were barred from participation in such matters in the men's Meeting. No women took part in the deliberations of the Yearly Meeting's Representative Committee. Largely as a result of proposals from rural meetings in Chester and Delaware counties, male hegemony in the business affairs of Hicksite Quakerism was ended in the seventies. The Yearly Meeting decided to admit women to the Representative Committee in its 1874 session. Two years of deliberation and discussion and a last-minute appeal by a prominent visiting Friend from more liberal New York in 1877 overcame conservative opposition to changes in the Monthly Meetings. A new edition of the Discipline stipulated that membership certificates for all Friends required the signature of both men and women, called for joint consultation on all Discipline violations, and permitted the preparation of separate epistles by the men's and women's Meetings. The resulting autonomy was, as one Friend put it, "according to the spirit of the present age."[2]

But even those steps toward autonomy struck some "as but pruning branches here and there instead of getting to the root of the matter." They believed the ultimate solution to the problem of inequality was to do away with the distinction between men's and women's Meetings altogether. Partitions in some Hicksite meetinghouses were being dismantled as early as 1880, particularly in rural areas where dwindling membership made joint meetings more practical. Bucks county Meetings, which moved early to erase distinction, had lost a third of their members between 1863 and 1899. In city Meetings these practical considerations were not as decisive because membership had been on the rise until 1881 and declined only an eighth in the last two decades of the century (Table 2). At Race Street a bastion of male dominance fell when women won the right to serve on the Monthly Meeting Property Committee in 1889. A decade later Race Street approved joint business meetings on a trial basis. While the men explained the experiment in terms of efficiency, it was the persistent logic of the women's demand for equality which had won the day. It took but a few months to convince the diehard conservatives that joint sessions were workable, as well as just. The Race Street Women's Monthly Meeting ceased to exist as a separate entity in 1900. If it did not immediately promote the unity in families which the women had argued would result, this change was a logical culmination of the Quaker testimony that "in Christ there was neither male nor female."[3]

The Orthodox in Philadelphia were several decades behind their Hicksite cousins in erasing this structural segregation between men and women. The dependence of women's Meetings upon men's remained a part of Orthodox practice until the twentieth century. Even the Library Committee of the Arch Street Monthly Meeting was without women members until 1890. The boards governing independent Orthodox philanthropies remained as exclusive as men's clubs beyond the turn of the century. The Board of Managers of the Institute for Colored Youth decisively rejected an 1895 proposal that women be included in its official deliberations. Young Friends such as Agnes Tierney began to call attention to the injustice which the Discipline perpetuated in denying women autonomy in the conduct of their business meetings. While she was willing to admit that such inequalities had arisen at first from rational causes, she suggested that Quaker practice in this regard had not kept pace with knowledge. Her appeal was to justice, and she argued that "only by equality in action can the fullest fruits of spiritual equality be realized."[4]

The turning point for Orthodox women came in the revised Discipline of 1910. It granted autonomy to the Women's Monthly Meetings and at the same time sanctioned the holding of joint sessions. Twelfth Street Friends had held occasional joint meetings to deal with specific problems seven years before the Discipline made it official. They did away with the separate women's Meeting entirely in 1918. The more conservative Arch Street Friends were slower still in granting women equality in the administration of that small body. And the 1914 Yearly Meeting granted women the right to sit as members of its executive arm, the Representative Meeting, fully forty years after the corresponding Hicksite body had admitted females. In speaking for this liberalization in the 1914 session, Joseph Elkinton insisted that "service, not sex" be the basis for representation on all committees. Yearly Meeting action had made the "males-only" rule of Orthodox philanthropy boards a real anomaly. The Institute for Colored Youth, newly named the Cheyney Training School for Teachers, appointed Anna Sharpless and Frances Garrett to its board in 1915.[5]

The crumbling of Philadelphia Orthodoxy's sexual segregation in the second decade of the twentieth century was but a part of the more general liberalization brought about by younger Friends' efforts. Because it was but one element in a larger transformation, it lacked the distinctiveness of the victories won for "the woman's cause" by Hicksite females in the seventies and nineties. Yet, like the Orthodox, Hicksites were still holding separate Yearly Meetings for women in 1920. Both branches cautiously united men and women in single Yearly Meetings six years later. Acknowledging their advanced thinking on the subject, the Hicksites named a woman, Jane Rushmore, to serve as the first clerk of the newly united Meeting. She held the position for several years in the decade that followed.[6]

What accounts for these differences on the woman question between Hicksite and Orthodox? The essentials of religious doctrine which divided the two branches offer meager explanation. Joseph John Gurney, who had a profound influence in Orthodox circles, had imbibed an opposition to women's rights along with religious ideas from the English Methodists and Anglicans. The pragmatic rationale supplied by some Friends—the need for internal unity, the desire to consolidate in the face of dwindling membership—applied to both branches to an equal degree. Women in Orthodox Meetings did offer vigorous challenges to the status quo. They promoted benevolent enterprises which men were tardy to support, and they were active in attempts to prevent past practice from governing the actions of the church. This troubled the cautious men who dominated the Orthodox Yearly Meeting, and it may have sustained their reluctance to grant women equality in the administration of Meetings at any level. Orthodox women began collecting clothing and other supplies to be sent to needy blacks in areas taken by the Union armies twenty months before a full-fledged collecting and dispatching agency, the Friends' Freedmen Association, was created by Orthodox males in late 1863. Orthodox women argued later in the century for the entrance of Friends into the foreign mission field. Denied official sanction by the men of the church, the women created their own association which supported extensive work in Japan. It took Orthodox men decades to reconcile themselves to this effort and give it their official support. In pushing for revisions in the Discipline which would soften the penalties for marrying outside of Quaker Meeting and which would permit Friends to attend such marriage ceremonies, the women of the Twelfth Street Meeting resumed their reformist agitation in 1891. It took them a decade to convert the men of the Twelfth Street Meeting to their thinking.[7]

Such vigorous internal reform work on the part of Orthodox women might explain the difference between the two branches on the woman question were it not for the fact that Hicksite women played a similar role within their own Meetings. They too began relief work for Southern blacks in April 1862 and carried the major share of the burden until January 1864, when the men of their branch created the Association of Friends for the Aid and Elevation of the Freedmen. Lucretia Mott initiated suggestions for revision of the endogamous marriage rule in the Women's Monthly Meeting at Race Street in 1879. Six years later the women persuaded their male counterparts to join them in requesting alteration of the Discipline to permit Friends "marrying out of Meeting" to be retained as members. The liberalized rule appeared in the 1894 Discipline. Hicksite women also pressed their Yearly Meeting to join the Union for Philanthropic Labor, which other Hicksite bodies had formed in 1881. Their arguments overcame quietest scruples and the Philadelphians joined this cooperative benevolent organization a decade later.[8]

The character of the 1927 Separation and the leadership of Lucretia Mott best explain the stronger support which the Hicksites gave to the woman question. Friends who became Hicksites had objected strongly to the attempts of the Philadelphia Meeting for Sufferings to determine what constituted heresy for all members of the Yearly Meeting. In trying to prevent Elias Hicks from speaking, the Orthodox leadership pushed his supporters into the role of defenders of religious liberty. This, as well as their initial economic inferiority to the Orthodox, prompted them to employ rhetoric suffused with the language of equality and democracy. While Hicks himself was a quietist, some of his supporters followed the inner light's directions into benevolent social causes. Lucretia Mott was one of these; her involvement in the anti-slavery crusade led her, as it did others outside Quakerism, into other reform movements such as the fight for women's rights. Mrs. Mott's latitudinarianism was hardly typical of Philadelphia Friends of either branch, yet she left an indelible mark upon her Hicksite colleagues. Her egalitarian views won the approval of only a handful of Race Street Friends, but this minority provided the catalyst for change in the status of women Friends.[9]

The Hicksites manifested this difference from the Orthodox rather early in their willingness to make available opporunities for higher education for women. When Swarthmore College was still in the planning stage, Edward Parrish, who was to become its first president, argued for a coeducational institution. Opposition to the plan arose more from fears about the social results of coeducation than over the right of Quaker women to receive collegiate instruction. Writing in 1866 to explain the rationale for the college's establishment, he put his finger on one of the more difficult problems for Victorian womanhood:

The mental attrition of the class-room is especially favorable to students forming a just estimate of each other's capacity, and thus losing false ideas of perfection in each other, the frequent source of romantic attachments. Constantly subjected to artless association and competition, they seldom exhibit that unnatural constraint and coyness which distinguish the unaccustomed intercourse of boys and girls, when first thrown together in what is called society. . . .

Whether or not Swarthmore succeeded in undercutting the nineteenth-century tendency to put women on pedestals, Parrish had enunciated an aim designed to appeal to adherents of equality and simplicity.[10]

Nearly two decades before the opening of Swarthmore, another institution had been founded in Philadelphia by a group anxious to give women a chance in the professions. The city's medical schools were the best in antebellum America, but none of them would admit women as students. The rejection of the applications of several young Hicksites prompted a Philadelphia group to found the Female Medical College in 1850. Never a sectarian educational establishment, the college attracted many women from diverse faiths and different parts of the country. But in the initial years of its operation, Hicksite Friends dominated the governing board and to a lesser degree the student body. Two of the early deans of the college were Hicksite doctors, Ann Preston and Clara Marshall, products of the same Quaker farming community in Chester county. Orthodox support for the institution, called the Women's Medical College of Pennsylvania after 1867, grew rapidly. Male physicians in both branches helped gain recognition for the college's graduates and the admission of women into the Philadelphia County Medical Society in the 1880s. While Orthodox and Hicksite Friends were equally active as supporters of the Women's Medical College by 1890, the Hicksites deserve the credit for its founding and early development.[11]

If the worthy Orthodox managers of Haverford College ever permitted the idea of making the institution coeducational to enter their heads, they dismissed it with scarcely a moment's thought. In spite of the fact that the most liberal of Orthodox Friends directed the men's college, their liberalism was insufficient to grant the undergraduates what Edward Parrish had called "the artless association" of classes with women. It took the individual concern of a New Jersey Friend, Joseph Taylor, a retired tanner and physician who had spent much of his working life outside Philadelphia, to create a separate college for Orthdox women. Taylor's will of 1877, which served as a charter for the development of Bryn Mawr College, reflected the founder's uncertainty about the kind of educational fare he wanted to make available. Some had advised him to provide for a "guarded education" according to Friends' principles. Others had encouraged a more liberalizing curriculum which would widen horizons beyond the limits of Quaker cuture. If Taylor's will was ambivalent on the nature of the curriculum, it was indisputably clear in its faith in the ability of women to benefit from education beyond the secondary level and to make intellectual contributions in diverse social roles. The college accepted its first class in 1885.[12]

The suspicion, if not hostility, with which conservative Orthodox Friends viewed the development of Bryn Mawr sprang from the early defeat of the guarded-education interpretation of Joseph Taylor's will. The all-Orthodox Board of Trustees was artfully guided in this decision by one of the most forceful personalities in American education. First as dean and then as president after 1894, M. Carey Thomas of Baltimore molded an institution competitive with the best universities in the nation. She wore her Quakerism very lightly indeed, and with one or two exceptions the excellent faculty she assembled lacked even her nominal ties with the church. Observing her wordly handiwork, one Quaker expressed regret that Haverford had not been made coeducational. As late as 1899 *The Friend* reprinted warnings against the noxious influence intellectual ambition could have upon women—that it would make them "cold, unloved, and unhelpful" instead of "joyous, affectionate, and unselfish." Conservatives among the Orthodox were not yet reconciled to higher education for men. If Haverford appeared to weaken the foundations of home, family, and meetinghouse, Carey Thomas's "pursuit of excellence" at Bryn Mawr seemed to threaten the very survival of those precious institutions upon which they thought the Society of Friends rested. Support for the new college came primarily from affluent, liberal Friends connected with the Twelfth Street Meeting. A goodly number of their daughters were in the first graduating classes.[13]

The Wilburite-Gurneyite quarrels within Orthodoxy had threatened to split the Yearly Meeting in the fifties. The two groups continued together uneasily for several decades in a conscious attempt to maintain unity. To achieve this the Orthodox focused their attention on internal matters and emphasized their estrangement from other groups in the social order. The Hicksites maintained an ideological anarchy. Lacking the clear polarization of the Orthodox, they showed less intolerance toward dissent and became far more open to outside influences. It was thus the combination of their own Quaker belief in equality and their susceptibility to reform ideas of other liberal groups which prompted them to move more rapidly toward a less discriminatory view of the role of women in the church and in society.

This susceptibility to outside influence prompted the Hicksite Yearly Meeting to respond far sooner than the Orthodox body to the demands of women that the rule requiring endogamous marriage be dropped. In the major rewriting of their Discipline in 1894 Race Street Friends allowed those who married others outside the faith to remain members as long as they attended meetings for worship. In part this provision was an acknowledgement of marriage trends long at work. As early as the sixties and seventies more than 40 percent of the Hicksites were choosing marriage partners outside of Quakerism (Table 56). Friends born in the sixties were making marriage decisions just before the new rule was adopted; more than half of this group "married out of Meeting." Hicksite "worldliness" was clearly a product of these conjugal patterns. The lower rate of exogamous marriage in both generations of Orthodox Friends helps explain the reluctance on the part of the conservatives to accede to demands for Discipline revision lest it lead to an increase in the phenomenon in their branch. The pressure for change from the liberals was substantial, but the traditionalist leaders stuck by their refusal to compromise.[14]

Women had initiated the demand for change in the Twelfth Street Meeting in 1891. The wider contacts and associations of these affluent Friends, some of whom were part of the city's aristocracy, prompted them to push for a less seclusive Quakerism. The conservatives denied their pleas and became more rigid when the Germantown Meeting added its voice for change. The question became so divisive that when the Yearly Meeting undertook to rewrite the entire Discipline in 1909, discussion of the marriage provisions was prohibited. Traditionalists claimed that religious unity within families remained the surest foundation for faith and the maintenance of Quaker testimonies. Some argued for automatic disownment of members "marrying out of Meeting" on the grounds that those who did so were nominal members who diluted the strength of Meetings anyway. The reformers retorted by expressing the view that there was no clear correlation between exogamous marriage and a diminished faith. The liberals won only a modest concession in 1916 when the new Discipline permitted marriages with non-Friends to take place under Quaker supervision. The Orthodox never compromised their insistence that endogamous marriage was preferable.[15]

The Orthodox conservatives had used the marriage question as the keystone of their effort to maintain Christ over culture. Examination of the institutional commitment of married Friends in this study shows that the traditionalists were correct. The 264 subjects who married other Friends and the eleven who soon converted their spouses to Quakerism were much more involved in their Meetings than the 215 who married persons whose loyalties remained outside the faith (Table 57–58). Close to 80 percent of those who "married out of Meeting" became Nominal Friends, while only a third of those who married within Quakerism fell into that category. The difference is striking. Meetinghouse activities were family based, and those who abandoned religious unity in their families were drawn away from institutional participation by the demands of non-Quaker wives and husbands. The difference between exogamous and endogamous marriage shows up much more dramatically among the Orthodox, who remained more rigid on this score than the Hicksites. The Orthodox attitude contributed to its healthier rates of institutional participation.

Despite the limitations placed on their autonomy and independence within the Society, women showed greater institutional commitment than men (Tables 59–60). Among Practicing Friends, women outnumbered men three to two. Data on other denominations reveals a similar propensity for women to dominate the institutional work of their churches.[16] The committee work women did was a valuable outlet for their initiative. They busied themselves also as representatives to Quarterly Meeting and as supervisors of marriages. They met new members and those transferring from other Meetings, and they prepared "minutes" which Friends leaving Philadelphia could take with them to other Quaker congregations. And married women produced the largest proportion of active members—58 percent—of all the groups in the study. Unmarried Friends of both sexes took less part in Meeting affairs than their married counterparts, confirming the view that family life built a significant foundation for Meeting involvement. The difference is even more striking among the men than among the women. The greater proportion of Weighty Friends among single women than among single men suggests that women were more likely to compensate for the absence of a family through religious activity than men, who had a wider set of outlets in the secular world.

In each of the three Meetings under study, the Nominal proportion of the membership was smaller among women than men (Table 61). And at Twelfth Street and Race Street, the Weighty proportion among women was higher than that for men. Only at tradition-bound Arch Street, where city-wide conservative leaders consciously congregated, did women show lower proportions in the leadership category. Different patterns of activity for women developed in the two branches. While Orthodox women were slow to gain quality in the administration of their Meetings, they continued to take an active part in the ministry of the church. Hicksite women, on the other hand, were rarely "called" to the ministry. Of the 356 women in this study, five became ministers; all five were Orthodox Friends. A few women did receive appointment as ministers at Race Street, but they represented a much smaller proportion of the congregation than ministers at the two Orthodox Meetings. Women of both branches did become elders in equal proportions to the total membership. While the ministry was obviously much more than a channel for independent activity, involving as it did elements of prophecy and inspiration, this calling provided opportunities for influence and individual expression otherwise denied to women.[17] The fact that the branch of Quakerism which afforded less chance for women to play a role in the administration of its Meetings was attracting the most women into the ministry is instructive indeed.

Rebecca Kite Masters was one of these ministers. Born a Friend in Philadelphia in 1843, the daughter of currier James Kite, she transferred her membership to the distant Muncy Meeting at the time of her marriage to James Masters, who lived in Millville near the coal country of northeastern Pennsylvania. They had met at the Westtown boarding school which they both attended in the early sixties. All three of their children were later schooled there, and Rebecca served on the Yearly Meeting Westtown Committee for seven years. The family had returned to Philadelphia, as many rural people were doing, in 1875, at which time James estabished a modest milk business. They settled in a home on Preston Street near the recently erected meetinghouse in West Philadelphia. In the Twelfth Street Meeting Rebecca began to assume religious responsibilities at the age of thirty-six. While she had a brief tenure on the Western District Colored School Committee, she did a great deal of visiting of applicants for membership and of Friends transferring from other Meetings.

A conservative, she opposed Bible classes, intellectual pursuits, and use of musical instruments. Yet she could be critical of those "who lay too much stress on mere traditions, on the letter which killeth" Rebecca Masters' gift in the ministry was soon apparent, and Philadelphia Quarterly Meeting approved her nomination as a minister late in 1885. Six times before her death ten years later she was authorized by her Meeting to make religious visits. In 1890 she responded to a calling to meet with the employees of the Pennsylvania Railroad and the workers on the city streetcars in West Philadelphia. She visited southern New York State twice, bearing minutes from the Twelfth Street Meeting, and on one occasion spoke at the Tunessasa Indian School on the Alleghany Reservation. Her diary offers no hint of her perception of her own gift in the ministry and how this might have given her a wider influence; it focused completely on her close relationship with the divine. Whatever the explanation for her ministry, she gained from her religious visiting a wider experience than was open to many Quaker women of the era.[18]

A more customary role for women was the dispensing of benevolence. Countless numbers of women Friends made gifts to the needy at certain times of the year. Lucretia Mott's habit of taking baked goods, candy, and turkeys to children's homes and institutions for the aged on holidays serves as the prototype for this individual philanthropy. Other Quaker women involved themselves with the poor by serving as volunteers in institutions located in the slum districts of the city. The House of Industry in Southwark offered an outlet for this individual effort. Since work for the destitute sometimes involved lengthy stays in such neighborhoods, a far greater number preferred genteel brushes with poverty at the conference table, where they served as advisors and funds raisers for Friendly philanthropies. These were instructive activities which not only gave them a first-hand look at the social problems of the city, but offered opportunities for independence and decision-making.[19]

Two-fifths of the women in Philadelphia Meetings never married. A natural outlet for many of these was teaching. Several who attended Westtown and Friends' Central stayed on as faculty members for a year or two after graduation. Twenty women in the membership sample chose careers in the classroom which were of more than a few years duration. Teaching seems to have borne the label "spinsters only"—only two of the five who married remained in the classroom after being wed. At least twelve of the twenty taught in Friends' schools, including the charity institutions run by various Meetings. The Raspberry Street School, which served young children in the city's Seventh Ward black community, depended on the Arch Street Meeting for its staff as well as its funding. Sarah Barton, Sarah Kennard, and Rachel Hall served successive terms as the school's principal between 1881 and 1918. All three were active in their Meeting and, like many Arch Street Friends, came from small rural towns. None of the three married nor did they stray outside the shelter of Quaker institutions as they gave expression to their Meeting's traditional concern for black people. Careers in the classroom were never thought to be inappropriate for women Friends. It was only through these teachers that the Meetings were able to provide a guarded education for young Friends.[20]

Nor could it have raised any eyebrows in the most conservative Orthodox Meeting to discover that young women were going into medicine by the end of the nineteenth century. This happy combination of science and service had attracted many women in both branches since the founding of the Woman's Medical College. Nine of the women in the membership sample became practicing physicians after receiving their degrees from that institution. Only one abandoned the profession to marry. Several had connections with the College in a teaching capacity and were residents at the Woman's Hospital in North Philadelphia or the West Philadelphia Hospital for Women. This last institution, which opened its doors in 1889, had as its president for many years one of the nine, Anna P. Sharpless. One of the prime movers in the institution's founding, she used funds inherited from her dye-manufacturer father to build and furnish an operating room in 1894. Her activity in the Arch Street Meeting as its treasurer and a member of the Committee on Friends in Necessitous Circumstances was paralleled by interests outside Quakerism.[21] Dr. Sharpless exercised her talents in an executive capacity; Amy S. Barton made her contribution as a teacher and researcher. This Arch Street Friend held a professorship in opthalmology at the College. Committed to her teaching and research, she never assumed any responsibilities in her Meeting. A strong advocate of clinical experience, she was a moving force behind the establishment of a small hospital and dispensary in a South Philadelphia slum from which developed the Woman's College Hospital.[22]

A surprising number of women from the conservative Arch Street Meeting entered the medical field in the late nineteenth century. Members of the same Meeting looked upon the higher learning at Bryn Mawr as a pernicious influence upon young Quaker women. Their enthusiasm for medical education resulted from its practicality. Training in medicine involved no contact with the "false notions" of literature and philosophy, no exposure to the contaminating influences of art and music. Medicine offered a natural outlet for women who possessed energy, intelligence, and independence, yet who hesitated to veer too sharply from the path of Quaker simplicity. In many fields Friends had resisted the trend toward professionalism; not so in medicine. Many Quaker men had become doctors during the nineteenth century; their familiarity with the pace of change in medicine and the necessity for professional training had overcome Friendly scruples in this field. But Quaker conservatives still regarded professionalism and organization in social benevolence as an interference with the promptings of the Divine in every man—and woman. As a result, few Orthodox women ventured into social work as the field began to take shape in the eighties and nineties. Hicksites did so more readily, but even their pioneering efforts were marked with hesitancy. If the new professionalism won them over, they tended to abandon their Quakerism.

The career of Hicksite Cornelia Hancock spanned nearly fifty years as a nurse, teacher, and social worker, first in the South and later at Point Breeze in South Philadelphia, where she and her colleague, Edith Wright, applied the principles of the English social worker Octavia Hill in rehabilitating the slum housing community. Her involvement with the social problems of Philadelphia's slums left her little time for more than nominal ties with the Race Street Meeting.[23] Another Hicksite activist, Susan Parrish Wharton, became a prime mover in the development of social settlements in Philadelphia. From a library on St. Mary's Street established to counteract the circulation of "debasing" literature among the young, she developed a center which bore all the marks of a social settlement before the name was ever applied. She also arranged for W. E. B. DuBois's appointment at the University of Pennsylvania in 1895 to conduct his study of the Seventh Ward black community. Like Miss Hancock, she retained her membership at Race Street but took no part in the Meeting's business.[24] The social worker who moved the furthest from Quaker culture in these years was Helen Parrish. A granddaughter of the prominent abolitionist Dr. Joseph Parrish, she began teaching in a kindergarten on St. Mary's Street at the age of twenty-three, before her cousin Susan Wharton had opened the library there. The six months she spent in London in 1888–89 observing the work of housing reformer Octavia Hill convinced her to join others purchasing homes in the St. Mary's Street area which could then be repaired and rented to the poor. Rent collecting provided her entrée into the daily lives of the tenants, whose habits and values she attempted to reform. The supervision Helen Parrish gave them was paternalism at its worst, and her style was abrupt and domineering, but it was all very Progressive. When the Octavia Hill Association was formed in 1896, she became active in managing its properties and devoted over forty years to supervising its rent collections. Formed as a limited-return corporation to purchase and rehabilitate homes in the city, the Association was capitalized at $10,000 and promised a respectable return to investors. Helen Parrish viewed the O.H.A. as a direct means of improving the quality of life and reforming the people living in the Fourth and Fifth Wards. Her zeal for housing reform became so great that she tried pressuring local Republican politicians to gain passage of a tenement house inspection bill before the state legislature. The pressure was ineffectual, but her willingness to approach Israel Durham and Boies Penrose was a measure of the distance she had travelled from the meetinghouse. She had resigned from the Society of Friends at the age of twenty-four. With her early active social concern, even the Race Street Meeting seemed too confining.[25]

In confronting the power of the slum environment Cornelia Hancock, Susan Wharton, and Helen Parrish had worked through ameliorative social institutions. They had left Quaker conservatism far behind in their methods to improve the lot of the city's poor, but they never challenged the economic system itself. Eschewing any ties with organized labor, Cornelia Hancock even worked with employers to prevent strikes. Helen Parrish made socialist friends on her visit to England and she read socialist authors, but she looked to them more for the diagnosis of social ills than for the cure. The only clear socialist product of Philadelphia Quakerism in these years was Helen Marot. The daughter of Hicksite bookseller Charles Marot, she was part of a small coterie of philosophical anarchists, socialists, and other dissenters who met at her father's shop. Making herself an expert on labor problems, she served as an investigator for the United States Industrial Commission and was secretary of the Women's Trade Union League from 1906 to 1914. A strike in the garment trades in 1909 found her among the protest leaders heading a parade of women workers in New York City. She had long since left uncongenial Philadelphia and Quakerism behind when she began writing for *The Masses* in 1916. It was as a writer that she had her greatest influence. Her *Creative Impulse in Industry* (1918) was widely used as a textbook in economics. Her last post was a three-year stint on the editorial board of *The Dial* beginning in 1917.[26]

The impulses which prompted Anna Sharpless to develop the West Philadelphia Hospital for Women, which led Susan Wharton to open her library on St. Mary's Street, and which encouraged Helen Marot to take up the cause of working women were very much the same. A deep social concern for the less fortunate had been a part of the Society of Friends from its earliest days. Quaker women had always been particularly responsive to human suffering and hardship. As professions in which benevolence could be channeled were opened to both sexes, talented and energetic young women in the Society of Friends found new outlets for self expression and independence. The careers and activities these women chose depended to a great extent on the Meetings from which they came. Medical practice attracted women Friends from both branches, but it seemed most suited to women from conservative Orthodox congregations. To cautious observers medicine appeared a matter of individual service to individuals in need—a style consonant with Orthodox Quietism. The growing field of social work which attempted to deal with larger group problems created by industrialization and urbanization attracted the more liberal Hicksites. The energies and impatience of those who entered this new work led often to their estrangement from the faith in which their social concern had been born. The cautious ambience of the

meetinghouse became too confining just as the wider culture outside of Quakerism seemed to offer more to reform-minded women
Friends.

Philadelphia Friends were no more anxious to press for woman
suffrage than they had been to grant women equality in the administration of their Meetings. While a handful of prominent
Quakers took forthright public stands in favor of extending the
right to vote to both sexes, organized official support was lacking.
The hesitancy which marked political involvement for men naturally served to keep the issue from making much progress in the
city's meetinghouses. Other social reforms in which Friends were
developing an interest diverted their attention from this cause
until the twentieth century. Even then agitation in support of the
right to vote became a near monopoly of the Hicksites. As a
group, the Quakers in Philadelphia had little to do with the
campaigns which culminated in the adoption of the Nineteenth
Amendment.

Before her death in 1881, Lucretia Mott, the city's best known
suffrage advocate, used her energies to attempt a reconciliation
of the two national organizations pushing for women's political
rights. She did not live long enough to see the union of the National and American Woman Suffrage Associations. Indeed the
cause was more hopeful in the era in which she lived than it
became at the end of the century. There is no evidence to suggest
that Mrs. Mott was pushing the Race Street Meeting to endorse
suffrage. In the seventies there were other battles to be fought
and the Meeting power structure seemed impregnable to conversion. While not becoming an earnest advocate of the cause, the
Friends' Intelligencer began to reprint numerous articles from the
Woman's Journal which were favorable to suffrage in 1887. The
Orthodox press, on the other hand, made clear its opposition.
The *Friends' Review* expressed the belief that speech making and
other brushes with public life might develop masculine habits in
women. The more conservative *Friend* maintained a policy of near
silence, refusing to print articles and letters on the subject.[27]

Although the spirited Hannah Whitall Smith expressed the wish
in 1880 that she might play an active, eloquent role in political
life, there were few others bold enough to join her in these sentiments. What few pronouncements there were came from men.

Joshua Baily argued against women voting, not just because of its effects on family life and chivalry, but because there would be a deterioration in the moral tone of women and because political life would become more bitter if women entered it. Charles Rhoads took a contrary view; he saw women's right to the ballot as a power for good, leading to the enactment of noble laws, the election of righteous legislators, and the development of strong law enforcement. But even Rhoads had doubts about some of the effects on social life, and he supported only those attempts to grant woman suffrage in school elections.[28]

The turn of the century and the momentum generated by the progressive movement brought the woman question into sharper focus and altered the responses of both branches. Among the Orthodox the cautious discussions of the nineties gave way to a conspicuous silence which continued for two decades. No Philadelphia Orthodox Meeting even acknowledged the issue between 1900 and 1920. Only a few women in these Meetings took part in the organized efforts to gain women their rights at the polls. Dr. Anna Sharpless served as treasurer of the Eastern District of the Pennsylvania Woman Suffrage Association in these years. But of fifteen identifiable Quaker patrons for a P.W.S.A. bazaar held in 1915, only four were Orthodox women. Certainly M. Carey Thomas of Bryn Mawr was a figure of national importance in the quest for women's rights. Her local activities were channeled through the Equal Franchise Society, an organization noted for its elite and aristocratic membership. Miss Thomas appears not to have used the college as a recruiting ground for suffragettes, although she herself was a strong supporter of the National American Woman Suffrage Association. Personally close to some Orthodox leaders, she had little or no influence in the Yearly and Monthly Meeting power structure.[29]

Hicksite circles became far more receptive to the suffrage drive. By the turn of the century Lucretia Longshore Blankenburg was in the midst of her sixteen-year presidency of the Pennsylvania Woman Suffrage Association, a post she had taken at the urgings of Susan B. Anthony, who even gave her lessons in public speaking. The liberal teachings at Swarthmore, as well as its own successful example of coeducation influenced increasing numbers of Hicksites to give open support to the cause. Professors Jesse

Holmes and William I. Hull were particularly instrumental in pushing for this altered stance. The former served as a patron of fund raising efforts, while the latter joined his wife, Hannah Clothier Hull, a P.W.S.A. vice president, in speaking on the subject. When in 1913 a recent Swarthmore graduate, Martha Moore, stood at the corner of Broad and Chestnut Streets in Center City hawking copies of the *Woman's Journal*, it provided ample testimony to the success of the educators' efforts. Philadelphians such as Joel Borton took an active role in pushing the question at the Chautauqua, New York, meeting of the Friends' General Conference in 1900. After predictable initial hesitancy, the Hicksite Yearly Meeting urged individual Friends to take an active part in supporting the cause, but it created no special Quaker instrumentality through which they could channel their efforts.[30]

If the sexes stood on the same footing in the Society of Friends, the Hicksites reasoned, it was only logical that women should have equal status with men in the affairs of government. Since it took the harmonious cooperation of men and women to make a perfect home, it seemed clear that a model government would result only from the combined efforts of men and women at the polls. Joel Borton struck a responsive chord when he suggested that native-born women, as natural lovers of country, were better "Christian citizens" than the alien men who could vote after only a few years' residence in the United States. Since many believed that there were few women among the lower class immigrants, they saw woman suffrage as a means of improving the "class" of voters and increasing sobriety at the polls. Few shared the fear of an Orthodox Friend that this reform would enable "machine bosses" in the cities to organize the vice districts as "adjuncts of corrupt politics." More practical arguments pictured woman suffrage as a means of achieving political and social changes in the new urban, industrial order; they reflected the influence of the wider progressive movement upon these Hicksites. Friends interested in temperance and the end of municipal corruption viewed women voters as a means to noble ends.[31]

Cautious as the Hicksite Yearly Meeting had been in urging its members to work for woman suffrage, it had sponsored several public meetings at Race Street which offered platforms to national figures in the movement. N.A.W.S.A. President Anna Howard

Shaw, who spoke in 1906, was probably the best-known orator. But on the eve of a vote on the issue in the Pennsylvania and New Jersey legislatures, the Yearly Meeting gave a rare official endorsement to the reform. Citing the advantages of "a full recognition of the dignity of women and her [sic] right to complete development," the 1914 statement defended the principles of equal suffrage on the grounds of justice—an argument little used since the nineteenth century. While individuals might employ arguments of expediency, the Yearly Meeting preferred a lofty idealism to justify its support of women's right to vote. But if its rhetoric was lofty, its actions were more practical. A subcommittee on Equal Rights worked with other organizations in lobbying for adoption of the suffrage amendments in Harrisburg and Trenton in 1915. The subcommittee's assessment of the reasons for the defeats suffered in both states reflected a healthy realism, as did its prediction of the growing support for a federal amendment in the years that followed.[32]

But there were paths in this movement which Quaker caution ruled impassable even for Hicksite liberals. Philadelphia Friends remained steadfast in support of the National American Woman Suffrage Association which employed only traditional lobbying and petitioning techniques. N.A.W.S.A.'s decision to seek the ballot for women through the gradual process of amendments in all forty-eight states had appeal to Quakers whose sense of decorum and style was sedate in the extreme. Ironically, the most extreme faction of the movement was led by a Moorestown, New Jersey, Friend and Swarthmore graduate, Alice Paul. Schooled in the passionate civil disobedience of English suffragette agitation directed by Emmeline Pankhurst during a stay abroad between 1907 and 1911, Miss Paul attempted to convince N.A.W.S.A. leaders to use more militant tactics and, when that failed, created the Congressional Union in 1913. Her charismatic leadership brought her a devoted following which paraded in Washington streets and picketed the White House during the Wilson administration on behalf of a federal amendment. While the C.U. gained quite a following in Philadelphia, most Friends balked at the use of such public displays and militance.[33]

Despite some seventeenth-century precedents for civil disobedience in Quakerism, the conservatism of Philadelphia Friends three centuries later prevented them from embracing Miss Paul and her approach. Only pacifism was likely to produce acts of civil disobedience by Quakers and recent decades had produced few issues of that nature. When news of the behavior of English suffragettes first reached Philadelphia, Hicksites were critical. Disapproving of one who had barricaded her house to prevent the collection of taxes, the *Friends' Intelligencer* suggested in 1906 that proper passive resistance would require her to permit the authorities to sell her goods to obtain the amount of the taxes she refused to pay. Friends raised objections to the Congressional Union long before Alice Paul and her cohorts were dragged off to jail in 1917. Wilmer Atkinson, a Green Street Friend who was president of the Pennsylvania Men's League for Woman Suffrage from 1915 to 1919, attacked the C.U. for its "destructive policy." Friends remained loyal to N.A.W.S.A. even when it pledged support for the war effort. Miss Paul remained truer to her pacifist upbringing when she refused to support the president's war policy. Yet even this won her no new support in the Quaker community in Philadelphia.[34]

Ratification of the Nineteenth Amendment by the Tennessee legislature in August 1920 was applauded by Friends in both branches. Yet only the Hicksites had given the movement their open backing. Already more advanced than the Orthodox in opening opportunities for women in their own Meetings, the Hicksites gave formal endorsement to woman suffrage in 1914—perhaps the only church body to do so in the United States. Less traditionbound than the Orthodox, they had absorbed much of the progressive reform spirit of the wider culture. New roles for women in a changing social order seemed less of a threat to Hicksite families than to Orthodox ones. For the liberal Twelfth Street Friends who believed that women should vote, the very style of agitation on the question—even by the conservative N.A.W.S.A. —seemed too deviant from the model of proper behavior for Quaker women. The frequent parading which was so much a part of the suffrage cause in Philadelphia must have alienated many a potential supporter accustomed to meetinghouse methods of avoiding confrontation and conflict. More practical assessments of the effectiveness of such public demonstrations no doubt influenced some to eschew open involvement in the cause. Yet even the

gentle art of epistle writing, so often used when Friends wanted
to give expression to a cause of conscience but remain out of the
controversy, was never once employed by the Orthodox to deal
with the woman question.

William O'Neill has suggested that the heavy burdens of the
conjugal family system fell upon women only in the nineteenth
century. The habit of Philadelphia Friends to freeze behavior
patterns of that era into firm rules and roles for its members was
the product of their own internal feuds and divisions. As increasing numbers abandoned their Quakerism and thereby threatened
the Society with extinction, the family appeared more and more
the key to survival. To tamper with the role of women might
drastically alter that key institution. The Orthodox Discipline continued to insist on "unity in religious belief [as] essential to the
full enjoyment of the blessings of married life" as late as the
1920s. The Hicksites never used language that explicit in their
marriage rules. Successful experience with coeducation at Swarthmore and the wider contacts with elements of the larger culture
schooled the Hicksites to view a changing role for women as less
threatening to their religious institutions. Philadelphia Quakerism
was not without supporters for the movement to free women from
the shackles of Victorian convention. But the leadership role in
social feminism often attributed to Friends must be qualified by
acknowledging the tardiness of their support and the wide varia-
tion of attitude on the question which existed in Philadelphia.

CHAPTER **8** | Winds of
Change

In losing more than a third of its members after the Separation of 1827 the Society of Friends faced the awesome responsibility that it might not survive in the very city it had founded. But the predictions of extinction which Yearly Meeting critics occasionally made never came true. While they posted no significant gains, Friends held their membership at a fairly constant level between 1899 and 1916 (Tables 62–63). City Meetings continued to sustain losses, but respectable gains appeared in those Quarters which included Philadelphia's growing suburbs. Concord and Haddonfield Quarters in both branches and the Orthodox Abington Quarter benefitted from this suburban trend most obviously. The more distant rural Quarters continued to lose members who moved to Philadelphia or its surrounding towns. The smaller and more seclusive Orthodox branch lost an inconsequential eleven members, while the more worldly Hicksites had 207 fewer in 1915 than they did at the turn of the century. It is a measure of the vitality of forces at work in the Society of Friends in the years after 1900 that the membership decline levelled off. Which of those forces prevented the extinction of the Society? Did the achievement result from a compromise of essential traditions or from a redirection based on neglected elements in the Quaker past?

Progressive Friends had always argued that membership losses could be tied to the strictness of the Disciplines. In their view, these outmoded rules placed unnecessary burdens on modern Friends who were anxious to deemphasize Quaker peculiarities. The progressives won significant victories between 1890 and 1920 as the influence of quietism diminished. Two totally rewritten

170

Disciplines appeared in these years—a very liberal one issued by the Hicksites in 1894 and a more moderate Orthodox edition in 1910. The very act of scrapping the old organization and rephrasing passages some of which dated to the 1720s was a significant break with the past. The Hicksite document redefined that body's attitude toward disownment by employing a purposeful ambiguity: "It is the desire of the Society that no one be disowned except when his retention would be to weaken our testimony for Truth, impair the good example we desire to set, or confuse our sense of right living." Meetings could still exclude Friends for violating testimonies relating to war, oaths, trade, diversions, and the ministry. But according to the new rules, they would give attention to an individual's circumstances and his attitude toward his error in determining his status in the Society. The revision dropped admonitions against attending other religious services, reading romantic literature, listening to music, or failing in business. One member of the Race Street Meeing viewed the changes as sufficient to warrant her resignation. She felt that she no longer belonged "in this branch of the Society."[1]

The old Disciplines had condemned "the world's people" for their religious errors in a tone which certainly lacked Friends' gentleness. Revision offered an opportunity to employ more conciliatory language. Compare the statements on plainness and simplicity made in the 1886 and 1894 editions:

Advised that all Friends both old and young keep out of the world's corrupt language, manners, and vain and needless things and fashions, in apparel, buildings, and furniture of houses: some of which are immodest, indecent, and unbecoming. And that they avoid immoderation in the use of lawful things, which though innocent in themselves may thereby become hurtful; also such kinds of stuffs, color and dress as are calculated more to please a vain and wanton mind than for real usefulness [1886].

The spirit of Truth which led our early Friends to lay aside things unbecoming the Gospel of Christ still leads in the same path all who submit to its guidance; we therefore earnestly encourage all Friends to watch over themselves in this respect and to seriously consider the plainness and simplicity which the Gospel enjoins, manifesting it in their conversation, apparel, furniture, buildings, salutations, and manner of living, exercising plainness of speech without respect to persons in all their converse among men, not balking their testimony by varying their language according to their company [1894].[2]

The more modest alterations the Orthodox made in the rewriting of their Discipline were, as the Meeting for Sufferings assured Friends, changes in tone more than substance. The phrase "Hireling ministry" had been the object of considerable debate for years. Substituting a more temperate explanation for opposing a "paid ministry," the 1910 version stated: "While we would not judge or condemn others to whom these truths have not yet been revealed, we should bear our testimony against that system which confines the ministry to a particular person." It also urged families to "discourage"—not "suppress"—the reading of plays, romances, and novels. Children could no longer be disowned for adopting worldly fashion, but parents were asked to reason with them about the moral dangers involved. The new Discipline reiterated its opposition to music, and most of the older causes for disownment were retained, including the controversial matter of marriage "out of Meeting." Diminished in numbers, the traditionalists accepted even these modest changes grudgingly. While they could admit, as one Arch Street minister did, that some of the older Quaker ways were merely useful or ornamental to their faith, they feared that abandonment of these "accidental" religious manifestations might eventually lead to a loss of "the fundamental."[3]

Some of these changes in the Orthodox and Hicksite rules were clearly moves to accommodate Quakerism to the demands of modern culture. They reflected a desire to interpret the testimony of simplicity more liberally. They also cut back the hedges which protected the community. With the exceedingly significant pacifist testimony they did not tamper. The essence of Quaker practice was certainly not compromised: assimilative American culture had merely eaten away at the edge of Friends' distinctiveness. It was up to a new generation to articulate patterns of behavior which proved that liberal interpretation of distinctiveness could succeed in perpetuating Quakerism in the twentieth century. The conjunction of liberalization of the Disciplines and a levelling off in the membership decline suggests that the changes could have been a factor in the new membership stability; some individuals may have decided not to leave Quakerism because of its altered climate after 1900. But the branch which most successfully brought its declension under control made the more modest changes in its Discipline and at a time which was too late to really have a major influence on developments between 1899 and 1916. The Hicksites, who made more significant alterations five years before, still lost nearly 7 percent of their adherents.

The altered language used to describe "the world's people" did not portend Quaker moves toward interdenominational cooperation. Habits of aloofness were too ingrained. But the new climate did prompt Friends to repair the fissures which had weakened their own Society internally. The Arch Street Yearly Meeting terminated its forty-year policy of isolation by renewing correspondence with other Orthodox bodies in 1897. Official visits from Quakers in other Yearly Meetings became more frequent once correspondence was resumed. By 1913 cordial ties with London had been restored assuring increased influence from a body which was growing increasingly liberal. Orthodox leaders made sincere efforts to restore trans-Atlantic contacts, though a critical reserve continued to characterize the Philadelphia attitude toward Evangelical Quakerism in the United States. When the Western bodies which eventually formed the Five Years Meeting met in Indianapolis in 1897 to write a Discipline which approved of a paid ministry and abandoned birthright membership, *The Friend* labelled them merely as "modern representatives of Friends." Even though the editors of that weekly still considered Philadelphia Yearly Meeting to be "conservative" in 1914, the body was changing rapidly because of its wider contacts.[4]

The walls which separated Orthodox and Hicksite also began to crumble. Local educational institutions on both the secondary and college level felt fewer restraints than the Meetings themselves. Swarthmore's President Magill often sought the counsel of his more experienced counterpart, Thomas Chase. In 1903 and 1910 the Orthodox Peace Association and the Westtown School felt free enough to invite Swarthmore professors Jesse Holmes and William I. Hull to address them. Haverford's Rufus Jones spoke occasionally at Swarthmore in these years. The Hicksite Friends' Central School named a mathematics teacher as its principal in 1909 even though he was a Twelfth Street Friend. The school committee found that W. Elmer Barrett's "intimate knowledge of the school's problems rendered him an acceptable candidate." This educational cooperation served as an important model for the rest of the Society. But for Orthodox Friends still seriously troubled by the Unitarian tendencies in the Race Street Yearly Meeting, it was far from reassuring to note that prominent Philadelphia Hicksites participated in a congress of the National Federation of Religious Liberals in 1909. The Federation was composed as well of Baptists, Jews, Universalists, and Unitarians.[5]

Both groups moved hesitantly in taking joint action to confront serious problems. When a martial spirit seemed to sweep the nation in the nineties it touched a nerve common to Hicksite and Orthodox alike. The Pennsylvania legislature considered a bill for universal military training in the high schools in 1895. Separate lobbying groups from both branches rushed to Harrisburg to dissuade the legislature from adopting the measure. The following year the Race Street Yearly Meeting announced it would "welcome any step which tends toward the cooperation of religious bodies as indicating a growth of Christian love and charity." This cautiously extended olive branch produced a jointly sponsored public meeting to support the arbitration treaty being considered by the U.S. Senate in February 1897. But not all Friends were ready for this cooperation as the caustic rejection of support by some indicates. Ten years later the Race and Twelfth Street Meetings made a joint appointment of a probation officer who worked through the juvenile court in Philadelphia. By that time the two branches were working together in the temperance movement. The Hicksites appeared more anxious to promote these joint ventures than the Orthodox and they celebrated them more joyfully in their official minutes. It is significant that the catalytic agent for renewed communications had been the most precious of Friends' testimonies, pacifism. The experience of the Great War was to do even more to provide a foundation for the eventual reunion of Orthodox and Hicksite Friends.[6]

It was difficult for older Friends to set aside views which they had embraced for decades. Therefore, initiation of renewed contacts between the branches was in part the work of young Quakers. The Hicksite Yearly Meeting had established an independent organization for youth which became a natural outlet for criticism of the traditional. This Young Friends' Association began a lecture series in 1895, not confined to religious topics, which fostered an open and questioning atmosphere. The Friends' Institute, next to the Twelfth Street Meeting, performed the same function for the Orthodox young. By the 1910s these youthful Friends were speaking out for modifications in the queries and increasing Orthodox-Hicksite cooperation in efforts to maintain neutrality and peace. The boldness with which they challenged their elders shocked many Quakers. Looking back on these events in the late twenties, an Orthodox Friend attributed this youth movement to a "Revival" which took place in 1905 as a result of the educational traditions at work at Twelfth Street. He called this tradition "the Haverford spirit."[7]

The label was not inaccurate. Much of the pressure to discard elements of the Quaker past which prevented active participation in the present came from a generation educated at the Friends' colleges. The rigor of their intellectual demands produced graduates who refused to accept many traditional assumptions. Several Swarthmore and Haverford professors—unlike those at Bryn Mawr—were thoughtful Friends who were out of step with the Philadelphia leadership. The wider contacts of these educators assured that they would be influenced by the Progressive movement. They wrestled openly with basic religious questions and social problems as they related to Christianity. Because they were effective teachers many of their students carried this questioning spirit back to Philadelphia Meetings as adults. If the colleges had lost all their religious influence and become simply worldly outposts, they would have turned out graduates willing to leave Quakerism to the quietists and the elderly. As it was they produced a generation which attempted to adapt the faith to the modern world.

The interconnection between reform and higher education was not confined to Quakerism. Several American colleges laid the foundations for the social justice movement at the turn of the century. Some of them even abandoned their religious affiliations in the process. Dartmouth, Williams, and Oberlin, which had been hotbeds of evangelism in the middle of the nineteenth century, channeled the enthusiasm of their students into reform and social justice after 1900. The Quaker institutions produced more cautions and restrained approaches to the Social Gospel. The curriculum at Swarthmore directed student attention toward social concerns early in the new century. Professor Frederick Spiers offered a course in "Industrial and Other Social Problems" in 1904, with the assistance of two pioneers in Philadelphia's social settlements, Mary Richmond and Anna Davis. Child labor reformer and capitalist critic Scott Nearing gave courses in "Current Economic Problems" and "The Social Cost of Economic Maladjustment" five years later. The Orthodox colleges were tardier in this regard. It was not until 1914 that Haverford named Frank Dekker Watson to a professorship in social work; Watson offered sociological studies of criminology and race problems as well as a course in case work. The following year Carey Thomas announced the creation of a graduate department of social economy and social research at Bryn Mawr.[8]

Three scholar-teachers in particular had a profound impact on the young in the college classroom and upon Philadelphia Meetings at which they spoke and in whose work they sometimes participated. Isaac Sharpless and Rufus Jones at Haverford and Jesse Holmes at Swarthmore introduced Friends to the progressive currents of thought alive in the wider culture and urged them to create Quaker outlets for those impulses. Holmes, who taught philosophy and religion, was a Quaker maverick and self-appointed gadfly whose views were shocking even to the liberal Hicksites. He believed that contemporary religious experience need not be expressed in terms of the life of Jesus, Paul, or George Fox, but "should be so stated as to plainly . . . form a part of twentieth-century life." He was an archcritic of the American emphasis on the rights of property, and his views on race relations were far more liberal than those of his contemporaries. Aware that he was teaching in a transition period of Quaker history "when old formulas have lost their power and the new faith is yet 'without form,' " he candidly helped students grapple with questions of religious significance.[9]

In 1910 Isaac Sharpless expressed the belief that the contemporary generation of Friends differed markedly from its predecessors.

It is more in touch with the world around, it is more open to new ideas, it is less inclined to accept as conclusive argument for itself that

Friends in the past followed certain customs. It is probably no less loyal to fundamental Quakerism; and it is much more hopeful that this will become, not the possession of a slowly dying though very respectable remnant, but a growing and vigorous organism adapting itself to the problems of its environment, and winning strength and confiidence by its real efficiency.

What he described was in part the result of his own handiwork. Though raised in a conservative Chester county Orthodox family, he was deeply influenced by Gurneyite evangelism and trained in the sciences outside the Quaker community at Harvard. First as dean and then as president of Haverford, Sharpless built upon the vigorous intellectual traditions established by his predecessors by gathering a faculty of the highest scholarly standards. To overcome the emptiness which he felt suffused late-nineteenth-century Quakerism, he prescribed for young Friends explorations in the ethical, sociological, and economic disciplines. He believed in Biblical criticism as "the only thing that can hold intelligent people to Christianity." Both through precept and policy Sharpless induced the Haverford students to put the tools of intellect to work in what he saw as a restoration of the faith.[10]

With the quietist leaders of Philadelphia Yearly Meeting he had ambivalent relations. They deplored the developments at Haverford as intellectual pretensions, but their antagonism was muted by the respect they had for his family and the artful way in which he handled matters of controversy. His tact and diplomacy eased the path of change in Orthodoxy. Some called him the recognized leader of the liberals in Philadelphia. A Weighty Friend, he served seventeen years on the Westtown Committee of the Yearly Meeting. While most of his own generation clung to the ways of the past, Haverford's president was interpreting social Christianity to Quakers when he was in his sixties. He fiercely resented the tendency of small groups of older Friends to control committee nominations as to bar younger members from participation. His criticism of the conservative weekly, *The Friend*, centered on its failure to promote discussion of varying opinions. He even called into question the "sense of the Meeting," which, he believed, placed control of Meetings in the hands of the least progressive members. Sharpless hoped that Friends would have the intelligence to see the proper relation between their principles and the human effort needed to solve urban problems. He urged Meetings to reach out to their needy neighbors with "creaturely activities" such as gymnasiums, adult schools, Bible classes, and other social work. Yet he was rarely able to persuade his fellow members at the liberal Twelfth Street Meeting to take such action. After his retirement in 1917, he admitted, "I am not a radical Socialist, though with an inclination thitherward, in the direction of land nationalization and some cooperative tendencies."[11]

A younger colleague of President Sharpless who taught philosophy and religion at Haverford and edited *The American Friend* had an even greater impact on Quakerism nationally. Rufus Jones was far less restrained in his attacks on the influence of conservatism. Broadened by European travel and intellectual friendships with such non-Quakers as Francis Peabody, Jones was deeply committed to enriching the Society of Friends with outside influences. He belabored the Yearly Meeting for its narrowness which he traced to an ignorance for which he prescribed large doses of intellectual training. "Philadelphia Friends believe they are a chosen and peculiar people, called to witness to special truths in a special manner," he complained soon after his arrival in the city. For his candor, he found two of his early writings excluded from the Friends' Library. Even the Haverford Meeting, which he frequently attended, censured or "eldered" him for "delivering a discourse" which struck some as being too much like a planned sermon. His constant pleas for a restoration of Quaker unity rankled Philadelphians with long memories. They were particularly irritated by his cooperation with the Western evangelicals who created the Five Years' Meeting in 1902.[12]

Jones provided the intellectual rationale for less rigid interpretations of the testimony of simplicity. The vigor with which he defended enjoyment of the arts aroused the hostility of the Wilburites. Jones believed there was nothing implicit in ficticious and imaginative writing which made it immoral or dangerous. "It depends," he argued, "wholly on whether the creation is pure and true to what is best in life, or whether it appeals to the baser passions of the reader." He saw no evil in gratification of the senses and he pointed to the enjoyment of flowers as an example of it which Friends approved. Noting the absence of rubrics against music in the Bible, Jones informed Philadelphians that the earliest Quaker Disciplines made no mention of it until the eighteenth century, which he branded "Friends' century of decadence." The erudition of his arguments and his knowledge of Quaker history posed a considerable threat to the traditionalists, some of whom retaliated by cancelling their subscriptions to *The American Friend*.[13]

For traditions Jones had little regard. As "petty peculiarities" which "smelled of mortality," they were in his view "only husk" and bound to disappear in time. He deplored the Quaker habit of living in the past. Emphasizing its creedlessness, he defined Quakerism more as a peculiar attitude toward God and a relationship to Him, instead of a fixed religion. He wanted Meetings to tolerate frank expressions of opinion and encourage discussion. His pleas for diversity had a Hicksite ring, but the yardstick by which he measured the Orthodox Yearly Meeting in Philadelphia was the corresponding body in London, not Race Street. He thought the guarded education had come to mean a fear of facing up to the whole truth, and he discerned it to be more in the Catholic than the Quaker tradition. "The moment one tries to 'fix' life and crystallize it into a set shape, it ceases to be life," he asserted in 1899. "The characteristic of life is its power to make its own form and expression, ever changing, ever developing, ever modifying its form, and yet kept to its essence."[14]

It would be incorrect to describe Jones simply as a Gurneyite. He thought earnestness and enthusiasm were manifestations of religious strength, while excitement indicated weakness. He affirmed that mystical religion had a positive role for man to play and that without it religion degenerated into nothing but asceticism, which offered no positive test of divine guidance. But he distinguished between what he called "negation mystics" and "affirmation mystics." The former attempted to transcend the finite, while the latter sought God's revelation in the world of man. Jones urged Friends to be active in human service for he regarded a faith which produced nothing practical as doomed: "we shall either surrender the heritage which has come down to us, or . . . we shall so bury it in a napkin to preserve it that it will neither grow at our hands nor enrich the world."[15]

The influence Jones had upon Haverford students from 1893 to 1934 was profound indeed. Many who were to guide the Society of Friends in the new century had struggled first with basic religious problems under his tutelage in "Phil. V" in a Chase Hall classroom. After graduation they often asked his advice on religious or personal matters. And they sought his guidance as they undertook careers in teaching or accepted responsibility for First-day school assignments in their own Meetings. As their professor had done, many of them built strong personal friendships with British Friends who epitomized the more active Quakerism liberals sought to foster in Philadelphia. Through his prolific speaking and writing, Jones brought meaningful religious messages to many who had once looked upon Quakers as an odd and peculiar people. An occasional worldly and lapsed Friend would read his work and end up in an intellectual and religious quest which led back to the meetinghouse. Jones penned twenty-one volumes between 1899 and 1920. The scholarly *Studies in Mystical Religion* (1909) and *Spiritual Reformers in the Sixteenth and Seventeenth Centuries* (1914) proved his academic credentials, while his shorter studies of "the inner light" had a greater influence in charting a course for Quakerism.[16]

As early as 1894 Jones evidenced support for those in other denominations, like Episcopal Bishop Henry Codman Potter of New York, who were applying Christian principles in their analysis of social and economic questions. An 1899 editorial in *The American Friend* reflected Jones' conversion to the Social Gospel: "Something is wrong when a company of worshipers meet week after week to enjoy communion with the Lord, and sit unconcerned about the multitudes who in the same city live in misery, in hunger, in squalor, in vice, and in sin." To the Quaker summer schools which met in alternate years after 1900 on the Haverford campus, Jones invited several spokesmen of this movement. Washington Gladden and Walter Rauschenbusch were among the more prominent participants. Jones matched performance with conviction by undertaking administrative responsibilities to promote social Christianity. Though both Yearly Meetings declined to join the Federal Council of Churches founded in Philadelphia in 1908, he became active in the local council and served for a time as chairman of the Commission on Social Service which coordinated investigations of social needs in the Quaker city. Evidence suggests that Jones was a moderate on the question of how far the church association could go in demanding alteration of the social order.[17]

The Social Gospel was a minority movement in all the denominations it affected. Among Friends in Philadelphia before the European war, the minority which professed concern about Christian solutions to the urban and industrial ills of the day was quite small. In 1908 the Orthodox Yearly Meeting received a proposal initiated by women in the Germantown Meeting recommending that a new set of questions be added to the queries which were read in each Meeting:

Are we as Friends of Christ, individually trying in some way to lighten the burden of Humanity by caring for the welfare of those less favored than ourselves?

Are we bearing a testimony against purchasing articles, made by underpaid labor or under conditions injurious to the health of those employed; and are we trying to cooperate with those throughout our country who are endeavoring to lessen these and kindred evils and patronizing stores where the health of those who serve us is considered?

A Philadelphia lawyer who was also a Weighty Friend argued against it as "socialistic." Referred to the Meeting for Sufferings, which by that time included several liberals, the suggestion met final rejection. The Meeting found it impossible to lay down rules which would apply equally to diverse communities. But it expressed the hope "that by the fidelity of our membership to individual duty in these things, the life of the church may be quickened and her service enlarged." Uniting also with the ideal of self-denial by which Friends could help the less fortunate, the Meeting included in its decision an attack upon the covetousness, selfishness, and mistrust which often characterized the economic system in the United States. Although no victory for the Social Gospel, the incident reflected the growing influence of the college-based progressives who looked to Holmes, Sharpless, and Jones for intellectual leadership.[18]

Local Quaker weeklies displayed increasing interest in social service. They encouraged efforts for better housing and schooling for all and suggested support for higher wages for working people to end labor exploitation. No longer fearful of government paternalism, they urged the city to take action to deal with pauperism and problems of public health. Yet *The Friend* continued to push for more than human effort to change material conditions: "The surest and quickest way to effect any of the various moral and social reforms is by conversion of the individual." The *Intelligencer* cautioned Friends against absolute judgments of the righteousness of the poor they were trying to help and suggested a greater concern for their own motives and intents. By 1911 the Hicksite Yearly Meeting lent official sanction to preventive social work which would undermine evils at the root even if it required major social reorganization. A majority at Race Street believed that philanthropic service was the essence of religion. After 1913 the Orthodox Yearly Meeting gave increasing attention to practical expressions of religious faith, although it continued to see social service as but one part of the larger responsibility of reaching the populace with a Christian message. As the city's unemployment rose in 1914 the Arch Street Women's Meeting shelved its quietism and created a permanent committee to provide poor relief.[19]

Not only had the anti-organizational values of the quietist period stifled efforts to deal with social problems, but they made bureaucratic efficiency unthinkable. Industrialization had swept such organization into fashion in the wider culture after 1900 and the new values conquered older Quaker norms with surprising ease. The committee tradition and anti-professional values in the structure of the Society of Friends appeared to stand in the way of bureaucratization. But demands for efficiency overcame these obstacles. Pressures on the Hicksite Committee on Philanthropic Labor and on the First-day School and Education Committees prompted the suggestion that a single agency undertake all clerical work, call meetings, and coordinate activities of the three committees. Established in 1912, the Central Bureau had a general secretary and two assistants. Four years later, when the Yearly Meeting assumed jurisdiction over it, the Bureau took on greater responsibilities and increased the size of its staff. The Monthly Meeting at Race Street approved appointment of a full-time secretary in 1914. Even the Orthodox succumbed; the first Yearly Meeting secretary began work in 1918. These were major adaptations for Quakers and they reflected the increase of philanthropic service carried on by the Meetings as well as the growing influence of forces outside the faith.[20]

The increasingly progressive climate in the Quaker community affected two institutions sponsored by Friends in the city slums inhabited by the foreign born. Orthodox Friends established North House on Marshall Street above Franklin Square in 1906; Isaac Sharpless headed the settlement's board. The institution offered clubs, athletics, industrial arts, and a library to the "stagnant backwater of humanity" living in the area, and later, after it moved to new quarters, courses in cooking, homemaking, and dress making. Its all-Quaker staff, including many young Quakers fresh from college, worked with the professionals who were reinvigorating the city's Society for Organizing Charity and absorbed some of its progressive views. The S.O.C.'s Mary Richmond prompted thoughtful discussion of the Quaker approach to the urban poor in 1908, when she discussed modern methods of philanthropy with the Twelfth Street Friends who sustained North House. But the settlement staff continued to emphasize personal influence and refused to keep "scientific" records which many social workers utilized.[21]

The Hicksites changed the name of their old mission on Fairmount Avenue and Beach Street to the Friends' Neighborhood Guild in 1901. Its programs were designed to keep children off the streets. The Guild ran a gymnasium, offered sewing and manual training classes, and provided baths for a minimal charge. It was having to turn away fifty children a night for lack of adequate quarters in 1906. After Philadelphia Quarterly Meeting's Philanthropic Committee took over its fund-raising activities, the Guild's budget rose from $1,729 in 1907 to $7,186 a decade later. When the Green Street Monthly Meeting moved to Germantown in 1913, its old meetinghouse at 4th and Green was sold to the Guild for a new center. Invested funds for older but defunct charities were funneled to the Guild by Friends increasingly anxious to strengthen the Hicksite effort in social service within the city.[22]

Located as they were in the ring around Center City and not far from the Delaware River, North House and the Friends' Neighborhood Guild dealt primarily with immigrants crowding into older, dilapidated housing. North House called itself "a Congress of Nations." Russian and Polish Jews dominated the area around both settlements, although small numbers of Germans, Hungarians, Italians, and Armenians could be found there also. Friends found the Jews to be dirtier than most groups and "possessed of many unlovely traits," but they admired these newcomers for their determination to better themselves and their ability to build up prosperous businesses from meager pushcart beginnings. Concern over Americanization of the immigrants prompted both settlements to offer English classes, and North House showed a notable interest in impressing American customs on its charges. The guild's report that young Jewish children under its care sang Christmas hymns with enthusiasm must have assured Race Street Friends it was doing its bit to assimilate the newcomers. The guild's headworker gave vent to different sentiments in 1918: "Any program of Americanization, however sweeping, must rest on the bed rock of friendly association—not on pamphlets, citizenship papers, or English lessons, but on the brotherhood of man." While Friends had altered many of their views on the urban poor after 1900, they retained ambivalent feelings toward the foreign born.[23]

It would be incorrect to view Quakers as reformers who wholeheartedly joined in the demand for changes in the American social, economic, and political fabric. Friends might disapprove of currents in American life, but the objects of their criticism differed from those of the Progressives. The old Quaker attack on the economic system focused more on irresponsible speculation and misuse of trust than exploitation of labor and the organization of national power. And as strong adherents of the work ethic, Friends had approached the question of poverty with condescension. What was familiar to Friends was the mental set of estrangement from the values of the social system. This did prompt some moves to gain Meeting support for reform, but the moves were tardy, hesitant, and primarily from the young. It is important to remember that Philadelphia Friends refused to join the Federal Council of Churches.[24]

The two settlement houses developed by Friends in these years reflected a mix of Progressive methods and older Quaker standards. Workers at North House and the Friends' Neighborhood Guild dissented from some aspects of the new professionalism in social work on the grounds that it was becoming too scientific and too impersonal. Many of them clung to an individualism in charitable endeavor for which *The Friend* continued to plead and which bore the mark of anti-organizational quietism. Most of the social workers of this era displayed a greater sympathy with the foreign born than one can observe among the Friends, hampered by years of inexperience with immigrant problems. The modest budgets of the two Quaker settlements suggest that their efforts in the slums did not produce an outpouring of financial support. Traditional hesitancy also prevented a rush to political action at the height of Philadelphia's reform enthusiasm. Friends were less involved in the successful Progressive mayoralty campaign of Rudolph Blankenburg in 1911 than they had been in the eighties and nineties. Through the middle of the 1910s, the Quaker attack on economic abuses under capitalism came primarily from those in their twenties who were taking their cue from the colleges. These were transitional years in which the young were forced to frame their arguments in terms designed to gain the support of their elders.[25]

In one area of philanthropy Friends deviated sharply from most Progressives. As they emerged from their quietist period and adopted views more consonant with active service, their first instinct was to channel their efforts in traditional directions. It was this that prompted them to take renewed interest in the plight of black Americans in the second decade of the twentieth century. The tempering of Friends' concern in the eighties and nineties had reflected an acceptance of the accommodationist philosophy most clearly articulated by Booker T. Washington. After 1910 Friends took an interest in promoting more militant organizations for Negro betterment. While the paternalism of their previous benevolence did not altogether disappear, it was balanced by a growing understanding of the need for black self-esteem and the initiatives which would promote it. In a return to a Quaker distinctiveness which had been compromised in the three decades following Reconstruction, Friends encouraged the examination of black culture and history at a time when few whites acknowledged their existence. An important factor in the renewal of Friends' concern was the increase during the Progressive Era of the grossest form of white oppression of blacks, the practice of lynching.[26]

In 1904 the Orthodox Meeting for Sufferings penned an address "On the Sacredness of Human Life" which attacked lynching on the grounds that men had no right to arbitrarily destroy what was a gift of God. But the authors were more preoccupied with the likelihood that impatience with the orderly process of law could lead to anarchy than they were with discussing the prime victims of the practice. The protest did not even mention blacks. But in 1911 the evil appeared very close to Philadelphia. An armed mob of four hundred masked men stormed a Coatesville hospital in nearby Chester county and lynched Ezekiel Walker, a black accused of murdering a policeman. A West Chester jury promptly freed the lynchers. An Orthodox Quaker asked if Friends had not become apathetic on the question of blacks; he concluded, "We cannot leave the Negro to himself." A Hicksite was dismayed that such a thing could happen in a town which was "practically in the hands of Friends." Cheyney principal Leslie P. Hill aroused considerable interest in the problem in a talk at Bryn Mawr College in 1918. Arch Street Friends demonstrated a reanimation of their concern over injustices to blacks the following year. They formed a joint committee with Race Street Friends to study the lynching evil and distributed the results of their investigation to clubs, schools, and other organizations. In open meetings they sponsored, Friends endeavored to educate the wider public on this problem.[27]

While a handful of Hicksites had been working since the eighties to rekindle interest in schools for blacks at Aiken and Mount Pleasant, South Carolina, they were unable to raise more than token aid in Philadelphia. Yearly Meeting–sanctioned appeals to thirty-one Monthly Meetings in 1898 produced only $207 from seven, despite ample publicity given the school's desperate financial situation. Martha Schofield, who had directed the school at Aiken since 1868, made annual pilgrimages to Philadelphia in a fruitess quest for support. Renewed interest did manifest itself in the 1910s. Financial contributions in 1911 had risen to four times the 1898 figure. The Hicksites centralized all their fund-raising activities for Negro education nationally in the Friends' General Conference under a superintendent for Colored Work in 1915. By this time regrets about the decline of interest in blacks after Reconstruction received frequent expression. The Yearly Meeting Philanthropic Labor Committee stated that Friends themselves had sustained a loss in failing to give "moral support to the cause of the Colored Race." It created a special subcommittee to deal with the problems of blacks in 1916.[28]

Discussions at the General Conference of 1912 indicated the persistance of views toward black Americans bred in the era of accommodation. One prominent Philadelphia Hicksite characterized the Friends' view of Negroes in the seventies as "sentimental gush." Calling black religion an "emotional spree," he asserted that Negroes failed "to understand that in religion the essential thing is character." In his view, "character" consisted of self-denial, perseverance, frugality, and industry. Another Philadelphian told the conference: "I confess that the thing about which I am most worried in the race prejudice as we meet it in individuals today, is not so much its effect upon the black man as its effect upon the white man." Many Friends were reading works by Thomas Dixon, and one asserted that contributions to the South Carolina schools had fallen off after *The Leopard's Spots* appeared on Philadelphia bookshelves. But when D. W. Griffith's classic rendering of another of Dixon's works appeared as the film "Birth of a Nation" in 1915, many Friends did protest its showing in the Quaker city.[29]

Perhaps because they had abandoned Negroes in the South and terminated their aid to schools so readily, the Hicksites' sense of guilt drove them to increase their philanthropy markedly. Under their auspices, new settlement houses made their appearance to serve black neighborhoods in Philadelphia. Founded in 1906, the Spring Street Settlement attempted to deal with the economic and social difficulties of blacks living in the slums around the red light district north of Race Street and east of Broad. Cornelia Hancock, who had been working with black problems since 1863, served at Spring Street as a teacher and continued to raise funds for many projects for Negroes. The settlement offered instruction in shoe-making and sewing, social activities for the young, and nursing care for all age groups in the neighborhood. A careful census of the residents of the district kept Friends in touch with the most recent migrants from the South. By 1920 demographic changes in the area prompted the settlement to consider moving to remain in touch with the black population. The personal zeal of Susan Wharton provided direction for the Starr Center, which served the blacks living near South Street east of Broad. When they moved westward from that area, Miss Wharton followed by creating the Whittier Center in 1916 to minister to the needs of blacks populating the 30th Ward. These institutions attempted to combine the personal benevolence of individual Friends with the standards of the growing profession of social work.[30]

After 1900 the conservatism of Booker T. Washington's leadership produced a strong countermovement by younger, more militant blacks such as W. E. B. DuBois. When a small band of liberal whites joined them in creating the National Association for the Advancement of Colored People in 1910, they undertook to press more forcefully for the end of legal discrimination and segregation. Orthodox Philadelphians who entertained the Tuskegee educator at the Quaker summer resort in Pocono Manor and who remained in his debt for securing Carnegie funds for the Christiansburg Industrial School were hesitant to praise DuBois. So it was more from liberal Hicksites that the local branch of the N.A.A.C.P. received encouragement. The group's annual meetings were held in the Race Street meetinghouse. This practice began in 1911, when DuBois and Oswald Garrison Villard made the principal addresses. At about the same time Orthodox Friends participated in the founding of an association to deal with black unemployment problems. The Armstrong Association, under the leadership of John T. Emlen, became a local affiliate of the National League on Urban Conditions among Negroes in 1913. The group assisted blacks in their attempts to break into the plumbing, carpentry, and roofing trades. It also held neighborhood meetings in Philadelphia and outlying towns to encourage civic action and particularly to seek improved housing conditions.[31]

Not only did Friends begin to retreat from their critical views of blacks, but they showed a greater sensitivity to the recipients of their benevolence as people. By 1910 the Western District Colored School sought to instill race pride in its students. The school paid principal attention to the prose and poetry of black authors such as Paul Lawrence Dunbar and to the lives of Negro leaders in student recitals. The Spring Street Settlement collected a special library of works by black authors. In a statement of purpose in 1914 the institution's board declared: "The Spring Street Settlement stands for *democracy*. Its officers, Head Worker, teachers and volunteers are continually in and among its people, not over and above them, but in close personal touch and sympathy with them." When the managers of the Institute for Colored Youth began discussions with Leslie P. Hill about his accepting the principalship at Cheyney, they consented to his request for courses in music. Yet their unwillingness to accept courses in drama at the same time showed a retention of a sense of stewardship governed by Quaker values. This new empathetic spirit prompted the Arch Street Meeting in 1916 to change the official name of its school on Raspberry Street to the Benezet School to honor its founder. They believed that the old title—The School for Black People and their Descendents—was offensive to Negroes.[32]

Quaker concern manifested a new realism in confronting the problems of blacks who were migrating to Philadelphia in such numbers during the World War. After visiting the South in 1912, Hicksite Henry Wilbur reported to concerned Philadelphians on the discriminatory interest rates which kept black tenant farmers in a constant cycle of indebtedness to white landowners. Wilbur believed that Negroes could not be expected to remain on farms below the Mason-Dixon line as long as they were caught in such an economic trap. With the assistance of Orthodox Friends, the Armstrong Association attempted to find employment for those who migrated to the Quaker city in fields other than domestic service to which they were so frequently confined. The Hicksite Yearly Meeting's special subcommittee on the Colored Race declared its intention to confront the social and economic problems of the migrants, and it pointed to goals of "industrial freedom" for Negroes. The demands of war prompted the Pennsylvania Railroad to hire hundreds of the newly arriving blacks. The Hicksite subcommittee pleaded with the railroad to give Negro laborers employment stability in 1918. Friends realized that the end of the hostilities would dramatically increase the availability of white labor, a condition which would jeopardize the jobs blacks had won in the restricted wartime labor market.[33]

The Hicksites joined other local progressives working for improved housing in the city, but they focused particularly on the slums into which the black migrants were compelled to move. The Spring Street Settlement badgered the city's building inspectors about unsafe dwellings Negroes inhabited in its neighborhood and protested dangerous slot gas meters installed in some of these dwellings by the United Gas Improvement Company. By 1918 housing conditions for blacks had worsensed as the migration from the South increased. The Hicksites sponsored a public meeting at the Race Street meetinghouse early in 1918 in which prominent black civic leaders and ministers were asked to discuss the housing situation. Friends demanded that a good portion of the federal funds in a housing bill pending before Congress be used for the improvement of Negroes' dwellings in cities such as Philadelphia. This was but the first of a series of public forums sponsored at the meetinghouse on this subject. By 1919 Friends expressed gratification over increased attention given Negro housing problems by the local press. Quaker interest in the city's black population complimented the interest in housing reform which local progressives supported through the Philadelphia Housing Association.[34]

As they emerged from the cocoon of quietism in the new century, Friends maintained certain lines of distinctive behavior which separated them from others in Philadelphia. The dangers of assimilation into the national culture, which even Rufus Jones had perceived when he began to open windows in Philadelphia meetinghouses, had not been realized. The power of the corporate community had exerted its influence to slow the pace of change as young and old worked together to adapt Quakerism to the realities of modern urban life. Even if Friends were not in the vanguard of reform activity, they had certainly raised their awareness of secular problems to a level which required organized responses. It is clear that a more positive outlook was generated in both Yearly Meetings. The progressive elements which looked to Haverford for direction created that vitality by their informed approaches to questions which had long vexed and divided Friends. In 1912 a Hicksite indicated that in his youth he had heard mostly about what Friends ought not do, while contemporary Friends talked only about what they could do.[35] The intellectual challenge and the focus given to Christian service by the progressive mood combined to transform Quakerism.

But through 1914 forces were lacking to fulfill the hope Rufus Jones had expressed a decade and a half earlier. He had spoken then about the need for the Society of Friends "to stand for something in particular" and to deliver a "fresh, vital message" to the world.[36] The increased philanthropy, positive though it was, did not offer a channel of expression particular enough to define a modern Quaker purpose. But in the terrible World War which followed, Friends seized upon their most precious testimony and, linking it to active service for the needy, charted a clear course for themselves in the new century.

CHAPTER **9** | The Anvil
of War

If the pacifist testimony was the most singular of Friends'
religious tenets, it was the least tested in the late nineteenth century, once the crisis of the Civil War was at an end. America's
isolationist policy had limited Quaker opportunities to demon-
strate their steadfastness to peace. That this testimony did not
atrophy for want of challenge at a time when other aspects of
their cultural and religious distinctiveness were being eroded is a
measure of its significance to Friends. This is not to say that the
entire community gave it unanimous support when the World War
compelled Philadelphia Quakers to take a stand. But the vitality
it showed in the face of the near hysteria for war found in practically all segments of American society offers ample testament to
its centrality in Quakerism. Save for the Mennonites and some
groups on the American Left, Friends stood alone in their objection to the war policy.

During the Civil War many Philadelphia Friends had refused
induction into the Union Army. Only four of the 150 drafted
into the military from Orthodox Meetings actually served in the
conflict. Not surprisingly, urban Friends were more susceptible to
enrollment than those in rural Meetings. The Hicksites were not
very strict about disowning those who had been soldiers and refused to acknowledge their error; they even retained a brigadier-
general in membership. Yet Race Street Monthly Meeting expelled at least one member who refused to condemn his own conduct, and Arch Street treated a similar case in the same way.
Twelfth Street disowned another, not for participation, but for
paying a $300 commutation fee. The retention in membership of

many participants, including 10 of the 177 men in our sample born in the 1840s, is attributable to the peculiar circumstances of the conflict. Because Friends were such staunch opponents of slavery, they were placed in a quandary as to which of their testimonies should take precedence in responding to a war directed against that oppressive institution. All Philadephia Friends were strong supporters of the Lincoln administration and they disavowed any connection with the political anti-war movement that was mobilized in 1863. The President showed considerable sympathy for Quaker pacifism, and those with scruples against participation received gentle official treatment as a result. Distraints on property made by local officials were more common in rural areas than in Philadelphia. Friends rejoiced at the outcome of the hostilities and in actions to free the slaves. As a test of pacifist mettle, the Civil War was not very demanding.[1]

In the postwar years, the question of peace remained comparatively dormant in Hicksite consciousness. The Representative Committee memorialized the Pennsylvania legislature early in the seventies when a state constitutional change appeared to threaten abolition of exemptions from militia requirements for pacifists. Hicksite women were more concerned about problems of military display than the men of the Yearly Meeting, who preferred cautions to the membership to public protests on such issues. Only after the women prodded them to do so did the Meeting write the Board of Education objecting to military training in the schools. The Orthodox devoted far more attention to the matter of the state militia exemption in Harrisburg. They worked successfully for its inclusion in the 1874 Constitution along with a stipulation that funds for military activities be drawn from the general treasury and not from a specific tax which Friends could never have paid in good conscience. They made frequent appeals to historical tradition, asking the constitutional convention to "restore our beloved State to the exalted position for religious toleration . . . which it occupied while under the control of William Penn." The growing Orthodox interest in foreign affairs was a departure from quietism, which eschewed involvement in government as leading to religious compromise. They sought to dissuade President Cleveland from using force against Canada in a dispute over fisheries in 1887, recommending arbitration, for which there was successful precedent in the *Alabama* claims settlement. They gave widespread distribution to appeals for arbitration of American disputes with Britain over the Venezuelan-Guiana boundary and with Spain over Cuba.[2] Increasing support for arbitration prompted many international lawyers and academicians in the legal profession to join the peace movement after 1900. Their interest in the 1899 Hague Conference, which created machinery for a Permanent Court of Arbitration, was mirrored by a hopeful enthusiasm. Pacifist appeals penned by both Philadelphia Yearly Meetings were distributed widely. Isaac Sharpless, Charles Roberts, and Isaac Clothier were among the prominent Friends who sponsored a public meeting to elicit support for international arbitration early that same year. Even before that, all sorts of Quakers had raised objections to the growing national muscle-flexing in which the United States engaged with weaker Latin American and Pacific states. Friends dominated Philadelphia committees for Philippine independence in 1904. Most had deplored the "splendid little war" against Spain, although few if any of their numbers were involved. The Orthodox Meeting for Sufferings had admitted to estrangement from national sentiment as early as 1887, when it noted a growing martial spirit in the land.[3]

The zeal of the authors of a 1900 Orthodox peace appeal led them to criticize presidential power. They accused McKinley of exercising dictatorial powers under the plea of military necessity, which they believed would prepare Americans to accept a kind of executive authority which was incompatible with republican institutions. "With a large standing army and powerful navy under his control, the President of the United States may cease to be an official deriving his high office from the free choice of his fellow countrymen." These were strong words—too strong for the Yearly Meeting, which had to approve publication. The revised version omitted the prescient sections on threats posed by presidential power and merely asked Americans to compare their individual professions of Christianity with the nation's growing interest in military action. In the quieter years that followed, Yearly Meeting leaders engaged in extensive correspondence and personal visits with Roosevelt, Taft, and Wilson in which they pressed for reduced armaments, urged the writing of arbitration treaties, and pleaded with the presidents to eschew specific actions inimical to peace. If they were too cautious to pen attacks on the dangerous potentials of the executive, Orthodox Friends at least agreed that the presidency was the governmental office most in need of pacifist influence. The Hicksites joined them in some of these appeals after 1900, but they remained less vocal in support of pacifism.[4]

Both branches entered the new century devoid of any regular standing committee to deal with challenges to the peace testimony. The Yearly Meetings did not create any until the European war confronted them with sizeable responsibilties. True to their isolation within Quakerism, Philadelphians had remained out of the Peace Association of Friends which several Orthodox bodies created in Baltimore in 1867. Its primary strength was among the Western Meetings and its tone was exceedingly evangelical. The Gurneyites in Philadelphia did respond by creating their own Peace Association, which held its annual meetings at Twelfth Street during Yearly Meeting week. And individual Friends joined wider-based associations such as the American Peace Society. Albert K. Smiley, a New York Quaker, began hosting the Lake Mohonk Peace Conferences in 1894. After 1900 those conferences, which at first attracted only churchmen and Mugwump reformers, worked for a greater catholicity in the choice of participants. Those efforts helped make pacifism very respectable in the years before the outbreak of the European war. As C. R. Marchand has shown, the nation's social, professional, and business elites swelled the ranks of the peace movement during the Progressive Era. Through the American Peace Society, the Carnegie Endowment for International Peace, and the World Peace Foundation, they supported pacifism in the abstract as a safe outlet for the reform impulse, but their advocacy required no real challenges to specifics of United States foreign policy. Swarthmore professor William I. Hull, the most active Friend involved in these associations, observed that a great number of the adherents were "nominal peace leaders."[5]

The outbreak of war in Europe decisively changed the complexion of the peace movement. Many in the popular associations declared that their interest in peace did not extend to the conflict then raging abroad. The journal of the American Peace Society announced in April 1915 that the organization had given up any idea of protesting the war and was little interested in the terms of the peace to follow. The response among Philadelphia Friends was quite different. News of the hostilities prompted Quakers to marshal their spiritual resources for the difficult task of enunciating pacifist doctrines in a war climate. Men and women at Twelfth Street united behind a statement the women had prepared:

Under a sense of disappointment and horror at the conditions existing in Europe in this present war, we desire as a body to take up our share of the responsibility for the ideals of our Society, to use every possible effort to make our opposition to the war felt, to unite in an expression of close sympathy with Friends in England who are feeling the testing of this distressing time and to express our belief that out of the chaos and conflict will come a strengthening of faith in righteousness and peace.

The Orthodox Representative Meeting offered strong commendation to President Wilson for his demand for neutrality, as well as for his peaceful overtures to the belligerents. These Friends hoped that a firm stand against militarism by the United States would set a valuable example for all nations.[6]

In having to meet the challenge of the preparedness advocates in the two years that followed, Philadelphia Friends were thrown on their mettle. They saw that it was time to speak out boldly against joining the arms race which they believed would certainly lead to American participation. They began major efforts to propagandize for neutrality and pacifism in 1915. In a widely distributed address, Isaac Sharpless urged Americans to "develop a universal feeling, to allay race and national prejudices and suspicions which often ripen into war," and to urge limitation of commercial ambitions so that the rights of others could be recognized. The Representative Meeting dramatically increased the number of public statements on the war it prepared for distribution early in 1915. Both branches in Philadelphia sent delegates to the Friends' National Peace Conference at Winona Lake, Indiana, in July, which formulated policies to aid Meetings in making peace appeals and petitioning congressmen. For many years out of touch with English Friends, the Hicksites penned a memorial to London praising Quakers there for their defense of principle against British military recruitment. When a prominent London Friend, Henry Hodgkin, came to Philadelphia later in the year, Orthodox and

Hicksites attended joint meetings held in both the Arch Street and Race Street meetinghouses to hear reports of the situation in Britain. The war was increasing cooperation between once-divided Friends.[7]

Hodgkin was instrumental in inducing Quakers to join with Y.M.C.A. leaders and social workers in forming the Fellowship of Reconciliation at a meeting in Garden City, Long Island, late that same year. The new organization, which sought to apply uncompromising religious principles to the question of war participation, attracted many who were disillusioned by the half-baked pacifism of the large popular peace societies. Two Philadelphia Friends, lawyer Edward Evans and banker Charles Rhoads, were officers of the Fellowship, and Rufus Jones exercised a profound influence over its direction. Lacking specific goals, its members met in small groups in private homes for discussions of the application of Christian teaching to the crisis at hand. Its emphasis on personal conscience and individual initiative reflected the values of the Friends who dominated it in the early years. In Philadelphia, Quakers used techniques much less in line with their traditions to bring their peace message to the wider public in 1916. Hicksites Lucy Biddle Lewis and Hannah Clothier Hull set up a "Peace Shop" in a Center City office building where they worked with Orthodox Friends to distribute posters and window displays as pacifist propaganda devices. The newly formed Orthodox Peace Committee contributed $500 to a national propaganda effort which was buying full-page advertisements in *The New Republic, The Outlook, The Survey,* and a number of metropolitan daily newspapers.[8]

The Peace Committee was undeterred by the unpopularity of its message. Its members made open air talks from automobiles all over eastern Pennsylvania, New Jersey, Delaware, and Maryland, and they set up peace booths at county fairs in the region.

It is significant that not many of those who listened would have ever heard our message, had it been given in our meetinghouses as has been our custom. For perhaps the first time . . . have the Friends of Philadelphia gone out to meet the workingmen in the factory, the crowd in the street, the "cracker barrel club" in the country store and the idler in the village square.

These were precedent-shattering days for Friends. They had brought Orthodox and Hicksite together in a common effort. Shelving quietist hesitancy, they employed worldly techniques from the political forum and the marketplace to spread their message. And they began to make more and more contacts with pacifists outside Quakerism. The enthusiastic activism of 1916 did not blind Friends to reality. American involvement in the war seemed increasingly likely. The Peace Committee drafted bills for national legislative consideration providing alternatives to military service for conscientious objectors. The Yearly Meeting urged young Friends of draft age to make up their minds in advance. A foreboding about American entry into the conflict pervaded its sessions in late March 1917. The group wired Wilson urging him to view a peaceful solution of American difficulties with Germany as "consistent with true patriotism."[9]

The climate for peace agitation between 1914 and 1917 was still a comparatively salutary one. While many of the nation's business and professional elite had lost their enthusiasm after Sarajevo, a visible and vocal contingent of social workers had taken their place. Thus, if Friends could no longer count on allies in the American Peace Society, they found new unity with the American Union Against Militarism, which grew out of a meeting at the Henry Street Settlement in the fall of 1914. Some of the new professionals in the social settlements saw war as ruinous to their hopes for social justice. These same years saw new recruits to the cause from the woman's movement and from segments of organized labor. And the Federal Council of Churches offered uncertain support to pacifism before 1917.[10] The participation of these groups helped shield Friends from attacks by preparedness zealots and those who equated patriotism with militarism. Once they brought their scruples of conscience out of the meetinghouse and onto public platforms, once their voices of protest ceased to be muted, they became susceptible to increased pressures if not hostility from majority elements in American society. This was one of the costs of accommodation with the larger culture. The full implications of these changes were not apparent until after Congress declared war on Germany in April 1917.

American entry into the First World War decimated the ranks of the peace movement. The effectiveness of allied propaganda and the mounting hysteria against Germany permeated all segments of the social order. Dissent from the militaristic consensus required conviction and courage. Many churchmen repeated tales of horror about the invasion of Belgium from their pulpits. The Federal Council of Churches gave its approval to the war policy. It asserted that the right of freedom of conscience should not be violated, but when asked by the Civil Liberties Bureau to aid conscientious objectors, the council refused. An adjunct of the council, the Church Peace Union, became an agent of the government's Committee on Public Information to "educate" the churches as to the "moral aims of the war." The American Peace Society even circulated pledges of national loyalty to its membership for signatures. As Friends looked about them they saw that only a few social workers in the American Union Against Militarism, some left-wing elements in the labor movement, and the Fellowship for Reconciliation remained on pacifist platforms. In this exposed position they had to present their defense of noncooperation with the war effort.[11]

Their response reflected this position. The Orthodox Representative Meeting showed a far greater concern for public reaction than was its habit. And in advising young draft-age Friends on how to answer demands for their service, it urged a similar caution. The Meeting professed the deep loyalty Quakers felt for the United States and its desire to contribute to the well-being of the nation and of the entire world as well. It also urged pacifists in the Quaker community to try to understand the noble motives which prompted most men to take up arms. Orthodox leaders tried to counteract the negativism of their opposition by linking their refusal to take up arms with positive hopes for a reconstruction of the world. The Representative Meeting promised that Friends did not intend to hide behind religious exemptions, but would perform alternative service. Unlike some of Friends' nineteenth-century stands, their previous pleas for a peaceful settlement did not turn into open criticism of the administration's decision for war. The national mood in 1917 dictated a prudent emphasis on conscience and courage.[12]

Friends cannot be faulted for being defensive. They seemed to sense the national concern about loyalty long before sedition and espionage became administration obsessions. Individual Quakers might be outspoken in their criticism of intervention; the Yearly Meeting had a sense of corporate responsibility which made it view such candor as hazardous indeed. But the Orthodox Yearly Meeting was uncompromising in its defense of principle. It reaffirmed the convictions of early English Friends who had declared in 1660: "We utterly deny all outward wars and strife and fighting with outward weapons, for any end or under pretence whatever." Maintaining that "religion and conscience are superior even to the State," the Orthodox explained that Christ's example of combatting wrong with love remained the precedent for their stand. To use means which violated love and defeated its ends was no way to overcome evil in the world. Their arguments were simplistic; they did not include those Rufus Jones had used to explain the Quaker position before 1917. The Haverford professor argued that war frustrated man's potential for the development of his spiritual stature and denied him the "diviner contacts" which fostered a truer ideal of manhood. He saw it also as interfering with the "processes of liberation" unleashed by democracy, which had brought mankind to "the dawn of a real human emancipation."[13] To the American president and his people war was the very means by which those gains could be preserved.

The Yearly Meeting took steps to assist those who intended to refuse military service and was zealous in its defense of their conscientious objection, in spite of the national climate. When the government decided in the summer of 1917 that all "C.O.s" must report to mobilization camps for noncombatant service, a contingent of Orthodox leaders travelled to Washington to lodge a protest with authorities. Some Quakers became ambulance drivers or joined medical teams in the Army. Others who refused these alternatives as too direct a contribution to the conflict were detained in camps where their civil liberties were abridged. Meeting representatives held countless discussions with War Secretary Newton D. Baker to iron out the thorny exemption problem. The government eventually decided those rejecting service under the Army could be examined by an impartial commission and assigned either to agricultural labor or European reconstruction work, if found to be sincere pacifists. Pressure to accept service under the military was intense, however, and some objectors received harsh treatment and prison sentences. Protests against violations of their civil rights came primarily from the Society of Friends.[14]

The Orthodox Yearly Meeting needed its courage in the defense of Christian scruples against war. From the Episcopal Church this pacifism brought a sharp attack: "Quakerism is sixteen hundred years too late to be entitled to the epithet Christian." An Episcopal organ, *The Living Church,* argued that Quaker rigidity would work against the abolition of war and a righteous peace. It hinted that Friends' pacifism was limited to the profits of neutrality. While the Philadelphians tried to emphasize the positive elements of their position, the outlook of the general public assured that these explanations would receive scant hearing. So intense was the hysteria for participation that countless numbers of American Friends wavered in their pacifist resolve. Among American Quaker bodies in the First World War, the Philadelphia Orthodox had taken the strongest anti-war stand. Nurture in exclusive quietism had preserved a distinctiveness on the peace issue less vulnerable to worldly accommodation than was found in the compromised Quakerism of the Midwest. Other East Coast Yearly Meetings left the matter to individual conscience and avoided official stands on the issue. As we shall see, Hicksite resolve was weaker than that of the Orthodox in Philadelphia. For all its defensiveness and attention to public opinion, the Arch Street Yearly Meeting provided a pacifist light undimmed by compromise.[15]

It was one thing for Friends to express positive hopes for world reconstruction, but what was needed was a vehicle for their realization. To convince critics of Quaker loyalty, leaders sought a positive outlet for Friendly principles. Hoping that Quakers might "redeem the time" and prove that "for this hour they are in the world," Rufus Jones had a solution. He organized on the Haverford College campus a service unit for young Quakers interested in relieving suffering caused by the hostilities. Directed by Jones and Dr. James Babbitt, the unit began training in the spring of 1917 for diverse forms of volunteer work. Less than a month after the declaration of war, representatives of the Orthodox Yearly Meeting, the Hicksite Friends' General Conference, and the Five Years Meeting met in Philadelphia to plan a per-

manent national organization for Quakers in the United States—
the American Friends' Service Committee. Through it they hoped
to mount European relief and reconstruction projects in which
those exempted from military service could engage in positive
efforts to heal the wounds of war. While there was a defensive
side to this, it was also the culmination of the trend toward activism already at work in Philadelphia Meetings. Jones and his
supporters wanted the A.F.S.C. to "inspire and unify the Society
of Friends and arouse it to its proper sense of mission in the
world crisis."[16]

The Haverford unit of 100 men trained through the summer,
learning French and gaining practice in ambulance driving, rescue
work, and fundamental relief activities. The unit embarked for
Europe in September under the aegis of the Red Cross. Working
with that organization and an English Friends' emergency relief
team already in the field, A.F.S.C. agents found specific tasks in
the Marne Valley in France. Morris E. Leeds and J. Henry Scattergood had completed the general planning in Paris before the
unit arrived. Tackling the reconstruction of several villages, the
Service Committee volunteers built portable houses some of which
were not far from the front lines. While the Red Cross provided
part of the materials for reconstruction, the A.F.S.C. had to
acquire the bulk of the supplies itself. The costs of the effort were
considerable, and the Service Committee spent around $2,000,000
in the first two years of its existence. Philadelphia Friends, regardless of their attitude toward the war, rose to the occasion.
Race Street Monthly Meeting alone contributed over $41,000 in
the first eighteen months of the Committee's work. In a single
year the Orthodox Yearly Meeting turned over $165,000 to the
A.F.S.C.[17]

Jones had taken the chairmanship of the Committee, while
Vincent Nicholson headed the administrative staff, which was
housed in the Friends' Institute on Twelfth Street. Funds began
to come in from non-Quaker sources interested in the projects.
Increasing numbers of volunteers from other faiths undertook
assignments for the Committee in Europe. Most Meetings in the
area participated in canning food and sewing garments to be sent
abroad. Articulate Friends travelled to Quaker communities to
keep supporters informed of the work being done by the A.F.S.C.

All of this generated an excitement in the Quaker community which had not been felt since the programs for the Indians and the freedmen in the sixties and seventies, but the activities now were accompanied by a new unity. The Arch Street meetinghouse was the site of cloth-cutting operations prefatory to the sewing of garments. Twelve blocks to the west, garments ready for shipment to France were sorted and repacked in one of the rooms of the Race Street meetinghouse. Seven years earlier Jones had expressed the hope of seeing "a whiff of inspiration sweep over us and a devotion possess us"; his A.F.S.C. was achieving just that.[18]

Jones was personally helpful in charting a course for individual Friends through the uncertainties of the war period. Many of his former students and others who merely knew him by reputation sought his counsel when they faced difficult decisions about their draft status. His plans for the A.F.C.S. sprang naturally from his familiarity with the troubled consciences of those who had written him for advice. Even before American involvement he had guided concerned young Quakers into ambulance units under English auspices. Jones conferred frequently with authorities in Washington on the question of C.O. exemptions, and he remained a vital force in the Fellowship of Reconciliation—the only important Protestant churchman to do so after 1917. So forceful had his leadership been through these years of trial that it prompted the Arch Street Yearly Meeting conservatives to acknowledge their gratitude for the strength and confidence he had given all Friends.[19]

Though Jones had inspired the two branches to cooperate, he could not overcome the traditions of accommodation which had been building for decades among the Hicksites. Their Yearly Meeting did announce its official support of pacifism, but it also openly declared that that testimony was not binding on the conscience of any individual. An Emergency Peace Committee it created assisted those unwilling to serve in the military. But the tones of Hicksite pacifism were far more muted than those at Arch Street. A peace meeting scheduled for the Race Street meetinghouse was cancelled when the Monthly Meeting Property Committee heard that authorities had prevented a similar function from taking place the night before at the South Street Theater. Early in 1918, when pacifist professor Jesse Holmes of Swarthmore requested permission to use the meetinghouse for a series of lectures on "Internationalism and the Great War," he was refused. Yet the same Property Committee authorized the building's use to lodge soldiers, sailors, and marines furloughed in the city. These were troubled times, and the Hicksite establishment displayed a marked nervousness over its pacifist affiliation.[20]

A major segment of that establishment actually favored the war. They did not think themselves to be inconsistent with the Quaker faith; they believed that Christ would not have remained neutral in the face of Germany's "organized savagery." So 120 prominent Hicksites—most of them Philadelphians—publicly pledged "loyalty to the cause of civilization and to the President of the United States" by approving the war effort. Eighty-one-year-old Isaac Clothier was among them; not only did he view the war as just, but he avowed that if younger he would have voluntarily joined the army. Arguing that they sought to avoid divisiveness, the directors of the *Friends' Intelligencer* restricted editor Henry Ferris, who wanted to speak out bodly against the war in its columns. Some wanted him to run a full-page Liberty Bond advertisement on its front page, and Horace M. Lippincott headed a group which sought Ferris' ouster from the journal. Attempts to get the 1918 Yearly Meeting to rescind its condemnation of "all wars" were, however, unavailing. Swarthmore was the only Quaker college in the country to have a Student Army Training Corps on its campus during the hostilities. One of its professors, William Forbush, told the graduating class at Friends' Central School in 1917 that "it was their duty in the war to perpetuate an America worthy of the men willing to die for it." Only when the persistent Henry Ferris interrupted the commencement exercises and expressed the hope that none of the graduates would be willing to kill for their country did Quaker pacifism get a hearing at the proceedings.[21]

There was hardly any "backsliding" on peace among the Orthodox. Their periodicals and Meeting policies remained emphatically pacifist. But the Orthodox were not impervious to popular pressure on war issues as a pre-armistice incident at Haverford indicated. Dismayed by the bellicosity of public opinion and the government's refusal to give credence to German peace feelers in the early fall of 1918, Professor Henry J. Cadbury penned a critical letter to the *Public Ledger:*

As a Christian and patriotic American, may I raise one cry of protest in your columns against the orgy of hate in which the American press and public indulges on the receipt of peace overtures from the enemy. Whatever the immediate result of the present German request for an armistice, the spirit of implacable hatred and revenge exhibited by many persons in this country indicates that it is our nation which is the greatest obstacle to a clean peace and the least worthy of it.

Cadbury concluded with a plea for moderation in the interest of a "safer and saner international fellowship" in the postwar period. A candid description of the national mood the letter may have been, but it produced a response which was far from peaceful. Cadbury was forced to appear before the U.S. Attorney, although he was eventually absolved of having violated the Espionage Act. A group of Haverford students sent a petition to President William Wistar Comfort condemning the letter. The Alumni Association labelled it "treasonable." The managers were closer to the truth; they called it "indiscreet," but they recommended an immediate leave of absence for the religion professor. While claiming to respect the right of academicians to dissent, the college repudiated his "intemperate and unjustified language." Cadbury had his defenders in the college community, but they were outnumbered. Rejecting offers of an administrative post with the Service Committee, he eventually taught at the Harvard Divinity School. Strained by their unpopular anti-war stand, Philadelphia Friends had sacrificed one of their finest young scholars on the altar of good relations with the wider culture.[22]

Overall, the First World War revealed that essential ambivalence in the Quaker personality between worldly ways and a conscientious distinctiveness. The extent of its accommodation with American culture was made manifest by the difficulty many Friends had in sustaining a strict pacifism through the conflict. In the process, witness against war became less a corporate stand for peace than a collection of individual acts of conscience. While the Yearly Meetings had issued their condemnations of all wars, they disowned no one for participation. In March 1918, of the 299 men of draft age in the Orthodox Yearly Meeting, 50 were in military service, although most of these were engaged in non-combatant activities. The Hicksites were less precise, as they were less rigid on the issue. But what the World War signalled was a fundamental change: Friends' Meetings were permitting diverse interpretations in the application of the most important testimony in the Quaker faith. While the Orthodox came closer to sustaining a corporate pacifism, they did not inquire as to the attitude of participants toward their conduct when the hostilities were concluded. The 120 Hicksites who had publicly supported the war had even cited New Testament passages to prove that Christ was not a pacifist. They and the younger men who entered the service received no censure from their Meetings. Despite these accommodations, Friends had, along with the Mennonites, remained among the nation's primary war opponents. They had sustained pacifist dissent at some hardship when its adherents were few. And their American Friends' Service Committee provided a new outlet for pacifist public witness of the most positive sort.[23]

The experience of World War I reoriented Philadelphia Friends and established new patterns of witness for the twentieth century. The work of the Service Committee was most significant in guiding Quakers away from the paths of quietism. But their attempts to protect conscientious objectors brought them into alliance with secular groups with which they had had little previous contact. Many of these were left-wing critics of the social and economic order. The Quakers encountered their ideas at the very time that many Friends were raising questions about the relationship between that order and the World War. The result was to give the Society of Friends the appearance of a community on the left. While much of the old conservatism and hesitancy continued to influence Quaker tactics, there was an appreciable increase in criticism of the socioeconomic system. Many became firm internationalists, viewing the League of Nations as an effective means of preventing the return of war. The world conflict was salutary for many groups which had not at first seen it in those terms. For social justice advocates it brought their crusade for domestic reform to fruition. It gave an impetus to the drive for church unity and transformed the Federal Council of Churches into the most influential organization in American Protestantism.[24] And for Quakerism in Philadelphia it ushered in a new period of activism at home and abroad.

When Meetings came to the defense of conscientious objectors during the war, they became strong defenders of civil liberties and even of cultural diversity. Even before American involvement the Orthodox were protesting attempts to censor and bar from the mails publications which featured religious articles deemed "objectionable" by the Postmaster General. In May 1917 the Hicksite Peace Committee noted the speed with which war had brought denials of free speech, suppression of freedom of action, and the growth of intolerance. The Orthodox deplored violations of First Amendment guarantees in the Sedition Act of 1918. The effectiveness of government propaganda and frequent invasions of personal liberty and property prompted the Representative Meeting to note that the United States seemed to be adopting modified forms of the very Prussian autocracy against which it had been fighting. Orthodox leaders on the Peace Committee warned that if free exchange of ideas was not allowed, it would result in national stagnation or political upheaval. They censured the New York legislature for denying seats to five duly-elected Socialists and opposed enactment of a permanent Sedition Law by Congress in 1920. The Peace Committee even sent funds to the Civil Liberties Bureau to aid in the defense of the Bill of Rights.[25]

If their interest in civil liberties was new, the Friends' concern over international affairs was not. The enthusiasm they had once expressed for arbitration was transformed to the League of Nations idea. Many Friends wanted to eschew pious generalities and work for concrete instrumentalities for world peace. Rufus Jones had encouraged the Fellowship of Reconciliation into advocacy of a League of Nations late in 1918. The Orthodox Peace Committee prepared lessons on internationalism and urged Friends to read widely on the subject. The following April it gave strong support to the League idea, although it did not specify the form the body should take. The Representative Meeting sent J. Henry Scattergood and Charles J. Rhoads to the Paris Peace Conference to press Friends' feeling about the League and the importance of disarmament. Claiming that the League was originally a Quaker proposal, the Hicksites rejoiced in the hope that it would substitute "human welfare for 'National interest' as a standard for measuring international righteousness." The hopes of those Orthodox Friends who wanted the Society to go beyond pious utterances were dashed, however, when the Yearly Meeting attempted to unite on the issue of the Versailles Treaty, which was then before the Senate. Differences on the issue were so wide that the Meeting was unable to forge a public statement to send to Washington.[26]

It was the Service Committee more than anything else which helped keep Friends in touch with international problems. Its work of reconstruction in the Marne Valley continued well beyond the armistice. Near Verdun a team of volunteers attempted to rebuild an area practically levelled by fighting early in the conflict. Other projects took Friends to Russia, Serbia, Austria, and the Ukraine, where teams distributed food and medical supplies in 1918 and 1919. Philadelphia participants in these projects returned home with what Howard Brinton called "high and liberal ideals about things in general." The Orthodox Yearly Meeting foresaw continued need for service, "not merely in the stress of wartime, but as an expression of a living and vital conception of Christianity." Late in 1919, at the behest of Herbert Hoover, the A.F.S.C. laid plans for a food distribution program for German children left destitute by four years of war. Rufus Jones suggested that young Friends from all parts of the United States might devote a year to work with the A.F.S.C. abroad or in community service at home. It was clear that the Service Committee was too important to be treated as merely an expedient wartime agency for alternative service. Sceptical Carey Thomas, who had originally viewed it as a means by which Quakers could "shirk . . . their patriotic duty," thought in 1920 it had become the purest kind of philanthropy. It even survived the complacent twenties, when the social service and reform aims of most Protestant churches went into a decline.[27]

Another effect of the war was to convince Friends of the need for change in the social and economic life of the nation. The Social Gospel had had some influence in Philadelphia Meetings, but when Quakers had read Francis Peabody and Walter Rauschenbush their innate caution tempered any enthusiasm for Christian reform. Yet in the 1916 presidential election the editor of the *Friends' Intelligencer* spoke favorably of the Socialist candidate and his platform. He caimed that many Friends had become Socialists because of the respect that political doctrine showed humanity as opposed to property. Quite a few British Friends had joined the Labour party and were espousing such schemes as corporate consumer organizations, communal property, and a cooperative garden city controlled by Quakers. But in Philadelphia it was the interpretation of the war as a clear manifestation of a sick society which caught the attention of more and more Friends. The linking of social evils to the hostilities compelled good pacifists to reexamine their economic and social views. Edward Evans was more conservative than most of his colleagues in the leadership of the Fellowship of Reconciliation. Yet he went along when that organization allied itself with several labor radicals and called for Christian remedies to the American industrial order.[28]

But even before the Fellowship began to criticize the economic system, Philadelphia Friends had taken steps to develop Quaker criticisms of that system. Impressed by the work of a committee of London Yearly Meeting, twenty-four Orthodox Quakers proposed the creation of a Social Order Committee at the 1917 Yearly Meeting. Expressing the belief that the European war proved that twentieth-century civilization fell far below Christian standards, the group "discovered the seeds of war in our own social order." These Friends hoped that through a committee structure they could devise practical steps the Society could take to apply Christian teaching to business, the home, and politics. The Yearly Meeting acceded to their request. In the years that followed the committee held several sessions with the Hicksite Committee for Peace and Emergency Service in a quest for higher standards for American social and economic life. The new committee turned to the academic community for assistance in framing questions for their discussions. Swarthmore professor Jesse Holmes suggested that the Orthodox group consider:

What is the wage system? What regulates it? Should we ever engage labor at less cost than that of a decent living? What alternatives are there to the wage system?

What is the competitive system? Does it involve willingness to gain by the loss of others? Does it involve willingness to monopolize opportunity? Should we live on incomes other than those from our own labor?

Is our present system of special privileges, which is so interwoven with our industrial system, in harmony with the Christian and Quaker ideal of democracy?[29]

The Social Order Committee encouraged wide reading and thought in the search for answers to Holmes' questions. It decided to publicize its organized introspection through letters, pamphlets, and items in *The Friend*. It also asked Monthly Meetings to co-operate in organizing discussions of social topics and to make books chosen by the Committee available in Meeting libraries. To these libraries it sent copies of Walter Rauschenbush's *Christianizing the Social Order* and *The Social Principles of Jesus,* Vida Scudder's *The Church and the Hour,* and Charles Elwood's *The Social Problem*—all staples in the Social Gospel diet. They also added *A Word of Remembrance to the Rich* by John Woolman, the New Jersey Friend whose thoughtful concerns had jarred the eighteenth-century Quaker community out of its lethargy on the slavery issue. Hicksite participation was limited by the same forces which had made their pacifism so lukewarm; those attending joint sessions with the Orthodox were warned to "avoid any propaganda of particular social panaceas in the name of the Yearly Meeting." Discussants in Social Order Committee meetings made thoughtful attempts to find distinctive Quaker opportunities to place Christ over culture, but in trying to deal with the concrete, they operated almost exclusively on the theoretical level. Their impact in the area they most wanted to affect was minimal. Their discussions engaged but a small proportion of Meeting members, and in this they were like the Social Gospelers in most Protestant denominations.[30]

The earliest sessions dealt with industrial questions. Samuel Allen expressed approval of minimum wages and maximum hours, public works in times of depression, and sick benefits and old-age compensation insurance. Morris E. Leeds proposed a modified profit-sharing plan. He thought the Social Order Committee could educate people as to the value of such changes. Fresh from a week with Lillian Wald, Vida Scudder, and Emily Balch in a social settlement camp, Agnes L. Tierney urged Friends to make common cause with workers and to examine the injustices of contemporary economic conditions. The discussants asked serious questions about the consistency with Christianity of a system which pitted self-interest against self-interest. And they criticized competition for the waste which duplicated effort produced. Many doubted the value of the Sherman Anti-Trust Act as a workable means of compelling competition.[31]

Some of the group's sessions produced practical proposals upon which individuals could act. In his analysis of "Unearned Increment," Henry Albertson recommended that Friends abstain from the purchase of land for speculative purposes. He later suggested that affluent Quakers should not leave money to the young who were given an unfair advantage over less fortunate youth. Agnes Tierney urged the investment of inherited wealth in worthy enterprises such as housing projects or "garden cities" in spite of their low return. Another reported that two such investment opportunities existed in the city; one was the Octavia Hill Association, which improved slum housing and then rented it to the needy at low rates, returning 4 percent to investors. A remedial loan association begun by two Friends which was aimed at the small and usually exploited borrower limited its stockholders to a 6 percent return. After examining the padrone system and looking into housing conditions of Italian laborers on Friends' property, the group decided the workers were being treated inhumanely. It also raised for consideration the housing, education, and community life of the employees at the Westtown School. An examination of the Friends' charity organizations in Philadelphia produced recommendations for consolidation and simplification.[32]

Meetings in 1919 and 1920 with Jane Addams, municipal reformer and immigration commissioner Frederic Howe, and Glenn Plumb, author of the plan for railroad consolidation, explored ethical questions in relation to contemporary social, political, and economic developments. Committee members and participants were not merely academic idealists. Manufacturer Morris E. Leeds and insurance executive M. Albert Linton were among the more vocal influences in the sessions. The former applied some of his own formulas for industrial democratization in his electronic instrument firm, Leeds & Northrop Company. It is, of course, difficult to tell the extent to which the committee's views won favor beyond its own membership. Older Friends may have found it difficult to accept many of the group's conclusions, but the committee itself was not merely a preserve of the young. By granting standing committee status to concerns about the social order and devoting significant portions of the annual sessions to reports on the subject, the Yearly Meeting gave it a sanction not lightly bestowed in the Quaker community. While the pronouncements of the Representative Meeting and the Yearly Meeting did not show support for specific committee suggestions, their tenor reflected the same "shaking up and serious examination of principles hitherto supposedly permanent." Particularly in the Orthodox branch, Friends were seeking contemporary applications for distinctive Quaker testimonies after 1917 as they had never done in the nineteenth century.[33]

In 1870 the Quakers of Philadelphia were a distinctive and peculiar people whose island community remained outside the mainstream of worldly culture. Half a century later this community continued to harbor Friends whose values differed significantly from those of most of the Americans around them. But five decades had altered the terms and the intensity of their estrangement from the larger society. From an exclusive, conservative community bent on rigid enforcement of simplicity which eschewed most initiatives in organized philanthropy, the Society of Friends was transformed into a progressive body of civil-libertarian pacifists who supported active domestic and international programs of social melioration. Distinctive Quaker testimonies had not changed in these years; what had changed was the interpretation and emphasis given to each of these attitudes. During the early years of the new century, as Friends adopted many progressive views, the Quaker outlook seemed enough like the general reformist mood of the nation to cast doubt on the survival of a distinctive cultural position. But the coming of the World War recalled Friends to their traditional estrangement and compelled them to find definitive expressions for their unique cultural position.

They had been interested in "doing good" in Philadelphia since the eighteenth century, when their withdrawal from the government had induced them to find opportunities for civic influence in avenues less compromising than politics. The interest they took in the neglected minorities of that era—Indians and Negroes—remained an important focus for their benevolence even in their least active years in the nineteenth century. They maintained benevolent efforts once they were established with a remarkable tenacity. But their quietism prevented them from initiating new philanthropic endeavors after the 1840s. Insisting that each

Friend empty himself of worldly experience to make way for Divine guidance, quietism bred an anti-organizational spirit in the Quaker community. Only the evangelical group took decisive action to meet Indian and black needs after the Civil War. Estranged by the city and the multiplicity of problems it spawned in the industrial era, Friends used existing agencies and their civic influence in attempts to control the behavior of the increasingly diverse population in Philadelphia. But they created few benevolent instrumentalities adapted to contemporary urban needs.

After 1900, as they grew closer to the reformist aims of the national culture and took direction from influences at work in their own colleges, they began to deal more effectively with the needs of Philadelphia's poor. At the same time, they became more aware of the special needs of blacks. But it was not until they found pacifist motives for social service in the First World War that they reanimated their philanthropy with a Quaker distinctiveness which made it more effective. The American Friends' Service Committee became a permanent effort to relieve suffering at home and abroad—an expression of what war's antithesis could accomplish in an active, positive way. The developments between 1900 and 1920 restored Friends to their habit of "doing good" which had faltered in the Gilded Age. And linked with the testimony of peace this benevolence became uniquely Quaker.

In the process of change they became more sensitive to their own testimony of equality. Habits of social condescension and class prejudice which had marked much of their earlier philanthropy erected barriers to social understanding. These attitudes came naturally to Quakers, constituting as they did an affluent elite in Philadelphia. Some joined the institutional network of the city's upper-class aristocracy or became involved in the gentlemanly reform effort of the Mugwumps. Their pious stewardship in philanthropy and politics was premised on assumptions about social hierarchy which were at odds with their own professions. Only in the wake of the Progressivism they absorbed did they begin to deal with the needy in human terms which reaffirmed their own belief in equality. In these same years they began to make more thoughtful applications of that testimony within their own community. Women gained a status in the Quaker organizational structure which was far more equitable than that to which they had been confined in separate Women's Meetings.

Changes in American society itself had recalled Friends to their egalitarian ideals, and accommodation with national cultural norms had weakened outward signs of simplicity. As Friends' educational institutions responded to influences from parents and students, an increasing number of whom came from outside the faith they abandoned the rigid rules of simplicity which traditionalists treasured. Quaker colleges created a climate in which stringent attitudes on this testimony could not exist. Social and economic connections drew Friends away from the rustic simplicity of the plain dress, introduced them to music and the theater, and prompted them to choose fashionable architectural styles for their homes. But while many of the older manifestations of simplicity had disappeared, it still manifested itself in habits of mind and action when Friends did things for themselves and others.

The Quaker notion of community was altered as well. Meetings ceased to demand endogamous marriage and less frequently disowned members for violations of the testimonies. The serious decline in membership through the nineteenth century persuaded the traditionalists to accede to these changes. As the community abandoned its willingness to enforce Quaker standards, cultural diversity and individualism developed to diminish the corporate unity for which earlier Friends had striven. This became evident in the World War, when Meetings permitted individual conscience instead of corporate stance to become the standard for decisions on military participation. "The sense of the Meeting" continued to work against this atomism, and Friends went on socializing primarily with other members of the Society. But the attitude toward "strangers" had changed radically as Friends grappled with social problems in the city and made alliances to work for peace. In one way, the community ideal was strengthened: the old divisions and isolation bred in the theological controversies of the nineteenth century gave way to increasing contact and cooperation through such agencies as the Service Committee.

It was the essential ambivalence in the Quaker personality which prompted many of these alterations. Friends had chosen not to withdraw from the larger social order by adopting a rural seclusiveness. Having done so, it was inevitable that their island community like others in America would be pressured by outside forces to abandon much of its cultural uniqueness. On some issues —particularly the pacifist one—they determined to put Christ over culture. But on many others, they adapted their religious views to see Christ as the representative of culture. The Society of Friends was much less like a sect at the end of the First World War than it had been half a century before. But their community survived the losses of the nineteenth century because it found unique outlets for service after 1917. That service afforded them continued opportunities to express the remaining elements of Quaker distinctiveness. Since then their pacifism, their philanthropy, and their worldly simplicity have continued to offer a critical alternative by which to judge the development of American culture.

Tables

The data on which these tables are based derive from the membership sample described in the Bibliography. In the interest of simplicity, tables are expressed in percentages. Raw numbers for the variables are provided only in column totals under the figure N. Most tables should be read horizontally and in those cases the percentage total of 100.0 is omitted. The percentage total is included only in those tables which should be read vertically; in those cases the 100.0 will be found at the foot of the column. Only Tables 1, 2, 62, and 63 deviate from these general rules; in those instances the figures presented are clearly explained in the tables themselves.

Table 1. Orthodox Yearly Meeting Membership Statistics, 1827–99

Quarter	1827 Total	1881 Total	1881 % of Total	1881–99 Change	1881–99 % Change
Philadelphia	2,642	1,601	28.3	− 266	−16.6
Abington	321	541	9.5	+ 23	+ 4.2
Concord	788	932	16.4	− 150	−16.1
Caln	557	259	4.6	− 56	−21.6
Western	454	560	9.9	− 137	−24.5
Bucks	489	257	4.5		
Burlington	800	530	9.4	− 361	−40.6
Haddonfield	789	795	14.1		
Salem	298	185	3.3	− 145	−14.8
TOTAL	7,344*	5,660	100.0	−1192	−21.1
City Meetings	N.A.	1,752	31.0	− 68	− 3.9

*Includes 205 from unlisted Quarters abandoned after 1827.

Table 2. Hicksite Yearly Meeting Membership Statistics, 1827–99

Quarter	1827 Total	1881 Total	1881 % of Total	1881–99 Change	1881–99 % Change
Philadelphia	2,676	3,344	24.6	− 459	−13.7
Abington	2,829	1,785	13.2	− 372	−20.8
Bucks	2,831	1,715	12.6	− 356	−20.7
Concord	2,573	1,735	12.8	− 156	− 9.0
Caln	921	295	2.2	+ 7	+ 3.6
Western	2,296	1,780	13.2	− 387	−21.7
Southern	501	217	1.5	− 39	−18.0
Burlington	1,049	617	4.5	− 71	−11.5
Haddonfield	821	821	6.0	− 81	− 9.8
Salem	1,238	1,064	7.8	− 122	−11.5
Fishing Creek	—	221	1.6	+ 28	+12.7
TOTAL	18,485*	13,584	100.0	−2008	−14.7

*Includes 1,251 from unlisted Quarters abandoned after 1827.

Table 3. Monthly Meeting Membership of Three Types of Friends

Monthly Meeting Membership	Types of Friends			N
	Weighty	Practicing	Nominal	
Arch Street	31.8	33.3	34.8	66
Twelfth Street	14.3	41.3	44.4	230
Race Street	9.7	28.7	61.6	414
TOTAL	13.2	33.3	53.5	710
N	94	236	380	710

Table 4. Birthplaces of Three Types of Friends

Birthplace	Types of Friends			N
	Weighty	Practicing	Nominal	
Urban	10.2	31.0	58.8	303
Rural	17.3	35.9	46.8	301
TOTAL	13.5	33.4	53.1	604
N	83	202	319	604

Table 5. Age of Arrival in Philadelphia of Three Types of Friends

| Age of Arrival | Types of Friends | | | N |
	Weighty	Practicing	Nominal	
Birth	9.1	27.2	63.8	265
Under 18	8.3	35.4	56.3	96
19–35	15.6	38.7	45.7	173
Over 35	21.1	38.9	40.0	90
TOTAL	12.5	33.3	54.2	624
N	78	208	338	624

Table 6. Generation of Three Types of Friends

| Generation | Types of Friends | | | N |
	Weighty	Practicing	Nominal	
1840s	12.2	32.5	55.3	360
1860s	14.3	34.0	51.7	350
TOTAL	13.2	33.3	53.5	710
N	94	236	380	710

Table 7. Monthly Meeting Membership and Generation of Three Types of Friends

| Monthly Meeting Membership and Generation | Types of Friends | | | N |
	Weighty	Practicing	Nominal	
Arch Street	(31.8)	(33.3)	(34.8)	(66)
1840s	35.3	26.5	38.2	34
1860s	28.1	40.6	31.3	32
Twelfth Street	(14.3)	(41.3)	(44.4)	(230)
1840s	13.7	38.5	47.9	117
1860s	15.0	44.2	40.7	113
Race Street	(9.7)	(28.7)	(61.6)	(414)
1840s	7.7	30.1	62.2	209
1860s	11.7	27.3	61.0	205
TOTAL	13.2	33.3	53.5	710
N	94	236	380	710

Table 8. Sex and Generation of Three Types of Friends

Sex and Generation	Types of Friends			N
	Weighty	Practicing	Nominal	
Male	(12.4)	(26.8)	(60.8)	(354)
1840s	10.2	26.0	63.8	177
1860s	14.7	27.7	57.6	177
Female	(14.1)	(39.6)	(46.3)	(356)
1840s	14.2	38.8	47.0	183
1860s	13.9	40.5	45.7	173
TOTAL	13.2	33.3	53.5	710
N	94	236	380	710

Table 9. Secondary Education of Friends in Three Monthly Meetings

Monthly Meeting Membership	Secondary Education		N
	Quaker	Other	
Arch Street	66.7	33.3	66
Twelfth Street	49.6	50.4	230
Race Street	19.1	80.9	414
TOTAL	33.4	66.6	710
N	237	473	710

Table 10. Secondary Education of Urban- and Rural-Born Friends

Birthplace	Secondary Education		N
	Quaker	Other	
Urban	35.6	64.4	303
Rural	39.9	60.1	301
TOTAL	37.7	62.3	604
N	228	376	604

Table 11. Secondary Education of Men and Women by Generation

Sex and Generation	Secondary Education		N
	Quaker	Other	
1840s	(27.8)	(72.2)	(360)
Male	35.0	65.0	177
Female	20.8	79.2	183
1860s	(39.1)	(60.9)	(350)
Male	39.5	60.5	177
Female	38.7	61.3	173
TOTAL	33.4	66.6	710
N	237	473	710

Table 12. Secondary Education of Three Types of Friends

| Types of Friends | Secondary Education | | N |
	Quaker	Other	
Weighty	50.0	50.0	94
Practicing	40.3	59.7	236
Nominal	25.0	75.0	380
TOTAL	33.4	66.6	710
N	237	473	710

Table 13. Friends' Secondary Education and Spouse's Religion

| Spouse's Religion | Secondary Education | | N |
	Quaker	Other	
Quaker	38.2	61.8	275
Non-Quaker	28.4	71.6	215
TOTAL	33.9	66.1	490
N	166	324	490

Table 14. Children's Education of Friends Who Attended Quaker and Non-Quaker Secondary Schools

| Secondary Education | Children's Education | | | N |
	Exclusively Quaker	Some Quaker	Non-Quaker	
Quaker	20.9	51.7	27.4	124
Other	11.0	44.5	44.5	218
TOTAL	14.6	47.1	38.3	342
N	50	161	131	342

Table 15. College Education of Two Generations of Friends

| Generation | College Education | | | N |
	Quaker	Non-Quaker	None	
1840s	5.0	6.7	88.3	360
1860s	9.7	8.3	82.0	350
TOTAL	7.3	7.5	85.2	710
N	52	53	605	710

Table 16. College Education in Three Monthly Meetings

Monthly Meeting Membership	College Education			N
	Quaker	Non-Quaker	None	
Arch Street	3.0	7.6	89.4	66
Twelfth Street	11.3	7.0	81.7	230
Race Street	5.8	7.7	86.5	414
TOTAL	7.3	7.5	85.2	710
N	52	53	605	710

Table 17. College Education of Three Types of Friends

College Education	Types of Friends			N
	Weighty	Practicing	Nominal	
Quaker college	9.6	30.8	59.6	52
Non-Quaker college	15.1	35.8	49.1	53
No college	13.4	33.2	53.5	605
TOTAL	13.2	33.3	53.5	710
N	94	236	380	710

Table 18. Estate Values of Three Types of Friends

Estate Value	Types of Friends			N
	Weighty	Practicing	Nominal	
Insolvent	6.3	50.0	43.7	16
Under $1,000	15.2	21.2	63.6	33
$1–10,000	14.9	27.7	57.4	94
$10–50,000	15.8	43.6	40.6	101
$50–100,000	19.5	41.5	39.0	41
Over $100,000	12.5	41.3	46.2	80
TOTAL	14.8	37.0	48.2	365
N	54	135	176	365

Table 19. Estate Values and Original Meeting Status

| Estate Value | Original Meeting Status | | | |
	Birthright Member	Received in Youth*	Convinced Adult	N
Insolvent	76.8	0.0	23.2	13
Under $1,000	75.0	16.7	8.3	24
$1–10,000	75.4	15.5	9.1	77
$10–50,000	74.6	12.7	12.7	87
$50–100,000	77.2	5.7	17.1	35
Over $100,000	85.7	8.6	5.7	70
TOTAL	77.8	11.4	10.8	306
N	238	35	33	306

*At parental request.

Table 20. Estate Values and Birthplace

| Estate Value | Birthplace | | N |
	Urban	Rural	
Insolvent	50.0	50.0	14
Under $1,000	44.4	55.6	27
$1–10,000	48.8	51.2	78
$10–50,000	58.2	41.8	91
$50–100,000	50.0	50.0	36
Over $100,000	67.6	32.4	74
TOTAL	55.6	44.4	320
N	178	142	320

Table 21. Estate Values and Age at Arrival in Philadelphia

| Estate Value | Age at Arrival | | | | N |
	At Birth	Under 18	19 to 35	Over 35	
Insolvent	35.6	14.5	28.5	21.4	14
Under $1,000	38.7	22.6	32.2	6.5	31
$1–10,000	38.1	13.1	25.0	23.8	84
$10–50,000	50.6	8.1	21.8	19.5	87
$50–100,000	40.0	25.7	22.9	11.4	35
Over $100,000	61.3	13.3	22.7	2.7	75
TOTAL	47.0	14.1	24.2	14.7	326
N	153	46	79	48	326

Table 22. Estate Values in Three Monthly Meetings

| Estate Value | Meeting Membership | | | | N |
	Arch St.	12th St.	Race St.	Total	
Insolvent	3.6	5.1	4.0	4.4	16
Under $1,000	3.6	5.1	12.5	9.0	33
$1–10,000	28.6	23.4	27.0	25.7	94
$10–50,000	50.0	28.4	24.0	27.6	101
$50–100,000	7.1	13.2	10.5	11.5	41
Over $100,000	7.1	34.8	22.0	21.9	80
TOTAL	100.0	100.0	100.0	100.0	365
N	28	137	200	365	365

Table 23. Estate Values of Orthodox and Hicksite Friends by Generation

| Estate Value | 1840s | | | 1860s | | | N |
	Orth.	Hicks.	Total	Orth.	Hicks.	Total	
Insolvent	4.2	0.9	2.6	5.7	7.1	6.5	16
Under $1,000	4.2	10.9	7.7	5.7	14.2	10.7	33
$1–10,000	17.8	26.9	22.3	32.9	27.2	29.6	94
$10–50,000	38.0	26.9	32.2	24.3	21.2	22.4	101
$50–100,000	11.6	11.9	11.7	12.9	9.1	10.7	41
Over $100,000	24.2	22.5	23.5	18.5	21.2	20.1	80
TOTAL	100.0	100.0	100.0	100.0	100.0	100.0	365
N	95	101	196	70	99	169	365

Table 24. Achieved and Ascribed Occupational Status

| Occupational Category | Achieved Status | Ascribed Status | | Total | N |
		Spouse	Father		
Major professions	16.1	9.2	5.1	13.0	76
Business executive	20.2	24.6	40.7	23.6	137
Lesser professions	16.4	9.2	1.7	12.9	75
Small business/skills	21.4	32.5	39.0	26.3	153
White collar/sales	20.6	19.0	8.5	18.9	110
Blue collar	4.2	5.5	5.1	5.3	31
TOTAL	100.0	100.0	100.0	100.0	582
N	360	163	59	582	582

Table 25. Achieved and General Occupational Status by Generation

Occupational Category	Achieved Status			General Status*		
	1840s	1860s	N	1840s	1860s	N
Major professions	15.3	16.8	58	12.6	13.8	76
Business executive	25.0	15.7	73	29.5	17.0	137
Lesser professions	11.9	20.6	59	8.0	18.1	75
Small business/skills	22.8	20.1	77	28.2	24.1	153
White collar/sales	18.7	22.1	74	17.0	20.9	110
Blue collar	6.3	4.3	19	4.7	6.1	31
TOTAL	100.0	100.0	360	100.0	100.0	582
N	176	184	360	300	282	582

*Includes both achieved and ascribed status.

Table 26. Occupational Status of Orthodox and Hicksite Friends by Generation

Occupational Status	1840s			1860s		
	Orth.	Hicks.	N	Orth.	Hicks.	N
Major professions	16.2	9.6	37	11.8	12.9	39
Business executive	35.8	25.5	89	16.8	17.2	48
Lesser professions	8.9	7.4	24	20.1	16.5	51
Small business/skills	24.4	31.0	85	25.2	23.3	68
White collar/sales	10.6	21.4	51	18.5	22.7	59
Blue collar	4.1	5.1	14	4.2	7.4	17
TOTAL	100.0	100.0	300	100.0	100.0	282
N	123	177	300	119	163	282

Table 27. Occupational Status of Three Types of Orthodox and Hicksite Friends

Occupational Status	Weighty		Practicing		Nominal		
	Orth.	Hicks.	Orth.	Hicks	Orth.	Hicks.	N
Major professions	22.5	5.6	12.9	10.5	15.0	12.4	76
Business executive	18.3	16.7	29.0	29.4	28.0	18.7	137
Lesser professions	18.3	19.4	18.3	11.6	10.5	12.9	75
Small business/skills	28.6	41.6	20.5	23.2	27.0	26.8	153
White collar/sales	12.3	13.9	12.9	17.9	17.0	25.4	110
Blue collar	0.0	2.8	6.4	7.4	4.0	6.2	31
TOTAL	100.0	100.0	100.0	100.0	100.0	100.0	582
N	49	36	93	95	100	209	582

Table 28. Occupational Status and Birthplace

Occupational Status	Birthplace		N
	Urban	Rural	
Major professions	52.1	47.9	71
Business executive	74.8	25.2	131
Lesser professions	50.8	49.2	65
Small business/skills	46.0	54.0	124
White collar/sales	37.7	62.3	90
Blue collar	17.4	82.6	23
TOTAL	52.2	47.8	504
N	263	241	504

Table 29. Occupational Status and Original Meeting Status

Occupational Status	Original Meeting Status			N
	Birthright Member	Received in Youth	Convinced Adult	
Major professions	72.8	18.8	9.4	64
Business executive	92.7	2.4	4.9	123
Lesser professions	72.4	10.4	17.2	58
Small business/skills	68.6	14.8	16.6	115
White collar/sales	68.5	14.1	17.4	92
Blue collar	52.1	17.4	30.5	23
TOTAL	74.8	11.7	13.5	475
N	356	55	64	475

Table 30. Occupational Status and Age at Arrival in Philadelphia

Occupational Status	Age at Arrival				N
	Birth	Under 18	19–35	Over 35	
Major professions	44.8	14.5	33.3	7.4	69
Business executive	67.9	13.1	16.7	2.3	131
Lesser professions	40.6	13.1	30.4	15.9	69
Small business/skills	36.7	14.9	29.7	18.7	128
White collar/sales	33.0	17.6	31.8	17.6	91
Blue collar	9.1	27.3	40.9	22.7	22
TOTAL	44.5	15.1	27.9	12.5	510
N	227	77	142	64	510

Table 31. Social Register Listing of Three Types of Friends

Social Register	Types of Friends			N
	Weighty	Practicing	Nominal	
Listed	5.3	23.7	71.1	76
Not Listed	14.2	34.4	51.4	634
TOTAL	13.2	33.3	53.5	710
N	94	236	380	710

Table 32. Occupational Status and Social Register Listing

Occupational Status	Social Register Listing			N
	Listed	Not Listed	Total	
Major professions	10.1	13.5	13.0	76
Business executive	68.1	17.5	23.6	137
Lesser professions	7.3	13.6	12.9	75
Small business/skills	4.3	29.2	26.3	153
White collar/sales	10.2	20.1	18.9	110
Blue collar	0.0	6.1	5.3	31
TOTAL	100.0	100.0	100.0	582
N	69	513	582	582

Table 33. Estate Values and Social Register Listing

Estate Value	Social Register Listing			N
	Listed	Not Listed	Total	
Insolvent	0.0	5.3	4.3	16
Under $1,000	4.9	9.9	9.0	33
$1–10,000	9.8	29.9	25.7	94
$10–50,000	16.4	29.9	27.5	101
$50–100,000	11.5	11.2	11.2	41
Over $100,000	57.4	14.7	22.3	80
TOTAL	100.0	100.0	100.0	365
N	61	304	365	365

Table 34. Social Register Listing and Original Meeting Status

| Social Register | Original Meeting Status | | | |
	Birthright Member	Received in Youth	Convinced Adult	N
Listed	84.5	9.9	5.6	71
Not listed	72.8	12.1	15.1	498
TOTAL	74.4	11.8	13.8	569
N	423	67	79	569

Table 35. Social Register Listing and Monthly Meeting Membership

| Social Register | Meeting Membership | | | | N |
	Arch St.	12th St.	Race St.	Total	
Listed	3.0	16.1	8.9	10.7	76
Not listed	97.0	83.9	91.1	89.3	634
TOTAL	100.0	100.0	100.0	100.0	710
N	66	230	414	710	710

Table 36. Social Register Listing and Birthplace

| Social Register | Birthplace | | N |
	Urban	Rural	
Listed	86.2	13.8	72
Not listed	45.3	54.7	532
TOTAL	50.3	49.8	604
N	303	301	604

Table 37. Social Register Listing of Two Generations of Friends

| Social Register | Generation | | | N |
	1840s	1860s	Total	
Listed	12.5	8.9	10.7	76
Not listed	87.5	91.1	89.3	634
TOTAL	100.0	100.0	100.0	710
N	360	350	710	710

Table 38. Social Register Listing and City Residence in the 1890s

	Social Register Listing			
Residence	Listed	Not Listed	Total	N
Center City, North	7.3	15.0	13.9	58
Center City, South	54.5	11.4	17.1	71
West Philadelphia	10.9	27.4	25.2	105
North Philadelphia	7.3	41.5	37.0	154
Germantown	22.0	4.7	6.7	28
TOTAL	100.0	100.0	100.0	416
N	55	361	416	416

Table 39. Monthly Meeting Membership and Residence in the 1890s

	Meeting Membership			
Residence	Arch St.	12th St.	Race St.	N
Center City, North	1.7	56.9	41.4	58
Center City, South	12.7	54.9	32.4	71
West Philadelphia	7.6	33.3	59.1	105
North Philadelphia	5.8	14.9	79.3	154
Germantown	0.0	42.9	57.1	28
Suburbs	7.5	28.3	64.2	106
TOTAL	6.8	32.9	60.3	522
N	35	172	315	522

Table 40. Residence of Three Types of Friends in the 1890s

	Types of Friends			
Residence	Weighty	Practicing	Nominal	N
Center City, North	22.4	41.4	36.2	58
Center City, South	8.5	22.5	69.0	71
West Philadelphia	21.9	43.8	34.3	105
North Philadelphia	13.0	37.7	49.3	154
Germantown	5.7	22.9	71.4	28
Suburbs	11.3	37.7	51.0	106
TOTAL	14.4	35.9	49.7	522
N	75	188	259	522

Table 41. Occupational Status and Residence in the 1890s

Residence	Occupational Status						
	Major Prof.	Bus. Exec.	Lesser Prof.	Sml. Bus.	White Coll.	Blue Coll.	N
Center City, North	23.5	33.3	11.8	19.7	7.8	3.9	51
Center City, South	17.5	42.8	12.7	17.5	7.9	1.6	63
West Philadelphia	8.4	20.0	14.7	30.6	22.1	4.2	95
North Philadelphia	12.1	10.6	8.5	34.1	27.6	7.1	141
Germantown	11.1	59.3	7.4	7.4	14.8	0.0	27
Suburbs	13.2	30.3	10.5	31.6	10.5	3.9	76
TOTAL	13.3	26.7	10.9	27.2	17.6	4.3	453
N	61	117	50	124	81	20	453

Table 42. Residence of Friends by Decade

Residence	Decade			
	1880s	1890s	1900s	1910s
Center City, North	17.2	11.1	10.3	4.7
Center City, South	10.9	13.6	10.7	11.3
West Philadelphia	19.6	20.1	23.9	21.6
North Philadelphia	33.6	29.5	21.0	15.3
Germantown	4.0	5.4	6.6	10.2
Suburbs	14.7	20.3	27.5	36.9
TOTAL	100.0	100.0	100.0	100.0
N	488	522	512	444

Table 43. Residence of Three Types of Friends in the 1910s

Residence	Types of Friends			N
	Weighty	Practicing	Nominal	
Center City, North	23.8	42.9	33.3	21
Center City, South	16.0	34.0	50.0	50
West Philadelphia	19.8	45.8	34.4	96
North Philadelphia	19.1	29.4	51.5	68
Germantown	4.4	26.7	68.9	45
Suburbs	18.3	43.2	38.5	164
TOTAL	17.3	38.9	43.8	444
N	77	173	194	444

Table 44. Residential Mobility of Three Types of Friends

Number of Adult Residences	Types of Friends				N
	Weighty	Practicing	Nominal	Total	
One	28.0	16.5	14.1	16.7	118
Two or three	47.2	54.2	53.6	53.1	373
Four or more	24.8	29.3	32.3	30.2	213
TOTAL	100.0	100.0	100.0	100.0	704
N	93	236	375	704	704

Table 45. Estate Values and Residential Mobility

Estate Value	Number of Adult Residences			N
	1	2 or 3	4 or more	
Insolvent	18.7	25.0	56.3	16
Under $1,000	18.2	39.4	42.4	33
$1–10,000	12.8	53.2	34.0	94
$10–50,000	24.0	44.0	32.0	100
$50–100,000	12.2	61.0	26.8	41
Over $100,000	21.2	60.0	18.8	80
TOTAL	18.4	50.6	31.0	364
N	67	184	113	364

Table 46. Occupational Status of Friends with Urban and Suburban Residences in the 1910s

Occupational Status	Residence			N
	City	Suburbs	Total	
Major professions	9.3	13.1	10.6	40
Business executive	27.3	28.2	27.5	104
Lesser professions	15.4	13.7	14.7	56
Small business/skills	25.6	22.1	24.4	92
White collar/sales	18.3	15.3	17.5	65
Blue collar	4.1	7.6	5.3	20
TOTAL	100.0	100.0	100.0	377
N	246	131	377	377

Table 47. Typology of Friends by Birthplace

| Types of Friends | Birthplace | | N |
	Urban	Rural	
Weighty	37.4	62.6	83
Practicing	46.5	53.5	202
Nominal	55.8	44.2	319
TOTAL	50.2	49.8	604
N	303	301	604

Table 48. Birthplace of Three Types of Friends by Generation

| Types of Friends by Generation | Birthplace | | N |
	Urban	Rural	
1840s			
Weighty	26.8	73.2	41
Practicing	49.6	50.4	95
Nominal	60.5	39.5	167
1860s			
Weighty	47.6	52.4	42
Practicing	43.8	56.2	107
Nominal	50.7	49.3	152
TOTAL	50.2	49.8	604
N	303	301	604

Table 49. Monthly Meeting Membership and Birthplace

| Meeting | Birthplace | | N |
	Urban	Rural	
Arch Street	31.8	68.2	66
Twelfth Street	48.7	51.3	224
Race Street	55.2	44.8	314
TOTAL	50.2	49.8	604
N	303	301	604

Table 50. Birthplace of Members of Three Monthly Meetings by Generation

Meeting Membership by Generation	Birthplace		N
	Urban	Rural	
1840s			
Arch Street	41.2	58.8	34
Twelfth Street	60.9	39.1	115
Race Street	48.7	51.3	154
1860s			
Arch Street	21.9	78.1	32
Twelfth Street	35.8	64.2	109
Race Street	61.3	38.7	160
TOTAL	50.2	49.8	604
N	303	301	604

Table 51. Original Meeting Status of Three Types of Friends

Original Meeting Status	Types of Friends			N
	Weighty	Practicing	Nominal	
Birthright member	12.5	31.7	55.8	423
Received in youth	10.4	19.4	70.1	67
Convinced adult	25.3	43.0	31.6	79
TOTAL	14.1	31.8	54.1	569
N	80	181	308	569

Table 52. Original Meeting Status of Men and Women by Generation

Original Meeting Status by Generation	Sex		N
	Male	Female	
1840s			
Birthright member	52.1	47.9	238
Received in youth	38.5	61.5	13
Convinced adult	37.0	63.0	27
1860s			
Birthright member	49.0	51.0	185
Received in youth	51.9	48.1	54
Convinced adult	57.7	42.3	52
TOTAL	50.6	49.4	569
N	288	281	569

Table 53. Original Meeting Status of Three Types of Friends by Generation

Original Meeting Status	Types of Friends			N
by Generation	Weighty	Practicing	Nominal	
1840s	(12.2)	(32.5)	(55.3)	(360)
Birthright member	11.8	30.3	58.0	238
Received in youth	15.4	30.8	53.8	13
Convinced adult	29.6	44.4	25.9	27
1860s	(14.3)	(34.0)	(51.7)	(350)
Birthright member	13.6	33.2	53.3	184
Received in youth	9.3	16.7	74.1	54
Convinced adult	23.1	42.3	34.6	52
TOTAL*	14.1	31.8	54.1	569
	(13.2)	(33.3)	(53.5)	(710)
N	80	181	308	569
	(94)	(236)	(380)	(710)

*Status data were unavailable on 141 members.

Table 54. Nature of Bequests of Orthodox and Hicksite Friends

Bequests	Branch of Quakerism			N
	Orthodox	Hicksite	Total	
Quaker charities only	6.3	4.2	5.2	20
Non-Quaker charities	3.4	0.9	2.0	8
Quaker and other charities	9.7	7.1	8.3	32
Individuals*	80.6	87.8	84.5	328
TOTAL	100.0	100.0	100.0	388
N	176	212	388	388

*Includes those who died intestate.

Table 55. Bequests of Two Generations of Friends

Generation	Bequests		N
	Charities	Individuals*	
1840s	13.7	86.3	211
1860s	17.5	82.5	177
TOTAL	15.5	84.5	388
N	60	328	388

*Includes those who died intestate.

Table 56. Spouse's Religion of Orthodox and Hicksite Friends by Generation

| Generation by Branch of Quakerism | Spouse's Religion | | N |
	Quaker*	Non-Quaker	
Orthodox			
1840s	67.0	33.0	97
1860s	62.3	37.7	98
Hicksites			
1840s	56.8	43.2	153
1860s	43.7	56.3	142
TOTAL	56.2	43.8	490
N	275	215	490

*Includes 11 who converted spouses to Quakerism.

Table 57. Spouse's Religion of Three Types of Friends

| Spouse's Religion | Types of Friends | | | N |
	Weighty	Practicing	Nominal	
Quaker*	22.6	44.8	32.6	275
Non-Quaker	3.7	17.2	79.1	215
TOTAL	14.3	33.9	51.8	490
N	70	166	254	490

*Includes 11 who converted spouses to Quakerism.

Table 58. Spouse's Religion of Three Types of Orthodox and Hicksite Friends

| Spouse's Religion by Branch of Quakerism | Types of Friends | | | N |
	Weighty	Practicing	Nominal	
Orthodox				
Quaker*	27.0	51.6	21.4	126
Non-Quaker	7.2	21.8	71.0	69
Hicksite				
Quaker*	18.8	43.0	38.2	149
Non-Quaker	2.1	15.1	82.8	146
TOTAL	14.3	33.9	51.8	490
N	70	166	254	490

*Includes 11 who converted spouses to Quakerism.

Table 59. Sex of Three Types of Friends

| | Types of Friends | | | |
Sex	Weighty	Practicing	Nominal	N
Male	12.4	26.8	60.8	354
Female	14.1	39.6	46.3	356
TOTAL	13.2	33.3	53.5	710
N	94	236	380	710

Table 60. Sex and Marital Status of Three Types of Friends

| | Types of Friends | | | |
Sex and Marital Status	Weighty	Practicing	Nominal	N
Male	(12.4)	(26.8)	(60.8)	(354)
Single	6.9	19.0	74.1	58
Married	13.6	28.1	58.3	295
Female	(14.1)	(39.6)	(46.3)	(356)
Single	10.6	36.9	52.5	141
Married	16.0	41.7	42.3	213
TOTAL*	13.1	33.3	53.6	707
	(13.2)		(53.5)	(710)
N*	93	235	379	707
	(94)	(236)	(380)	(710)

*Marital data were not available for 3 members.

Table 61. Sex and Monthly Meeting Membership of Three Types of Friends

| Sex and Monthly Meeting Membership | Types of Friends | | | |
	Weighty	Practicing	Nominal	N
Arch Street	(31.8)	(33.3)	(34.8)	(66)
Males	39.2	17.9	42.9	28
Females	26.4	44.7	28.9	38
Twelfth Street	(14.3)	(41.3)	(44.4)	(230)
Males	13.9	33.9	52.2	115
Females	14.8	48.7	36.5	115
Race Street	(9.7)	(28.7)	(61.6)	(414)
Males	8.1	24.2	67.7	211
Females	11.3	33.5	55.2	203
TOTAL	13.2	33.3	53.5	710
N	94	236	380	710

Table 62. Orthodox Yearly Meeting Membership, 1899–1916

Quarter	1881–99 % Change	1899 Total	1916 Total	1899–1916 % Change
Philadelphia	−16.6	1,335	1,205	− 9.7
Abington	+ 4.2	564	645	+14.3
Concord	−16.1	782	864	+10.5
Caln	−21.6	203	207	+ 1.9
Western	−24.5	423	315	−25.5
Bucks-Burlington	−40.6	426	303	−28.9
Haddonfield-Salem	−14.8	735	918	+24.9
TOTAL	−21.1	4,468	4,457	− 0.2
City Total	− 3.9	1,663	1,461	−12.1

Table 63. Hicksite Yearly Meeting Membership, 1899–1915

Quarter	1881–99 % Change	1899 Total	1916 Total	1899–1915 % Change
Philadelphia	−13.7	2,885	2,221	−23.0
Abington	−20.8	1,413	1,243	−12.0
Bucks	−20.7	1,359	1,209	−11.1
Concord	− 9.0	1,579	1,896	+20.1
Caln	+ 3.6	302	291	− 3.6
Western	−21.7	1,393	1,273	− 8.6
Southern	−18.0	178	163	− 8.4
Burlington	−11.5	546	490	−10.2
Haddonfield	− 9.8	740	873	+18.0
Salem	−11.5	942	959	+ 1.8
Fishing Creek	+12.7	249	175	−29.8
TOTAL	−14.7	11,586	10,793	− 6.8

Notes

All citations use the short-title form. Complete facts of publication can be found in the Bibliography, which also explains the membership sample cited in the text. The following abbreviations appear in the notes:

AECFIA Associated Executive Committee of Friends on Indian Affairs (Orthodox)

AEF Friends' Association for the Aid and Elevation of the Freedmen (Hicksite)

AMM Philadelphia Monthly Meeting [Arch Street] at 4th and Arch Streets (Orthodox)

DR The Department of Records of Philadelphia Yearly Meeting of the Religious Society of Friends, 302 Arch Street, Philadelphia, Pa.

FFA Friends' Association of Philadelphia and Vicinity for the Relief of Colored Freedmen, later called the Friends' Freedmen Association (Orthodox)

FHL The Friends' Historical Library, Swarthmore College, Swarthmore, Pa.

HD *Rules of Discipline of the Yearly Meeting of Friends Held in Philadelphia* (Hicksite)

HRC The Representative Committee of Philadelphia Yearly Meeting (Hicksite)

HSP The Historical Society of Pennsylvania, 1300 Locust Street, Philadelphia, Pa.

HYM Philadelphia Yearly Meeting (Hicksite) Held at 15th and Race Streets

ICY Institute for Colored Youth, later called the Cheyney Training School for Teachers (Orthodox)

OD *Rules of Discipline of the Yearly Meeting of Friends for Pennsylvania, New Jersey, Delaware and the Eastern Part of Maryland* (Orthodox)

OMS Philadelphia Meeting for Sufferings (Orthodox)

OSOC   Philadelphia Yearly Meeting Social Order Committee (Orthodox)
OYM   Philadelphia Yearly Meeting Held at 4th and Arch Streets (Orthodox)
QC   The Quaker Collection in the Haverford College Library, Haverford, Pa.
RMM   Philadelphia Monthly Meeting [Race Street] at 15th and Race Streets (Hicksite)
TMM   Philadelphia Monthly Meeting for the Western District [Twelfth Street] on Twelfth Street below Market (Orthodox)

Introduction

1. Wiebe, *Search for Order*, pp. 11–44.
2. Clebsch, *From Sacred to Profane*, pp. 188–200; Handy, *Christian America*, pp. 63–64, 95–116, 190–97; Gutman, "Protestantism and the American Labor Movement."
3. Clebsch, *From Sacred to Profane*, pp. 1–14; Berthoff, *Unsettled People*, pp. 162–73, 377–95.
4. Among the studies of colonial Quakers are Tolles, *Meeting House*; James, *People among Peoples*; and Nash, *Quakers and Politics*. Recent investigations of Quakers in the peace movement include Chatfield, *For Peace and Justice*, and Whittner, *Rebels against War*. The standard history of the Quaker city is still Scharf and Westcott, *History of Philadelphia, 1609–1884*; recent works on modern Philadelphia are Baltzell, *Philadelphia Gentlemen*; Warner, *Private City*; Davis and Haller, eds., *Peoples of Philadelphia*; and Clark, *Irish in Philadelphia*.
5. Hopkins, *Rise of the Social Gospel*; Abell, *Urban Impact on American Protestantism*; May, *Protestant Churches*.

Chapter 1. Division and Declension

1. Mead, *Lively Experiment*, pp. 103–33; Wiebe, *Search for Order*, pp. xiii–xiv, 44–75.
2. Jacob Elfreth, Diary, May 21, 1871, Elfreth Papers; Barbour, *Quakers in England*, pp. 31–41, 240–43; Jones, *Quakers in the Colonies*, pp. 533–38
3. Nash, *Quakers and Politics*, pp. 168–75; Tolles, *Meeting House*, pp. 3–11, 230–43; Niebuhr, *Christ and Culture*, pp. 56–57, and *Social Sources*, pp. 17–21, 48–56.
4. *OD, 1869*, pp. 44–57, 73–78, 104–8, 144–47.
5. *Ibid.*, pp. 10–16, 79–93, 96–98; Marietta, "Delinquency," p. 25.
6. *OD, 1869*, pp. v–vi, 17–21, 42–43, 62, 131–34; *HD, 1869*, pp. 3–4, 8–13, 32–33, 111–14.
7. *OD, 1869*, pp. 34–37, 39–42, 59, 94–95, 101–2, 120–24; *HD, 1869*, pp. 25–28, 30–31, 42, 69–72, 77–78, 84–86, 102–3.
8. *OD, 1869*, pp. 37–38, 58–59, 61–72, 76–78, 103, 110–15; *HD, 1869*, pp. 23, 28–29, 41–42, 45–53, 86–87, 96–100.

9. *OD, 1869*, pp. 60, 80–87, 117–19, 136–43; *HD, 1869*, pp. 61–66, 73–76, 87–88, 116–22.

10. Gordon, *Assimilation*, pp. 23–30, 34–41; Wiebe, *Search for Order*, pp. xiii–xiv, 44–75; Hostetler, *Amish Society*, pp. 48–69, 262–69.

11. Jones, *Later Periods*, I, 457–58; Russell, *History of Quakerism*, pp. 301–14; Brinton, *Friends*, pp. 187–96; Doherty, *Hicksite Separation*, pp. 33–50.

12. OMS Mins., Mar. 15, 1867, pp. 283–94; Sept. 20, 1872, pp. 427–31; Oct. 25, 1872, pp. 432–33; Speakman, *Divisions*, 3rd ed., pp. 34–43.

13. *Friends' Review*, XXII (May 22, 1869), 617–18; OMS Mins., Apr. 17, 1868, pp. 326–28; Dec. 20, 1872, pp. 433–37; Mar. 16, 1883, pp. 231–32; and Apr. 13, 1894, pp. 120–22.

14. Hodgson, *Society of Friends*, I, 121; *Friend*, LVI (Oct. 21, 1882), 87; OMS Mins., Apr. 13, 1894, p. 125; Ahlstrom, *Religious History*, pp. 356–59, 774–83; Hutchinson, ed., *American Protestant Thought*, pp. 1–4.

15. Speakman, *Divisions*, pp. 3, 71; Janney, *Separation*, pp. 10–18, 139–69, 227–31.

16. *Friends' Intelligencer*, XXIX (May 11, 1872), 168–69, and (May 12, 1872), 185; Isaac Eyre to Isaac Hicks, May 12, 1880, Eyre Papers; John C. Parry to George Mitchell, Apr. 13, 1895, Mitchell Family Papers; RMM Mins., May 23, 1883, pp. 186–89; Walton, *Diaries*; HYM Mins., May 13, 1885, p. 265 (for the quotation), and May 16, 1896, p. 245.

17. Janney, *Separation*, p. 257; Doherty, *Hicksite Separation*, pp. 6–14, 77–89; HYM Mins., May 19, 1899, p. 372. On Hicksite prosperity after the Civil War, see Chapter 3.

18. *Friend*, XLIV (Mar. 11, 1871), 230–31, and XLVIII (Sept. 26, 1874), 47; *Friends' Review*, XXVIII (Oct. 10, 1874), 113–14; *Friends' Intelligencer*, XXXI (June 13, 1874), 248–49, and (Nov. 28, 1874), 632–33; XXXIII (Jan. 6, 1877), 724–25; and XLIV (Jan. 1, 1887), 3–5; Ahlstrom, *Religious History*, p. 768; Carter, *Spiritual Crisis*, pp. 3–20.

19. Smith, *Unforgotten Years*, p. 31; Elizabeth Yarnall, "The Other Branch," in Brinton, ed., *Then and Now*, p. 183; Isaac Eyre to Isaac Hicks, Oct. 14, 1877, Eyre Papers; Jonathan Rhoads to Joseph S. Elkinton, June 12, 1884, Elkinton Family Papers; Philadelphia *Public Ledger*, May 15, 1899, p. 15; Jacob Elfreth, Diary, May 15, 1865, May 14, 1866, May 31, 1874, May 21, 1871, and Apr. 22, 1874, Elfreth Papers; Joshua Baily to Charles Rhoads, Feb. 19, 1897, Baily Papers.

20. Joshua L. Baily, "Account of Yearly Meeting, Apr. 23, 1874," Baily Papers; Swift, *Joseph John Gurney*, pp. 14–15, 51–59, 150–51, 186–204, 213; Jones, *Later Periods*, II, 869–89; Russell, *History of Quakerism*, pp. 349–50.

21. Brinton, *Friends*, pp. 66, 192–94; Russell, *History of Quakerism*, pp. 355–56; [Lytle], "Some Account of Philadelphia Yearly Meeting—1856."

22. Jacob Elfreth, Diary, Aug. 26, 1867, and Jan. 24, 1872, Elfreth Papers; Joshua Baily, "Account of Yearly Meeting, Apr. 23, 1874," Baily Papers; Robson, *English View*, pp. 141–44; Jones, *Later Periods*, II, 893–

905; Henry Hartshorne to David Updegraff, Oct. 9, 1875, and Nov. [?], 1875, Hartshorne Papers.

23. *Friend*, XLV (Oct. 7, 1871), 54–56; (Dec. 30, 1871), 151–52; (Jan. 20, 1872), 175; and (Feb. 3, 1872), 191; Samuel Morris to David Sampson, Oct. 23, 1888, Morris-Sansom Papers; OMS Mins., Mar. 19, 1886, pp. 371–81.

24. Brinton, *Seventy-five Years*, pp. 10–11; TMM Mins., Nov. 24, 1875, p. 328; Jan. 24, 1894, pp. 75–77; Apr. 28, 1897, p. 233; Edward Scull to Thomas Chase, Dec. 13, 1880, and Jan. 17, 1882; James E. Rhoads to Chase, Dec. 10, 1887; and Edward Bettle, Jr., to Chase, Nov. 14, 1889, all in Chase Papers; Isaac Sharpless to [?], Dec. 31, 1894, Sharpless Papers.

25. Brinton, *Friends*, p. 193; AMM Mins., Apr. 28, 1881, p. 235; June 28, 1883, p. 275; Nov. 25, 1886, pp. 29–30; and Nov. 23, 1893, p. 159; Elkinton, *Selections*, pp. 345–46.

26. Jacob Elfreth, Diary, Apr. 25, 1873, and Apr. 18, 1904, Elfreth Papers; Isaac Eyre to Isaac Hicks, Jan. 19, 1881, Eyre Papers; *Friend*, LXXIV (Oct. 13, 1900), 97.

27. Jones, *Later Periods*, I, 471; HYM Mins., May 18, 1900, p. 48; Thomas, *History of Friends in America*, pp. 116–67, 195; *American Friend*, II (Jan. 31, 1895), 105–6; Isichei, *Victorian Quakers*, pp. 112–17.

28. Matlack, *Brief Sketches*, I, 435–538; Jones, *Later Periods*, I, 471; "Census of Philadelphia Yearly Meeting, 1881, 1899," MS. in TMM Membership Book, 1882–1912; "Census of Philadelphia Yearly Meeting, 1881," MS. in FHL; HYM Mins., May 18, 1900, p. 48.

29. Thernstrom and Knights, "Men in Motion"; TMM Membership Book, 1882–1912.

30. TMM Membership Book, 1882–1912.

31. For a discussion of the membership sample see the Bibliography.

32. Fichter, *Urban Parish*, pp. 26–27; Ringer, "Parishioner," pp. 1–12.

33. Moberg, *Church as a Social Institution*, p. 417.

34. Ringer, "Parishioner," pp. 24–49, shows that women dominate the institutional work of the Episcopal Church.

Chapter 2. Worldly Ways and the Guarded Education

1. Smith, ed., *Philadelphia Quaker*, pp. 36–37; Jacob Elfreth, Diary, Jan. 24, 1872, Apr. 17, 1872, and Apr. 17, 1883, Elfreth Family Papers; Geo[rge] Scattergood to Henry Hartshorne, Aug. 17, 1874, Hartshorne Papers.

2. Joshua Baily to J. Henry Bartlett, Feb. 10, 1911, and "Biographical Sketch of Joshua Baily," pp. 170–71, Baily Papers; *Friends' Review*, XXV (Mar. 23, 1872), 489–91; Henry Hartshorne to George Scattergood, Aug. 27, 1874, Hartshorne Papers; Jacob Elfreth, Diary, Apr. 17, 1872, Apr. 17–18, 1876, and Apr. 22, 1879, Elfreth Papers.

3. *Friends' Intelligencer*, XXIX (Sept. 21, 1872), 472–73, and XL (Jan. 5, 1884), 744–45; Isaac Eyre to [?], Jan. 22, 1872, Eyre Papers; HYM Mins., May 16, 1895, p. 199.

4. Tolles, *Meeting House*, pp. 129–30; OMS Mins., Feb. 10, 1882, pp. 193–94, and Mar. 16, 1894, p. 105; Edward L. Scull to Thomas Chase, Nov. 15, 1866, Chase Papers.

5. RMM Mins., Jan. 16, 1879, p. 280; Burt, *Perennial Philadelphians*, pp. 335–37.

6. Philadelphia *Public Ledger*, Oct. 15, 1916, p. 11; Harbeson, "Philadelphia Victorian Architecture," p. 264; King, *Philadelphia and Notable Philadelphians*, pp. 69, 75, 92.

7. Tatum, *Penn's Great Town*, pp. 73–74, 113, 196; King, *Philadelphia*, pp. 8, 13, 14, 17, 24A, 24B, 24C; Harbeson, "Victorian Architecture," pp. 258–59; Edward L. Scull to Thomas Chase, [May 1875], Chase Papers; Meigs, *What Makes a College?* p. 30; OYM Mins., Apr. 18, 1889, p. 425.

8. Tatum, *Penn's Great Town*, pp. 118–20, 198–99; King, *Philadelphia*, pp. 61, 65, 75, 79, 82, 88, 90–92, 98, for residences of Friends.

9. OYM Mins., Apr. 25, 1873, pp. 112–13, and Apr. 22, 1881, p. 280; OMS Mins., Mar. 20, 1885, p. 321; *Friend*, LX (Nov. 27, 1886), 135; Elliston P. Morris to Herbert Welsh, Sept. 9, 1910, Welsh Papers; Bispham, *Quaker Singer's Recollections*.

10. *Friend*, XLV (Aug. 10, 1872), 407–8; *Friends' Intelligencer*, XXIX (May 4, 1872), 152–53; TMM Mins., Feb. 18, 1880, p. 428; OMS Mins., Feb. 10, 1882, pp. 194–97; HYM Mins., May 15, 1893, p. 136, and May 13, 1901, p. 71.

11. Elkinton, *Selections*, p. 282; Philadelphia *Inquirer*, July 11, 1944, p. 9; OMS Mins., Dec. 17, 1875, pp. 41–42, and Dec. 16, 1881; HRC Mins., Dec. 18, 1868, p. 94, and May 15, 1893, p. 196; Jacob Elfreth, Diary, Apr. 17, 1905, Elfreth Papers.

12. Magill, *Educational Institutions*, pp. 1–35; Brinton, *Quaker Education*, pp. 8–22, 27–37.

13. Parrish, *Essay on Education*, pp. 6–9; *Friend*, LII (Mar. 22, 1879), 255; OYM Mins., Apr. 22, 1875, p. 145, and Apr. 20, 1876, p. 172; HYM Mins., May 15, 1873, pp. 329–31, and May 15, 1878, p. 96.

14. OYM Mins., Apr. 21, 1887, pp. 375–76, and Apr. 16, 1912, pp. 88–89; HYM Mins., May 12, 1887, p. 320; AMM Mins., June 25, 1874, pp. 110–11; Sept. 27, 1877, pp. 168–69; and Mar. 27, 1890, pp. 87–88; RMM Mins., Feb. 19, 1868, pp. 30–31; Sept. 17, 1890, pp. 376–77; and Sept. 17, 1913, p. 84.

15. RMM Mins., Mar. 20, 1878, p. 223; AMM Mins., Feb. 25, 1886, p. 20; Mar. 26, 1891, pp. 106–8; and Feb. 22, 1900, p. 267; Willcox, "History of the Friends' Central School System," pp. 30–48; Rufus Jones to [George Newman], [1907?], Jones Papers.

16. Hole, *Westtown*, pp. 91, 152, 173, 291, 299–302; Dewees, *Century of Westtown*, pp. 104–5, 155–58; Mohr *et al.*, *History of George School*, pp. 33, 104–5; HYM Mins., May 13, 1889, p. 374; McLachlan, *American Boarding School*, pp. 168, 229, 261.

17. OYM Mins., Apr. 19, 1872, pp. 88–89; Apr. 18, 1866, p. 315; Apr. 22, 1887, p. 387; and Apr. 24, 1903, p. 291; Dewees, *Century*, p. 114–15,

178; Hole, *Westtown*, pp. 151–52, 166, 213–14, 289–90; Samuel Morris to Charles S. Taylor, Nov. 20, 1886, Morris-Sansom Papers; McLachlan, *Boarding School*, pp. 164–67, 254–56.

18. Hole, *Westtown*, pp. 199–200, 376–77; HYM Mins., May 19, 1905, p. 324, and May 14, 1915, p. 287; OYM Mins., Apr. 20, 1899, p. 202; McLachlan, *Boarding School*, pp. 169–71, 283–85.

19. OYM Mins., Apr. 23, 1896, p. 119; Apr. 22, 1909, p. 12; and Apr. 21, 1910, p. 39; Mohr, *George School*, pp. 17–18; AMM Mins., Mar. 29, 1894, pp. 166–68, and Nov. 28, 1912, p. 258; *Thirty Schools Tell Their Story*, pp. 320–76.

20. Mohr, *George School*, p. 33; OYM Mins., Apr. 19, 1871, pp. 68–70; Apr. 17, 1882, p. 287; and Apr. 23, 1896, p. 119; AMM Mins., Feb. 24, 1887, p. 35; McLachlan, *Boarding School*, pp. 114–16, 256–57; Board of Public Education, First School District of Pennsylvania, *72nd Annual Report*, pp. 38–317.

21. Alumni records for Westtown, Friends' Central, and George School have been kept with some care, but those for Friends' Select in the mid-nineteenth century are lacking; for a discussion of the woman question, see Chapter 7.

22. Brinton, *Quaker Education*, pp. 37–38; Jones, *Haverford*, pp. 1–6; Parrish, *Essay on Education*, pp. 30–46; Elkinton, *Selections*, pp. 113–14; Babbidge, "Swarthmore," pp. 1–15; Meigs, *What Makes a College?* pp. 6–29; *Friend*, LIV (Oct. 30, 1880), 95, and LV (Oct. 8, 1881), 71–72.

23. Jones, *Haverford*, pp. 13, 33–36, 60–64; Babbidge, "Swarthmore," pp. 77–99, 110–13, 139–46, 211; Henry Hartshorne to James Whitall, Feb. 13, 1871, and Hartshorne to the Board of Managers, Mar. 14, 1871, Hartshorne Papers; Peterson, *New England College*, p. 137; Haverford College *Bulletin*, II (Oct. 1903), 15–16; Meigs, *What Makes a College?* pp. 29–30, 72.

24. Peterson, *New England College*, p. 147; Sharpless, *Story of a Small College*, pp. 98, 105–7; Corporation of Haverford College, *Reports, 1894–95*, pp. 4–7; Haverford College, *Bulletin*, XIV (Oct. 1915), 4–6, 12; Swarthmore College, *Twelfth Annual Catalogue, 1880–81*, p. 58; Swarthmore College, *Minutes of 31st Annual Meeting of Stockholders, 1894–95*, pp. 7–9, 18; Swarthmore College, *Bulletin*, XII (Mar. 1915), 7–10, 28; Bryn Mawr College, *President's Report, 1894–95*, pp. 430, 445; *ibid., 1914–15*, pp. v–xiv, 1, 19; Fuess, *Amherst*, p. 269; T. Wistar Brown to Rufus Jones, Apr. 14, 1909, Jones Papers.

25. OYM Mins., Apr. 17, 1882, p. 287, and Apr. 19, 1901, p. 244; Jones, *Haverford*, pp. 35–40; Magill, *Twenty-five Years*, pp. 187–90; Clark, *Distinctive College*, pp. 171–80; Meigs, *What Makes a College?* p. 217.

26. Haverford College, *Report of the Managers, 1865*, pp. 11–12; *ibid., 1876*, pp. 18–20; *ibid., 1885*, pp. 26–28; Corporation of Haverford College, *Reports, 1892–93*, pp. 14–16; Haverford College, *Bulletin*, IV (Oct. 1903), 18–20; IX (Oct. 1910), 20–21; and XII (Oct. 1913), 18–19; Jones, *Haverford*, pp. 71–78, 169–71.

27. Jones, *Haverford*, pp. 39–48; Chase, *Liberal Education*; Henry Hartshorne to Henry T. Coates, Dec. 21, 1865, and Hartshorne to James E. Rhoads, Feb. 18 and 21, 1885, Hartshorne Papers; Bryn Mawr College, *President's Report, 1884–85*, pp. 11–12; *ibid., 1914–15*, p. 59; Haverford College, *Bulletin*, XIII (Oct. 1915), 16.

28. Swarthmore College, *Eighth Annual Catalogue, 1876–77*, p. 45, and *Ninth Annual Catalogue, 1877–78*, p. 49; Cromwell, *Lucretia Mott*, p. 204; Babbidge, "Swarthmore," pp. 157–58, 166–67, 170; Swarthmore College, *Curricular and Special Meeting of the Stockholders and 18th Annual Meeting, 1881*, p. 14; Clark, *Distinctive College*, pp. 174, 177–80.

29. Babbidge, "Swarthmore," pp. 118–19, 218; Peterson, *New England College*, p. 82; Darlington, *Memoirs*, I, 103–11; Magill, *Twenty-five Years*, pp. 198–202, 208–10; Clark, *Distinctive College*, pp. 180–82; Jones, *Haverford*, pp. 120–39; Sharpless, *Small College*, p. 189; Corporation of Haverford College, *Reports, 1888–89*, pp. 15–16; Haverford College, *Bulletin*, XI (Mar. 1913), 58–59, and XIII (Nov. 1914), 67.

30. Haverford College, *Report of the Managers, 1867*, p. 6; Jones, *Haverford*, pp. 20, 97–102, 202–5; Sharpless, *Small College*, pp. 132, 183.

31. Clark, *Distinctive College*, p. 178; Barnard, *From Evangelism to Progressivism*, pp. 109–27.

Chapter 3. In the Marketplace

1. Lief, *Family Business*.

2. Barbour, *Quakers in England*, pp. 91–93, 246–49; Tolles, *Meeting House*, pp. 45–49, 85–123; Warner, *Private City*, pp. 79–98.

3. *OD, 1873*, pp. 124–31; *HD, 1869*, pp. 104–11; Tolles, *Meeting House*, pp. 46–49.

4. Rhoads, *Business Ethics*, pp. 5–6; OMS Mins., Apr. 18, 1890, pp. 457–59; Elliston P. Morris to Joshua Baily, Sept. 1, 1909, and Baily's Diary, Dec. 31, 1890, Baily Papers.

5. HYM Mins., May 17, 1867, p. 164, and May 15, 1891, pp. 60–61; OYM Mins., Apr. 22, 1904, p. 322; Rhoads, *Business Ethics*, p. 13; Jacob Elfreth, Diary, Jan. 12 and 14, 1865, and Feb. 20, 1865, Elfreth Family Papers.

6. Rhoads, *Business Ethics*, p. 10; OMS Mins., May 19, 1906, p. 419; *Friend*, XLVI (Jan. 11, 1873), 167–68, and LXXIV (Mar. 16, 1901), 273, for the quotation; May, *Protestant Churches*, pp. 52–54, 130–32.

7. OYM Mins., Apr. 24, 1891, p. 36; HYM Mins., May 16, 1896, p. 244; May, *Protestant Churches*, pp. 132–35; Philadelphia *Public Ledger*, Dec. 11, 1905, p. 7; Francis X. Sutton, "The Motivations and Rewards of the Business Executive," in Rischin, ed., *Gospel of Success*, p. 346.

8. Rhoads, *Business Ethics*, p. 7; OYM Mins., Apr. 22, 1887, p. 390.

9. Frederic Cople Jaher, "The Boston Brahmins in the Era of Industrial Capitalism," in Jaher, ed., *Age of Industrial Capitalism*, pp. 188–243. Quietists Joseph Elkinton and Charles Rhoads were a soap manufacturer

and a real estate dealer respectively, while Samuel Morris and Joseph Scattergood were farmers by choice (see Evans, Dictionary of Quaker Biography).

10. Jaher, "Boston Brahmins," pp. 228–32; Ashbrook, *Fifty Years*, pp. 11–26; Scharf and Westcott, *History of Philadelphia*, III, 2112–13, 2122.

11. Ashbrook, *Fifty Years*, pp. 26–27, 34–43, 79, 85–87; Douglass North, "Capital Accumulation in Life Insurance between the Civil War and the Investigation of 1905," in Miller, ed., *Men in Business*, pp. 238–53.

12. Lief, *Family Business*, pp. 13–18, 29–39, 46–47, 104.

13. *Ibid.*, pp. 95, 130–32, 147.

14. Isaac Eyre to Isaac Hicks, June 2, 1878, Eyre Papers; Jacob Elfreth, Diary, Apr. 16, 1907, Elfreth Papers; TMM Mins., Apr. 15, 1885, p. 79, and July 22, 1885, pp. 98–99; Joshua Baily to Edward and Henry Bettle, July 31, 1884; Horace G. Lippincott to Henry Bettle, Aug. 7, 1884; and John T. Morris to Edward Bettle, Aug. 29, 1884, all in Bettle Family Papers.

15. RMM Mins., Aug. 16, 1893, p. 60; AMM Mins., July 26, 1877, p. 162; Sept. 27, 1877, p. 163; Oct. 25, 1877, p. 165; June 25, 1885, p. 301; July 30, 1885, p. 302; and Aug. 27, 1885, p. 303.

16. Moberg, *Church as a Social Institution*, p. 415.

17. See for example, Stephan Thernstrom, "Immigrants and WASPs: Ethnic Differences in Occupational Mobility in Boston, 1890–1940," in Thernstrom and Sennett, eds., *Nineteenth Century Cities*, pp. 125–64.

18. Doherty, *Hicksite Separation*, pp. 42–66. When one considers that money values declined in the twentieth century, it is apparent that Friends born in the 1860s were even less prosperous than those born in the 1840s, whose larger estates were recorded during times in which the dollar bought more and taxes were fewer.

19. On the relative importance of different Philadelphia banks see *Banker's Directory*, pp. 348–50.

20. Scharf and Westcott, *History of Philadelphia*, III, 2252; Burt, *Perennial Philadelphians*, pp. 143–50; Glazier, *Peculiarities of American Cities*, p. 387.

21. Eleanor Bernert, "Changes in Occupational Structure in Chicago, Philadelphia, and the United States, 1910 and 1940," in Hatt and Reiss, eds., *Reader in Urban Sociology*, pp. 326–43.

22. Moberg, *Church as a Social Institution*, p. 415; cf. Ringer, "Parishioner," pp. 71–81.

23. Francis W. Gregory and Irene D. Neu, "The American Industrial Elite in the 1870s: Their Social Origins," and William Miller, "The Recruitment of the American Business Elite," in Miller, ed., *Men in Business*, pp. 193–211, 329–37; C. Wright Mills, "The American Business Elite," in Mills, *Power, Politics, and People*, pp. 110–39. For a discussion of intergenerational mobility among Friends, see Membership Sample in the Bibliography.

24. Baltzell, *Philadelphia Gentlemen*, pp. 264–73.

25. *Ibid.*, pp. 17–24.

26. Barbour, *Quakers in England*, pp. 163–67; *HD, 1869*, p. 96; *OD, 1893*, p. 136; Burt, *Perennial Philadelphians*, pp. 453–81.

27. Jaher, "Boston Brahmins," pp. 223–28; Baltzell, *Philadelphia Gentlemen*, pp. 35–39.

28. Baltzell, *Philadelphia Gentlemen*, pp. 177, 181–87; Burt, *Perennial Philadelphians*, pp. 529–32.

29. Morley, *Travels in Philadelphia*, p. 67; Tatum, *Penn's Great Town*, pp. 112, 125–27; Burgess and Kennedy, *Centennial History of the Pennsylvania Railroad*, pp. 431–32.

30. Thernstrom and Knights, "Men in Motion." On Friends' social contacts see, for example: Jacob Elfreth, Diary, Elfreth Papers, and Mott Papers; Axelrod, "Urban Structure and Social Participation"; Litwak, "Geographical Mobility and Extended Family Cohesion"; Stein, *Eclipse of Community*, p. 112.

31. *Twelfth Census of the United States, Taken in the Year 1900: Population*, I, 677; Matlack, comp., *Brief Historical Sketches*, I, 435–538; RMM Mins., June 3, 1869, p. 153; AMM Mins., Sept. 27, 1888, pp. 59–60; William Harbeson, "Yesteryear in Our Town," in White, ed., *Philadelphia Architecture*, p. 10; Baltzell, *Philadelphia Gentlemen*, pp. 264–73; Jonathan E. Rhoads to Joseph Elkinton, Oct. 25, 1894, Elkinton Family Papers.

32. Weaver, *West Philadelphia*, pp. 45–50, 101–8, 128–48; Baltzell, *Philadelphia Gentlemen*, pp. 193–95; Urban Traffic and Transportation Board, *History of Public Transportation in Philadelphia*, ch. 13; Matlack, *Historical Sketches*, pp. 435–538; *Thirteenth Census of the United States, 1910: Population*, III, 605–8; AMM Mins., Nov. 28, 1878, p. 190.

33. Thernstrom and Knights, "Men in Motion," pp. 29–35; *OD, 1873*, p. 28; Benjamin F. Whitson, Journal, Vol. II (1897–1903).

34. Urban Traffic and Transportation Board, *Public Transportation*, chs. 4–6; Burgess and Kennedy, *Pennsylvania Railroad*, p. 545; Baltzell, *Philadelphia Gentlemen*, pp. 202–5; Hilton and Due, *Electric Railways*, pp. 297, 306–7.

Chapter 4. Response to the City

1. Tatum, *Penn's Great Town*, pp. 109, 193–94; Burt, *Perennial Philadelphians*, pp. 361–62; Steffens, *Shame of the Cities*, pp. 134–61.

2. *OD, 1873*, pp. 32–33; *HD, 1869*, p. 24; Tolles, *Quakers and the Atlantic Culture*, pp. 36–54. *Friend*, XLIX (Nov. 29, 1875), 111–12; *Friends' Intelligencer*, LIX (Feb. 1, 1902), 70. The Quaker mayor in 1856 was Richard Vaux, a Democrat; the two Friends in the city councils are discussed below; Smedley Darlington of West Chester and A. Mitchell Palmer of Stroudsburg were the two Quaker congressmen from Pennsylvania in this period.

3. Thomas Speakman, "How Far Should Friends Take Part in Public Affairs?" *Friends' Intelligencer*, XLIV (Jan. 28, 1887), 65–66; *American*

Friend, II (Feb. 21, 1895), 173, and (Mar. 7, 1895), 220, for Jones' attitude; Isaac Sharpless, "Quakerism and Government," MS. of speech given in Berkeley, Calif., Apr. 3, 1909, Sharpless Papers; Sproat, *Best Men*, pp. 60–66.

4. Dusinberre, *Civil War Issues*, pp. 33–39, 48–50; Jones, *Later Periods*, II, 729; [Joseph Grinnell?] to Hamilton Fish, Oct. 24, 1872, Bettle Family Papers; Edward H. Magill to John Wanamaker, June 3, 1898, reprinted in *City and State*, IV (June 9, 1898), 640–41. Political analyst Samuel Lubell indicates that he has "yet to find an area of Quaker settlement which has not been unswervingly Republican" (*Revolt of the Moderates*, p. 271n).

5. Joshua Baily, Diary, Feb. 27, 1885, Baily Papers; Coben, "Northeastern Business and Radical Reconstruction," pp. 68–77; Charles Richardson to N. DuBois Miller, Sept. 10, 1890, and Francis R. Cope to Herbert Welsh, June 6, 1891, Welsh Papers; *Citizens' Republican Committee of Philadelphia to the Voters of Pennsylvania*, pp. 22–23.

6. McLachlan, "Genteel Reformers," p. 103; Blodgett, *Gentle Reformers*, pp. 1–18.

7. Bradley, *Henry Charles Lea*, pp. 15–16, 177–78, 189–94; Bryce, *American Commonwealth*, II, 406–14; Reform Club of Philadelphia, *Constitution, By Laws, Charter, Rules, Officers and Members*, pp. 4–39; E. Dunbar Lockwood to Henry C. Lea, Jan. 27, 1876, Lea Papers; Garrett, *Party Politics*, p. 20.

8. Scharf and Westcott, *History of Philadelphia*, I, 849, III, 1716; Disbrow, "Progressive Movement in Philadelphia," pp. 4–7; Vickers, *Fall of Bossism*, pp. 81–153; McClure, *Old Time Notes*, II, 460–61.

9. Vickers, *Fall of Bossism*, pp. 212–13, 231; Disbrow, "Progressive Movement," pp. 7–8; Richard Vaux to Henry C. Lea, Dec. 25, 1880, Lea Papers; Jacob Elfreth, Diary, Feb. 16, 1881, Elfreth Family Papers.

10. Joshua Baily, Diary, Jan. 19, 1886, and William H. Jenks to Baily, Nov. 13, 1893, Baily Papers; Henry C. Lea to Philip Garrett, Feb. 21, 1884, and Lea to [?] Cope, June 16, 1884, Lea Papers.

11. Hoogenboom, *Outlawing the Spoils*, pp. 195–96; *Friends' Intelligencer*, XXIX (Dec. 28, 1872), 696; *Friend*, LVI (Jan. 27, 1883), 199; Joseph Parrish to Herbert Welsh, July 23, 1889, Welsh Papers; Samuel Morris to R[utherford] B. Hayes, Dec. 1, 1877, in the Morris-Sansom Papers.

12. Civil Service Reform Association of Pennsylvania, *Tenth Annual Report of the Executive Committee*, pp. 15–21, and Joshua Baily to Herbert Welsh, Mar. 13, 1913, Welsh Papers; *City and State*, II (Dec. 17, 1896), 1; VI (Apr. 27, 1899), 273; XIV (Mar. 19, 1903), 226–28; and XV (Dec. 17, 1903), 402.

13. Henry C. Lea to Joel J. Baily, Feb. 10, 1887, Lea Papers; Citizens' Municipal Association, *2nd Annual Report* (1888), pp. 29–30, for the quotation, and 35ff; *4th Annual Report* (1890), pp. 30–36; *9th Annual Report* (1895), pp. 56–63; *20th Annual Report* (1906), pp. 42–44; *City and State*, XIV (Mar. 12, 1903), 207; Edwin H. Fitler to Joshua Baily, Oct. 5, 1887, Baily Papers.

14. Woodruff, "Municipal League"; *City and State*, II (May 14, 1896), 6; IV (Mar. 3, 1898), 363; and XIV (Jan. 29, 1903), 84–85, 93.

15. Stewart, *Half-Century of Municipal Reform*, pp. 19–20, 29–30, 51; *City and State*, I (Nov. 21, 1895), 2; Charles Richardson to Herbert Welsh, Jan. 7, May 23, 25, June 5, 1891, Welsh Papers; Richardson to Henry C. Lea, May 25, 29, 1899, Lea Papers.

16. *Journal of the Common Council of the City of Philadelphia, 1886–1887*, I, 49, 301, 339, 358, app. 339–50; *ibid., 1890–1891*, II, 23, 54, 172, 203, 353, 358, 372, 376, 414, 519; *ibid., 1894–1895*, I, 79, 85, 104, 122, 168, 170, 194, 206–11, 244, 260, 287, 314–15; II, 22, 115, 148, 251, 325, 377, 429, 462, 492, 498, 515, 542, 549; *City and State*, IV (Nov. 11, 1897), 81; (Jan. 27, 1898), 273; and XII (Jan. 30, 1902), 69.

17. *City and State*, IV (Oct. 21, 1897), 34; (Apr. 14, 1898), 481; and (May 12, 1898), 553; William G. Huey to Herbert Welsh, Feb. 11, 1895, Welsh Papers; McClure, *Old Time Notes*, II, 592–93; Philadelphia *Public Ledger*, Dec. 4, 1894, p. 12, and Sept. 7, 1912, p. 1; *Republican Club Book 1904*, p. 29.

18. Lists of members of the Lincoln Independent Republican Committee, of the executive committee of the Honest Government party, and of contributors to the Swallow campaign are in the Welsh Papers; Joshua Baily, "Speech given at the Academy of Music, Philadelphia, Oct. 20, 1890," Baily Papers; *Republican Committee . . . to the Voters*, pp. 22–23; Charles Richardson to Herbert Welsh, Oct. 20, 1898; Isaac Clothier to Welsh, Nov. 12, 1898; and James E. Rhoads to Welsh, Oct. 7, 1891, all in Welsh Papers.

19. Disbrow, "Progressive Movement," pp. 13–19; Committee of 70, *Report of the Executive Board, 1905*, pp. 23, 26–30; Abernathy, "Insurgency in Philadelphia."

20. Friends' Institute, Programs, 1903–1907; Ellis Yarnall to Henry C. Lea, June 9, 1905, Lea Papers; HRC Mins., Mar. 17, 1905, p. 78; *American Friend*, XII (Nov. 9, 1905), 736, for Jones' comments, and (Dec. 21, 1905), 848–51, for those of Sharpless; Philadelphia *Public Ledger*, Sept. 19, 1905, p. 2; Sept. 29, 1905, pp. 1–2; Oct. 11, 1905, p. 2; Oct. 12, 1905, p. 2; and Oct. 22, 1905, p. 10; Charles F. Jenkins, "The People's Party in the Twenty-second Ward," Jenkins Papers; Woodward, "Triumph of the People."

21. Disbrow, "Progressive Movement," pp. 20–26; Jenkins, "People's Party," p. 4; Committee of 70, *Report of the Executive Board, 1912*, pp. 4–13; Philadelphia *Public Ledger*, magazine section, Dec. 7, 1913.

22. Philadelphia *Public Ledger*, Sept. 6, 1911, p. 2; Oct. 2, 1911, p. 1; Oct. 11, 1911, p. 2; and Oct. 19, 1911, p. 2; Disbrow, "Progressive Movement," pp. 49–95.

23. Joshua Baily to Herbert Welsh, Nov. 4, 1891, and Walter Cope to Welsh, Nov. 13, 1890, Welsh Papers; Joseph Parrish to Henry C. Lea, May 29, 1885, Lea Papers; McFarland, "New York Mugwumps," p. 58.

24. Blodgett, *Genteel Reformers*, pp. 19–29; McFarland, "New York Mugwumps," pp. 43–58; Hays, "Politics of Reform," pp. 160–69.

25. *OD, 1880*, pp. 138–39; RMM Women's Mins., Apr. 19, 1899, pp. 350–52; TMM Mins., Nov. 15, 1905, p. 301.

26. *Friends' Intelligencer*, XXIX (Oct. 5, 1872), 504–5; Edward L. Scull to Thomas Chase, Oct. 22, 1872, Chase Papers; White, *Intellectual*, pp. 21–35; OYM Mins., Apr. 23, 1907, p. 180, and Mar. 30, 1916, p. 271; Hole, *Westtown*, pp. 269–73; *Friend*, LXXII (Sept. 3, 1898), 55.

27. *Friend*, XLVI (July 5, 1873), 367–68; HYM Mins., May 11, 1915, p. 238; OYM Mins., Apr. 13, 1919, pp. 47–49; White, *Intellectual*, pp. 12–20; Atkinson, *Autobiography*, pp. 157–69; Weygandt, *Philadelphia Folks*, p. 18.

28. *American Friend*, II (July 4, 1895), 639; *Independent*, LII (Jan. 4, 1900), 31; *Friends' Intelligencer*, LXI (Feb. 13, 1904), 102.

29. *Friend*, LV (June 10, 1882), 351–52; *Friends Intelligencer*, XXIX (June 15, 1872), 248–49, and LI (July 12, 1894), 472; Jacob Elfreth, Diary, June 26, 1872, Elfreth Family Papers.

30. G. Justice Mitchell to J. Howard Mitchell, July 28, 1877, Mitchell Family Papers; *Friends' Review*, XLI (Nov. 24, 1887), 264–65; Mackey, "Law and Order, 1877"; *American Friend*, I (July 19, 1894), 6, and (July 26, 1894), 29; and XVII (Mar. 3, 1910), 131; Joshua Baily to Herbert Welsh, Mar. 2, 1910, Baily Papers.

31. May, *Protestant Churches*, pp. 55–63, 101–11; *Friends' Intelligencer*, XL (Apr. 14, 1883), 136; LIX (Aug. 30, 1902), 550, and (Oct. 25, 1902), 678; Rhoads, *Business Ethics*, pp. 11–12.

32. Cross, ed., *Church and the City*, pp. xxxvi–xxxix, 331–52; Abell, *Urban Impact on American Protestantism*, pp. 147–61; AMM Mins., Nov. 23, 1893, p. 159; TMM Women's Mins., Feb. 18, 1891, pp. 109–110; "Biographical Sketch of Joshua Baily," Baily Papers; *Friends' Review*, XXVI (Nov. 9, 1872), 185.

33. Isichei, *Victorian Quakers*, pp. 113, 258–79; HYM Mins., July 21, 1886, p. 43; May 12, 1896, p. 248; and May 12, 1902, p. 155; TMM Mins., Jan. 24, 1894, pp. 75–77; Apr. 15, 1896, pp. 194–95; and May 20, 1914, pp. 44–45; TMM Women's Mins., Nov. 20, 1912, p. 136; RMM Mins., May 23, 1883, pp. 186–89, and May 22, 1901, p. 189; Edward Bettle, Jr., to Thomas Chase, Nov. 14, 1889, Chase Papers; *American Friend*, I (Dec. 12, 1895), 1236.

34. Jones, *Later Periods*, II, 915–20; Isichei, *Victorian Quakers*, pp. 123–34, 173–74.

35. OMS Mins., Dec. 19, 1873, pp. 6–7; Dec. 19, 1884, p. 305; June 24, 1876, pp. 68–70; Sept. 19, 1876, p. 72; Dec. 18, 1891, pp. 62–65; Mar. 16, 1894, p. 106; and Apr. 18, 1919, p. 5; AMM Mins., Aug. 25, 1887, p. 43, and Dec. 29, 1887, pp. 45–46; HYM Mins., May 14, 1915, p. 287, and May 15, 1917, p. 388; OYM Mins., Mar. 31, 1920, p. 135, and Apr. 24, 1896, p. 130; Pivar, "New Abolitionism," p. 162; Schlesinger, *Rise of the City*, pp. 333–35.

36. Anthony Comstock to Joshua Baily, Apr. 17, 1875 and Feb. 6, 1902, Baily Papers; Goodchild, "Social Evil in Philadelphia"; HYM Mins., May

12, 1902, p. 162; May 11, 1903, pp. 230–31; May 16, 1905, p. 312, for the quotation; May 9, 1910, p. 470.

37. Timberlake, *Prohibition*, pp. 4–12, 17, 29–30; Gusfield, *Symbolic Crusade*, pp. 45–50, 102–8; *Friends' Intelligencer*, XXXV (May 18, 1878), 200; *American Friend*, V (Mar. 17, 1898), 244.

38. *Friend*, LXXXVIII (Dec. 24, 1914), 304, and (Jan. 7, 1915), 328–29; TMM Mins., Jan. 22, 1868, p. 107, and Jan. 27, 1892, pp. 369–70; "Biographical Sketch of Joshua Baily," pp. 172–173, Baily Papers; Jacob Elfreth, Diary, Apr. 17, 1882, Elfreth Family Papers; HYM Mins., May 16, 1879, pp. 120–21, and May 9, 1887, pp. 302–3.

39. Gusfield, *Symbolic Crusade*, pp. 72–85; Samuel Morris to Francis L. Swift, Nov. 13, 1884, Morris-Sansom Papers; Joshua Baily, Diary, Dec. 30, 1888, Baily Papers.

40. "Biographical Sketch of Joshua Baily," pp. 172–82, 234; Neal Dow Joshua Baily, Aug. 16, 1877, and Oct. 29, 1880; Baily to Dr. [?] Dunn, Nov. 15, 1899; Baily, undated MS. speech on Temperance, all in Baily Papers.

41. OMS Mins., Feb. 17, 1879, pp. 114–19; Mar. 19, 1880, pp. 153–55; and Mar. 20, 1885, pp. 322–24; *Friends' Review*, XXXVI (Apr. 28, 1883), 603, and XLI (Dec. 15, 1887), 311; for the work of the Temperance Association see also Friends' Institute, Programs, Apr. 18, 1905, and Apr. 12, 1907; Yearly Meeting Tea Fund, Treasurer's Account, Apr. 18, 1911; *American Friend*, II (May 2, 1895), 429.

42. HYM Mins., May 19, 1882, p. 192; May 18, 1883, p. 217; May 17, 1884, p. 236; May 14, 1885, p. 266; May 17, 1889, pp. 391–92; May 16, 1890, p. 33; and May 15, 1893, p. 135.

43. *Ibid.*, May 10, 1898, p. 314; May 13, 1901, p. 69; May 12, 1902, pp. 157–58; May 16, 1905, p. 311; May 10, 1909, p. 435; May 12, 1913, p. 110; and May 15, 1917, p. 382; OYM Mins., Apr. 23, 1914, pp. 187–188, and Mar. 27, 1918, p. 369.

Chapter 5. Benevolence Near and Far

1. Rosenberg, *Religion*, pp. 1–11; Huggins, *Protestants*, pp. 5–13. See also review article: Singleton, "Mere Middle Class Institutions."

2. *List of Organizations Managed . . . by Members of the Society of Friends*; James, *People among Peoples*, pp. 193–215.

3. Civic Club, *Directory*, passim and specifically pp. 114–46, 347; Northern Association, *Annual Reports*, 1865, 1890, 1900, 1910, and "Report of Survey made of Women Employed by the Northern House of Industry by the Bureau of Social Research," all in the Northern Association Papers; Penn Sewing School, History, 1868–1888, and Minutes, 1894–1906, Northern Association Papers.

4. Civic Club, *Directory*, pp. 30, 50, 59–60, 110, 140, 156.

5. *Ibid.*, pp. 171, 186, 318; Friends' Mission No. 1, *Annual Report* 1880, and Friends' Neighborhood Guild, *Report* 1901, Friends' Neighborhood Guild Papers.

6. Civic Club, *Directory*, pp. 26, 31, 37, 39–40; Burt, *Perennial Phila-delphians*, pp. 220–27.

7. Civic Club, *Directory*, pp. 63, 134–35, 155; Rosenberg, *Religion and the Rise of the American City*, pp. 186–224.

8. Isaac Sharpless, "Editorial—Are We Liberal Givers?" *The Westonian*, XV (Nov. 1909), 201–3; Curti *et al.*, "Anatomy of Giving"; *Friends' Review*, XXVI (Mar. 29, 1973), 504.

9. *Friends' Intelligencer*, XXV (Mar. 9, 1878), 40–41; Civic Club, *Digest*, pp. xlii–xlviii; Huggins, *Protestants against Poverty*, pp. 57–79.

10. *Friends' Intelligencer*, XXV (June 22, 1878), 280–81; *Friends' Review*, XXXII (Oct. 26, 1878), 169; Huggins, *Protestants*, p. 62; *Monthly Register*, I (Dec. 15, 1879), 4; (May 15, 1880), 2; (June 15, 1880), 3; II (Nov. 15, 1880), 3; (Jan. 15, 1881), 6; and IV (Dec. 15, 1882), 16.

11. Kelsey, *Friends and the Indians*, pp. 19, 165–67; HRC Mins., Mar. 15, 1867, p. 76, and Dec. 13, 1867, pp. 83–85; OMS Mins., Jan. 23, 1869, pp. 365–68.

12. Fritz, *Movement for Indian Assimilation*, pp. 72–76; Priest, *Uncle Sam's Stepchildren*, pp. 29–30; Joseph Powell to Albert L. Green, Sept. 26, 1869, Green Papers.

13. D. W. Hunt to John B. Garrett, July 2, 1869, Garrett Papers; Kelsey, *Friends and the Indians*, pp. 170–76, 187–89, 197; HYM Mins., May 18, 1871, p. 265; *Friend*, XLIV (Nov. 12, 1870), 93, and XLVI (Feb. 1, 1873), 190–91.

14. Hannah [?] to Mary Lightfoot, Oct. 28, 1870; Deborah Wharton to Mary Lightfoot, Aug. 12, 1869, and July, 1873; Mary Jeanes to Mary Lightfoot, Sept. 2, 1870, all in Lightfoot Papers; Mary H. Child to Albert Green, July 8, 1869, Green Papers.

15. John Saunders to Albert Green, Dec. 14, 1871, and April 13, 1872, Green Papers; Fritz, *Indian Assimilation*, pp. 19–31; AECFIA, *3rd Annual Report, 1872*, pp. 8, 15.

16. Samuel Jeanes to Thomas Lightfoot, Dec. 10, 1870, Dec. 13, 1871, and Dec. 25, 1871, and Thomas Lightfoot to Howard White, n.d., Light-foot Papers; Kelsey, *Friends and the Indians*, p. 192; HYM Mins., May 17, 1872, p. 301.

17. William Canby Biddle to Albert Green, Oct. 5, 1871, and John Saunders to Green, Mar. 21, 1870, Green Papers; HYM Mins., May 17, 1872, pp. 301, 305; Mary Lightfoot to [?], Aug. 28, 1871, Lightfoot Papers.

18. AECFIA, *3rd Annual Report, 1872*, pp. 2, 11, 12; Thomas Lightfoot to [Indian Aid Association], n.d.; Mary Jeanes to Mary Lightfoot, Aug. 10, 1870, and Aug. 25, 1871, Lightfoot Papers.

19. Tatum, *Our Red Brothers*, pp. 114–18; Thomas Lightfoot to General C. C. Auguer, Mar. 27, 1871, Lightfoot Papers; Kelsey, *Friends and the Indians*, pp. 184–87; Priest, *Uncle Sam's Stepchildren*, pp. 36–41; Fritz, *Indian Assimilation*, pp. 114–30.

20. Jones, *Later Periods*, II, 620; OYM Mins., Apr. 19, 1865, pp. 292–98; Apr. 22, 1869, pp. 32–35; Apr. 28, 1913, pp. 151–54; Apr. 24, 1914, pp.

193–96; AMM Mins., Aug. 28, 1884, p. 290; TMM Women's Mins., Sept. 17, 1890, p. 92; Jacob Elfreth, Diary, Apr. 25, 1913, Elfreth Family Papers.

21. OMS Mins., Jan. 6, 1879, pp. 108–13; Mar. 21, 1879, pp. 128–29; Apr. 3, 1891, pp. 1–51; June 19, 1891, p. 59; Fritz, *Indian Assimilation*, pp. 202–10; *Proceedings of the Seventh Annual Meeting of the Lake Mohonk Conferences*, pp. 127–34; HYM Mins., May 14, 1895, pp. 203–4; May 15, 1899, p. 373; May 13, 1901, p. 68; and May 12, 1896, p. 248; Kelsey, *Friends and the Indians*, pp. 169n, 257, 259; Hagan, *American Indians*, pp. 111–12; Pratt, *Battlefield and Classroom*, pp. 235–36, 331, 333.

22. Fritz, *Indian Assimilation*, pp. 87–102, 167–68; OYM Mins., Apr. 22, 1868, pp. 11–12, and Apr. 20, 1893, p. 62; Priest, *Uncle Sam's Stepchildren*, pp. 31–34.

23. Woodcock and Avakumovic, *Doukhobors*, pp. 62–68, 84–137; OMS Mins., June 17, 1898, pp. 238–39, and Apr. 14, 1899, p. 248.

24. *American Friend*, VII (July 12, 1900), 660; Woodcock and Avakumovic, *Doukhobors*, pp. 19–22, 136; OMS Mins., Apr. 13, 1900, p. 276; Elkinton, *Selections*, pp. 383–91.

25. *Ibid.*, pp. 400–410, 433–44; OMS Mins., Apr. 17, 1903, p. 352; June 19, 1903, p. 356; Mar. 15, 1907, pp. 434–35; Apr. 12, 1912, pp. 104–6; and Mar. 21, 1919, pp. 464–65.

26. Woodcock and Avakumovic, *Doukhobors*, pp. 155–59; Elkinton, *Doukhobors*, pp. 62–63, 78–79, 95, 112–13; OMS Mins., Apr. 18, 1902, pp. 333–38; Joseph S. Elkinton, "Notes on a visit to Canada," June 24, 1900, Elkinton Family Papers.

27. Elkinton, *Doukhobors*, pp. 49–50; Woodcock and Avakumovic, *Doukhobors*, pp. 191–98, 204–9, 220–29; OMS Mins., Mar. 15, 1918, pp. 391–92.

28. OMS Mins., Apr. 17, 1908, p. 460; Apr. 12, 1912, p. 103; Apr. 17, 1914, pp. 189–91; and Mar. 19, 1915, pp. 243–44; Elkinton, *Doukhobors*, pp. 46–51; Woodcock and Avakumovic, *Doukhobors*, pp. 44, 214.

29. Sears, "Growth of Population in Philadelphia," pp. 60–87; U.S. Bureau of the Census, *Religious Bodies: 1916*, I, 470; Higham, *Strangers in the Land*, pp. 77–105.

30. Solomon, *Ancestors and Immigrants*, pp. 106, 122–23; Mrs. Solomon's claim that a Philadelphia branch was formed in November 1894 is not supported by the Minutes of the Immigration Restriction League, I, 1894–1902, Hall Papers (see particularly Oct. 2, 1901) or by *Reports of the Executive Committee of the Immigration Restriction League*; Philadelphia newspaper editorials, I.R.L. Collection of Endorsements and Opposition, 1894–1900, Hall Papers; Pennell, *Our Philadelphia*, pp. 468, 474.

31. *Friend*, XLVIII (Nov. 14, 1874), 100.

32. *Ibid.*, XLII (Sept. 26, 1868), 38–39; LII (Mar. 22, 1879), 223; and LV (Apr. 1, 1882), 271; *Friends' Review*, XXXII (Mar. 8, 1879), 472; XXXIX (Sept. 19, 1885), 105–6; and XLIII (July 17, 1890), 808; May, *Protestant Churches*, pp. 123–24. Similar concern over missionaries in Japan prompted Friends to defend the immigrants from that nation in the

new century; see Isaac Sharpless, "The Japanese Question," *Present Day Papers*, I (Apr. 1914), 109–12.

33. Billington, *Protestant Crusade*, p. 230; Samuel Morris to Peter Lynch, July 19, 1876, Morris-Sansom Papers; *Freedman's Friend*, I (Dec. 1870), 2; AMM Mins., Nov. 24, 1904, p. 43; Joshua Baily, undated speech on Temperance, Baily Papers; *Friends' Intelligencer*, XXXV (Mar. 16, 1878), 57; *Friends' Review*, XLIII (Nov. 21, 1889), 264, and XLVI (Feb. 2, 1893), 435.

34. Solomon, *Ancestors and Immigrants*, pp. 59–81; *Friend*, LXXII (Oct. 1, 1898), 81, and LXXIV (Jan. 19, 1901), 209; *American Friend*, VI (May 4, 1899), 412; for evidence of Friends' anti-imperialism see *City and State*, VI (May 25, 1899), 343–44; XVI (Mar. 10, 1904), 151, and (Apr. 28, 1904), 265; HYM Mins., May 15, 1906, pp. 332–35; Garrett, "Immigration to the United States," p. 188; Corporation of Haverford College, *Reports 1892–93*, p. 16; *American Friend*, II (July 4, 1895), 650; AMM Mins., Nov. 27, 1890, p. 97, and Dec. 25, 1890, p. 98.

35. Garrett, "Immigration," pp. 190–92; Atkinson, *Autobiography*, pp. 169–70; *Friends' Intelligencer*, XL (Apr. 28, 1883), 168; Hofstadter, *Age of Reform*, pp. 177–78.

36. *Friends' Review*, XLI (Nov. 24, 1887), 264–65, and XLVII (Nov. 16, 1893), 260; *American Friend*, I (Aug. 16, 1894), 101; Hopkins, *Rise of the Social Gospel*, pp. 102–6.

37. HYM Mins., May 14, 1909, p. 456; Disbrow, "Progressive Movement in Philadelphia," pp. 215–16; Philadelphia *Public Ledger*, Apr. 9, 1913, p. 14, and Jan. 20, 1916, p. 1; TMM Mins., Oct. 30, 1918, pp. 356–57; *Friends' Intelligencer*, LXXII (Dec. 11, 1915), 795.

Chapter 6. Tutoring the Freedmen

1. Drake, *Quakers and Slavery*, pp. 11–12, 51–62, 133–66, 172–74, 185–96; Zilversmit, *First Emancipation*, pp. 61–83, 156–67, 202–8; Jones, *Quakers in the American Colonies*, pp. 394–400.

2. Civic Club, *Directory*, pp. 70–71, 83, 364–65; Shelter for Colored Orphans, *Annual Report, 1867, 1892, 1900, 1914*; Philadelphia Home for Destitute Colored Children, *Annual Report, 1866, 1869*; RMM Women's Mins., Apr. 15, 1896, pp. 148–49.

3. Lucretia Mott to Martha Lord, [?, 1879], Mott Papers; DuBois, *Philadelphia Negro*, pp. 47, 230; Philadelphia Home for Aged and Infirm Colored Persons, *Annual Report, 1866, 1871, 1892*; Bacon, *History of the Pennsylvania Society*, pp. 22–27.

4. AMM Mins., Mar. 26, 1868, pp. 217–19; Civic Club, *Directory*, pp. 85–86; Penn Sewing School, History, 1868–1888; Brown, "Pennsylvania and the Rights of the Negro," pp. 47–48; *A Brief Narrative of the Struggle for the Rights of the Colored People in the City Railway Cars; Report of the Committee Appointed for the Purpose of Securing to the Colored People in Philadelphia the Right to the Use of the Street Cars*; *Friend*, XXXV (Apr. 5, 1862), 247–48; HRC Mins., Mar. 15, 1867.

5. Rose, *Rehearsal for Reconstruction*, pp. 3–62, 75–79; AEF, *Report of the Executive Board, 1864*, pp. 4–5; *Friend*, XXXVI (Oct. 4, 1862), 35, and (Dec. 27, 1862), 134; Jaquette, ed., *South after Gettysburg*, pp. 32–35.

6. Jones, *Later Periods*, II, 600; *Friend*, XXXVII (Dec. 19, 1863), 127; FFA, *Annual Report of the Executive Board, 1864*, pp. 5–6; Cope, *Report of a Visit*, pp. 4–6, 17; FFA, *Statistics of the Operation of the Executive Board, 1864*, pp. 2, 9–14.

7. FFA, *Annual Report, 1864*, pp. 4, 9–14; AEF, *Annual Report, 1864*, pp. 6–15; *ibid., 1865*, p. 4; *Friend*, XXXVII (Dec. 5, 1863), 110; [Garrett], *Memories of Philadelphia*, pp. 22–23; Lucretia Mott to Martha Wright *et al.*, Jan. 21, 1864, and Jan. 17, 1865, Mott Papers.

8. *Friend*, XXXVIII (June 17, 1865), 31, and XL (Dec. 22, 1866), 135; AEF, *Annual Report, 1864*, pp. 6–7; *ibid., 1866*, p. 14; FFA, *3rd Annual Report, 1866*, pp. 5, 11; FFA, *4th Annual Report, 1867*, p. 8; McPherson, *Struggle for Equality*, pp. 407–16; mortgage records, FFA, Mins., 1872–80; Warner, *Yardley Warner*, p. 285.

9. FFA, *Annual Report, 1864*, pp. 18–20; FFA, *2nd Annual Report, 1865*, pp. 15–17; FFA, *3rd Annual Report, 1866*, p. 9; FFA, *Statistics of the Operation of the Executive Board, 1864*, p. 17; *Friend*, XXXVII (Oct. 24, 1863), 63, and (May 28, 1864), 309; and XXXIX (Jan. 27, 1866), 175; AEF, *Annual Report, 1866*, pp. 7–8; Bentley, *History of the Freedmen's Bureau*, pp. 80–86; Jaquette, *South after Gettysburg*, p. 38.

10. Cope, *Report of a Visit*, p. 18; *An Appeal to Friends and Others on Behalf of the Destitute Freedmen of the South; Friends' Intelligencer*, XX (Feb. 29, 1864), 794–95; *Friend*, XXXVII (Sept. 12, 1863), 15, and (May 28, 1864), 309; FFA, "Dear Friends: The urgent needs of the freed people. . . ."

11. FFA, *4th Annual Report, 1867*, p. 10; FFA, *8th Annual Report, 1871*, p. 14; Rose, *Rehearsal*, pp. 368–69; *Friend*, XXXVII (Sept. 12, 1863), 15, and XXXIX (Nov. 4, 1865), 77; *Friends' Intelligencer*, XXI (Apr. 9, 1864), 76; Morrow, *Northern Methodism and Reconstruction*, pp. 159–60; Drake, "Freedman's Aid Societies," p. 181; *Freedman's Friend*, I (May 1875), 1.

12. *Friends' Intelligencer*, XXI (Apr. 9, 1864), 77–79; AEF, *Annual Report, 1867*, pp. 11–13; FFA, *Annual Report, 1864*, p. 10; FFA, *11th Annual Report, 1874*, p. 10; *Friend*, XXXVIII (December 31, 1864), 143–44; *Freedman's Friend*, I (Dec. 1867), 4.

13. FFA, *3rd Annual Report, 1866*, p. 10; FFA, *6th Annual Report, 1869*, p. 11; FFA, *8th Annual Report, 1871*, p. 5; AEF, *Annual Report, 1866*, pp. 6–11; AEF, *Annual Report, 1869*, pp. 3–4, 18; *Freedman's Friend*, I (Jan. 1876), 1; Murray, *Presbyterians and the Negro*, p. 165; Warner, *Yardley Warner*, pp. 65–69, 91–92; Jaquette, *South after Gettysburg*; Martha Schofield to Lucretia Mott, Apr. 7, 1877, Mott Papers; Patterson, *Martha Schofield, passim*.

14. Rose, *Rehearsal*, pp. 78, 316, 390–92, 402–3; Pearson, ed., *Letters from Port Royal*, pp. 223–24, 228, 250–51, 306, 321; Simkins and Woody, *South Carolina during Reconstruction*, pp. 125–26, 203–6, 428–29; Reynolds,

Reconstruction in South Carolina, pp. 107, 109, 123, 223; *New York Nation*, XV (Aug. 29, 1872), 130; Norwood, "Negro Welfare Work in Philadelphia," pp. 169–70.

15. FFA, *5th Annual Report, 1868*, p. 12; FFA, *8th Annual Report, 1871*, pp. 10–11; FFA, *9th Annual Report, 1872*, p. 5; FFA, *10th Annual Report, 1873*, p. 9; FFA, *11th Annual Report, 1874*, p. 6; FFA, Executive Board Mins., Nov. 11, 1873; Morrow, *Northern Methodism*, p. 173; Drake, "Freedmen's Aid Societies, p. 182; AEF, *Annual Report, 1872*, p. 1; *Friends' Intelligencer*, XXXIII (Dec. 9, 1876), 665; XXIV (Mar. 3, 1877), 26; and XXVI (Jan. 14, 1879), 265.

16. *Freedman's Friend*, 1 (Jan. 1877), 7; (Nov. 1877), 2; and (June 1880), 2; *Friend*, L (Mar. 10, 1877), 235; (Mar. 17, 1877), 245; (Mar. 31, 1877), 259; and (Apr. 21, 1877), 281; FFA, Executive Board Mins., Apr. 13, 1880.

17. *Brief Sketch of the Schools for Black People and Their Descendants Established by the Religious Society of Friends in 1770*, pp. 3–32; AMM Mins., Feb. 27, 1873, pp. 80–81; Beehive School, Mins., 1865–88; ICY, Managers' Mins., Feb. 19, 1889; Civic Club, *Directory*, pp. 323–24, 552.

18. *History of the Association of Friends for the Free Instruction of Adult Colored Persons*, pp. 3, 5, 22–27.

19. ICY, Managers' Mins., May 8, 1866, May 11, 1869, Oct. 11, 1871, Oct. 19, 1875, Mar. 27, 1876, and Mar. 20, 1888; ICY, Annual Report, 1860, p. 1; Coppin, *Reminiscences*, pp. 13, 19–22; Fletcher, *History of Oberlin*, pp. 534–535.

20. FFA, *11th Annual Report, 1874*, p. 10; Elkinton, *Selections*, pp. 173–76; AMM Mins., Feb. 26, 1880, p. 213; ICY, Managers' Mins., Nov. 12, 1867, Nov. 19, 1872, Oct. 15, 1878, and May 21, 1901.

21. ICY, Managers' Mins., Dec. 17, 1872, May 19, 1874, Mar. 18, 1884, Apr. 28, 1885, Sept. 21, 1886, and Mar. 15, 1892; Coppin, *Reminiscences*, pp. 23–37.

22. McPherson, "White Liberals and Black Power in Negro Education"; AEF, *Annual Report, 1871*, p. 4; FFA, Executive Board Mins., Mar. 9, 1875, and Apr. 8, 1879; William Polk, Jr., to the Friends' Freedmen Association, June 7, 1890; Leah Dore to [W. H.] Haines, Dec. 1, 1888, and Dec. 10, 1888; Leah Dore to E. M. Wistar, Jan. 5, 1889; Louise S. Dorr to E. M. Wistar, May 4, 1891, and Feb. 27, 1892, all in FFA MSS.; FFA, *25th Annual Report, 1888*, p. 7. More solid evidence on Christiansburg in the eighties is lacking because of a gap in the extant minutes of the FFA.

23. C. S. Shaeffer to Richard Wood, Jan. 7, 1889, FFA MSS.; *Friends' Intelligencer*, XLI (Mar. 15, 1884), 73–74; *Friend*, LXI (July 21, 1888), 404–5, 407; LXII (June 29, 1889), 383; LXV (Nov. 14, 1891), 127, and (Apr. 23, 1892), 310; LXXII (Aug. 27, 1898), 42; Hirshson, *Farewell to the Bloody Shirt*, pp. 123–29; Rose, *Rehearsal*, pp. 403–4.

24. Van Dusen, "Exodus of 1879"; Elizabeth Comstock to Joshua Baily, Dec. 22, 1879, and Feb. 23, 1880; Baily to Wistar Evans, June 14, [1880], Baily Papers; *Friends' Review*, XXXIII (Jan. 3, 1880), 330–31; FFA, Executive Board Mins., Apr. 13, 1880; Coben, "Northeastern Business and

Radical Reconstruction: A Reexamination," pp. 82–90; DuBois, *Philadelphia Negro*, p. 45.

25. FFA, Executive Board Mins., Nov. 22, 1898, and Apr. 20, 1914; *Freedman's Friend*, II (1904), 73–74, 78; III (1908), 154–56; ICY, Managers' Mins., Nov. 18, 1902, and June 16, 1903.

26. ICY, Managers' Mins., Jan. 20, 1885, Nov. 20, 1888, Mar. 19, 1889, June 18, 1889, Nov. 19, 1889, and Mar. 15, 1898; Coppin, *Reminiscences*, pp. 29–30; FFA, Executive Board Mins., Apr. 3, 1896, Apr. 20, 1896, Apr. 19, 1897, June 11, 1901, May 1, 1906, and Oct. 1, 1912; Fredrickson, *Black Image in the White Mind*, pp. 283–319; Meier, *Negro Thought*, pp. 100–118.

27. Bullock, *History of Negro Education*, pp. 150–54; Coppin, *Reminiscences*, p. 30; ICY, Managers' Mins., Feb. 18, 1902, Sept. 16, 1902, May 17, 1904, Oct. 16, 1904, Apr. 19, 1905, Nov. 15, 1910, May 16, 1911, Oct. 20, 1914, Apr. 17, 1917, Mar. 19, 1918, and Feb. 17, 1920.

28. FFA, Executive Board Mins., Nov. 12, 1901, and Oct. 7, 1902; ICY, Managers' Mins., Feb. 18, 1902, Feb. 21, 1905, and Sept. 16, 1913.

29. ICY, Managers' Mins., Dec. 9, 1902, May 19, 1903, and Oct. 20, 1903; *Association for Adult Colored Persons*, pp. 29–30; Beehive School, Mins. 1865–88; AMM Mins., Sept. 28, 1893, p. 157; Sept. 27, 1900, pp. 274–76; Nov. 29, 1900, p. 280; and Jan. 24, 1918, p. 126; Wright, *Negro in Pennsylvania*, p. 126.

30. TMM Mins., Mar. 19, 1884, pp. 39–40; TMM Women's Mins., Sept. 20, 1893, pp. 189–92; Oct. 17, 1894, pp. 15–17; Oct. 21, 1896, pp. 82–86; Oct. 20, 1897, pp. 111–15; Oct. 18, 1899, pp. 172–77; Oct. 16, 1901, pp. 48–49; Dec. 16, 1903, pp. 160–61; Dec. 17, 1913, p. 188; and Nov. 15, 1916, pp. 133–34.

31. Wright, *Negro in Pennsylvania*, p. 166: OYM Mins., Apr. 3, 1919, pp. 41–43; Darlington, *Memoirs*, I, 125–26, 133; Friends' General Conference, *Proceedings 1912*, pp. 54–58. The Swarthmore board denied a proposal to admit a black as late as 1932; it was not until the late forties that Negroes were admitted (Hunt, *Revolt of the College Intellectual*, pp. 101–5). Haverford admitted a black from the West Indies in the twenties (Archibald MacIntosh to the author, June 1973).

32. Joshua L. Baily to Wistar Morris, June 14, 1880; Baily to Hutchins Inge, Apr. 29, 1870, and Sept. 25, 1876; Baily to [his sons], Mar. 15, 1891, all in Baily Papers; FFA, Executive Board Mins., Nov. 14, 1905, and June 5, 1906; FFA, *36th Annual Report, 1899*, pp. 1–4; Bullock, *Negro Education*, pp. 124–26.

Chapter 7. Quaker Women and Social Feminism

1. Barbour, *Quakers in England*, pp. 132–33; Jones, *Later Periods*, I, 113–18; James, *People among Peoples*, pp. 50–52.

2. HYM Mins., May 13, 1867, pp. 148–50; May 14, 1874, p. 364; May 19, 1876, p. 55; May 18, 1877, p. 83; Isaac Eyre to Isaac Hicks, May 6, 1877, and June 3, 1877, Eyre Papers; *Hicksite Discipline, 1877*, pp. 19, 41.

3. *Friends' Intelligencer*, XXX (Mar. 20, 1875), 52; Isaac Eyre to [?], Dec. 5, 1880, Eyre Papers; RMM Mins., June 20, 1883, p. 195; Mar. 20, 1889, p. 229; Mar. 22, 1899, pp. 378–79; and May 23, 1900, pp. 86–87.

4. AMM Mins., Mar. 27, 1890, p. 89; ICY, Managers' Mins., Dec. 17, 1895; Agnes L. Tierney, "The Spiritual Equality of Men and Women Friends . . . ," *Friend*, LXXII (Mar. 25, 1899), 281–82.

5. *OD, 1910*, pp. 43–44, 60; TMM Mins., Jan. 21, 1903, p. 135, and May 15, 1918, p. 330; AMM Mins., Oct. 27, 1910, p. 197; OYM Mins., Apr. 25, 1914, p. 190; Philadelphia *Public Ledger*, Apr. 21, 1914, p. 15; ICY, Managers' Mins., June 29, 1915.

6. *Faith and Practice: Orthodox [Discipline], 1926*, p. 65; Johnson, *Under Quaker Appointment*, pp. 149–53.

7. *Friend*, XXXVI (Oct. 4, 1862), 35; Jones, *Later Periods*, II, 911–12; TMM Women's Mins., July 22, 1891, p. 120; TMM Mins., Oct. 16, 1901, p. 59.

8. AEF, *Report of the Executive Board, 1864*, pp. 4–5; RMM Women's Mins., Jan. 22, 1879, p. 344, and Feb. 19, 1879, p. 347; RMM Mins., Jan. 7 and 16, 1885, pp. 323–28; *HD, 1894*, pp. 81–92; HYM Mins., May 17, 1889, p. 398, and May 13, 1892, pp. 89–90.

9. Doherty, *Hicksite Separation*, pp. 16–32; Cromwell, *Lucretia Mott*, pp. 123–70.

10. Babbidge, "Swarthmore College in the Nineteenth Century," pp. 47–58; Parrish, *Essay on Education*, pp. 62–63.

11. Alsop, *History of the Woman's Medical College*, pp. 1–44, 60–74, 145; Marshall, *Woman's Medical College*, pp. 54–67.

12. Meigs, *What Makes a College?* pp. 6–29; O'Neill, *Everyone Was Brave*, pp. 110–14.

13. O'Neill, *Everyone Was Brave*, pp. 47–50, 66–73; Henry Hartshorne to James Rhoads, Feb. 21, 1885, Hartshorne Papers; *Friend*, LXXII (July 8, 1899), 403.

14. *HD, 1894*, pp. 81–92; OYM Mins., Apr. 24, 1903, p. 282. The Orthodox argument about the marriage question makes it sound as if no women married out of Meeting, which the statistics show to be false. Actually, Meetings were often warned in advance of wedding plans with non-Friends, and when they were satisfied that this would not prevent attendance of meeting for worship, they accepted the situation.

15. TMM Mins., Dec. 16, 1891, p. 361, and Oct. 16, 1901, p. 59; AMM Mins., Aug. 29, 1878, p. 185; OYM Mins., Apr. 21, 1909, pp. 6–7, and Apr. 20, 1910, pp. 33–34; Samuel Morris to S[amuel] Emlen, Jan. 21, 1877, in the Morris-Sansom Papers; *OD, 1916*, pp. 109–10.

16. Ringer, "Parishioner," pp. 15–20; Fichter, *Urban Parish*, pp. 100–117.

17. The role of ministers and elders in Quakerism is summarized in Brinton, *Friends for 300 Years*, pp. 83–98; RMM Mins., June 15, 1898, p. 340.

18. Rebecca K. Masters, Diary, 1880–83, Journal; Rebecca Masters to Rufus Jones, May 7 and 13, 1894, Jones Papers.

19. Lucretia Mott to Martha [Lord], [Dec. 1879?], Mott Papers; Jacob Elfreth, Diary, Jan. 8, 1867, and Jan. 6, 1868, Elfreth Family Papers; Civic Club, *Directory*, pp. 83, 145, 154, 347.

20. AMM Mins., Feb. 24, 1881, p. 233; Sept. 26, 1895, p. 191; and Sept. 28, 1916, p. 102.

21. Alumnae Association of Woman's Medical College, *Transactions, 1900–1901*, p. 111; Katzenstein, *Lifting the Curtain*, p. 81.

22. Fell, *Woman's Medical College*, pp. 156–61; Alumnae Association of Woman's Medical College, *Transactions, 1900–1901*, p. 113.

23. Jaquette, ed., *South after Gettysburg*, pp. 35–36, 194–95, 214; *Friends' Intelligencer*, XXXII (Feb. 5, 1976), 788–89; Bacon, *Quiet Rebels*, pp. 120–21; Society for Organizing Charity, *Monthly Register*, I (Dec. 15, 1879), 4, and II (Jan. 15, 1881), 6; Sutherland, "City of Homes," pp. 39–42, 58, 62–63; Cornelia Hancock to Henry C. Lea, Jan. 14, 1904, and Jan. 14, 1906, Lea Papers.

24. Sutherland, "City of Homes," pp. 45–63; Susan P. Wharton to Jane Addams, July 11, 1897, Addams Papers; Johnson, *Under Quaker Appointment*, pp. 59–65.

25. Sutherland, "City of Homes," pp. 45–51, 119–31; Davis and Sutherland, "Reform and Uplift among Philadelphia Negroes"; RMM Mins., Apr. 18, 1883.

26. Pratt, *I Learn from Children*, p. 18; Boone, *Women's Trade Union League*, pp. 80, 107.

27. Flexner, *Century of Struggle*, pp. 216–19, 361; *Friends' Intelligencer*, XLIV (Apr. 30, 1887), 286; (May 14, 1887), 319; and (Dec. 17, 1887), 815; *Friends' Review*, XXV (Feb. 17, 1872), 408–9; *Friend*, LXVIII (May 4, 1895), 327.

28. Smith, ed., *Philadelphia Quaker*, pp. 49–50; Joshua Baily, Diary, Aug. 26, 1894, Baily Papers; *Century*, XLVIII (Aug. 1894), 613–23; *Friend*, LXXI (Sept. 11, 1897), 62–63.

29. Katzenstein, *Lifting the Curtain*, p. 81; *Keystone State Bazaar in Aid of the Pennsylvania Woman Suffrage Association, February 25, 26, 1915*; Krone, "Dauntless Women," pp. 17–18, 157.

30. Blankenburg, *Blankenburgs of Philadelphia*, pp. 115–16; Katzenstein, *Lifting the Curtain*, pp. 96, 129; Krone, "Dauntless Women," p. 37; Friends' General Conference, *Proceedings, 1900*, pp. 164–65; HYM Mins., May 13, 1901, pp. 67–68; May 15, 1906, p. 334; and May 13, 1912, p. 50.

31. *Friends' Intelligencer*, LXIV (Feb. 16, 1907), 104–5; Friends' General Conference, *Proceedings, 1900*, pp. 160–65; *Friend*, LXXXVI (June 12, 1913), 396–97; Kraditor, *Ideas of the Woman Suffrage Movement*, pp. 43–74.

32. HYM Mins., May 15, 1906, p. 334; May 10, 1909, p. 436; May 14, 1914, p. 209; May 10, 1915, p. 233; May 16, 1916, pp. 309–310; and May 13, 1919, p. 57.

33. Flexner, *Century of Struggle*, pp. 262–70; Krone, "Dauntless Women," pp. 40–55; O'Neill, *Everyone Was Brave*, pp. 126–30; Katzenstein, *Lifting the Curtain*, pp. 184–85.

34. *Friends' Intelligencer*, LXVIII (June 2, 1906), 349; Wilmer W. Atkinson, "A Statement, A Comparison, and an Appeal" (Philadelphia, 1914) and "Heading Toward Hidden Rocks" (Philadelphia, n.d.), pamphlets in FHL; Krone, "Dauntless Women," pp. 57–60; Flexner, *Century of Struggle*, pp. 283–87.

Chapter 8. Winds of Change

1. *HD, 1894*, pp. 35–36, 46, 55–59, 65, 105, 115–19; RMM Women's Mins., Nov. 20, 1895, p. 117.

2. *HD, 1886*, p. 88; *HD, 1894*, pp. 38–40.

3. OMS Mins., Mar. 22, 1910, pp. 42–43; *OD, 1910*, pp. 16, 21–22, 96, 100–101, 115; *Friend*, LXXXX (Aug. 18, 1910), 47.

4. OYM Mins., Apr. 23, 1897, pp. 153–58; Apr. 22, 1913, p. 126; and Apr. 24, 1913, p. 134; Jones, *Later Periods*, II, 930–34, 971–79; *Friend*, LXXI (Nov. 27, 1897), 151, and LXXXVII (Feb. 5, 1914), 373.

5. Edward H. Magill to Thomas Chase, Dec. 2, 1879, and Mar. 9, 1885, Chase Papers; Friends' Institute, Programs, 1903–1907; OYM Mins., Apr. 21, 1910, p. 38; Joseph Swain to Rufus Jones, Apr. 26, 1904, Jones Papers; RMM Mins., Oct. 20, 1909, p. 200; *Unity of Spirit*, pp. 222–27, 267, 277–79.

6. OMS Mins., Apr. 12, 1895, pp. 154–57; HYM Mins., May 16, 1896, p. 243; May 10, 1897, p. 278; and May 13, 1907, p. 369; John Dillingham to Rufus Jones, Feb. 10, 1897, and Asa Wing to Jones, Feb. 11, 1897, Jones Papers; Joshua Baily to Charles Rhoads, Feb. 19, 1897, and Baily to David Scull, Feb. 4, 1907, and Feb. 13, 1907, Baily Papers. Official reunion of the two Yearly Meetings in Philadelphia was not accomplished until 1955.

7. RMM Mins., Sept. 18, 1895, pp. 176–77; *City and State*, XIV (June 11, 1903), 464; Friends' Institute, Programs, 1903–1907; Jacob Elfreth, Diary, Mar. 21, 1916, Elfreth Family Papers; Francis Taylor, "The Development of the Activities of the Yearly Meeting (1827–1927)," *Friend*, CI (Oct. 13, 1927), 191–93.

8. Peterson, *New England College*, pp. 152–53, 174–77; Barnard, *From Evangelism to Progressivism*, pp. 3–33, 115–27; Swarthmore College, *Bulletin*, I (Mar. 1904), 73, and VII (Dec. 1909), 86–87; Disbrow, "Progressive Movement in Philadelphia," pp. 199–206, 278; Haverford College, *Bulletin*, XIII (Jan. 1915), 66–67, and XIV (Jan. 1916), 62; Meigs, *What Makes A College?* pp. 90–92.

9. *Friends' Intelligencer*, LXVI (Nov. 27, 1909), 753–54; *Friend*, LXXXIV (Jan. 5, 1911), 209; Darlington, *Memoirs*, I, 133; Jesse Holmes to Rufus Jones, Dec. 13, 1904, Jones Papers.

10. *Westonian*, XV (June 1909), 129–130, and XVI (Oct. 1910), 305–8; "Report to the Board of Managers, 1892," Sharpless Papers, Jones, *Haverford*, pp. 60–63, 73–93.

11. Jones, *Trail of Life in the Middle Years*, pp. 26–27; Isaac Sharpless to [?], Dec. 31, 1894, Sharpless Papers; *American Friend*, XVII (Nov. 10,

1910), 715–16; Isaac Sharpless, "The Quaker Boy at School," *Independent*, LXV (Sept. 3, 1908), 543–46; John H. Dillingham to Rufus Jones, Nov. 27, 1898, Jones Papers; Isaac Sharpless, "Quakerism and Moral Reform," MS. of speech given in Berkeley, Calif., Apr. 4, 1909, Sharpless Papers; Sharpless to Henry T. Brown, June 15, 1912, and to [Henry T. Brown?], Mar. 3, 1918, Sharpless Papers; Philadelphia *Public Ledger*, July 18, 1910.

12. Vining, *Friend of Life*, pp. 63–80; Jones, *Trail of Life in College*, pp. 106–24; *American Friend*, II (Apr. 25, 1895), 389; IV (Apr. 15, 1897), 339–40; and XVII (Feb. 24, 1910), 115; Rufus Jones to [George Newman], [1907?], and Coleman Nicholson to Jones, Oct. 8, 1909, Jones Papers.

13. *American Friend*, I (July 26, 1894), 30–31; II (Feb. 21, 1895), 172; George Vaux, Jr., to Rufus Jones, Aug. 16, 1894; Charles Rhoads to Jones, Sept. 24, 1894; Rebecca K. Masters to Jones, Nov. 15, 1894, all in Jones Papers; Rufus Jones to Josiah Leeds, July 3, 1894, Leeds Papers.

14. *American Friend*, IV (Jan. 14, 1897), 28–29; (Mar. 25, 1897), 268–69; (Dec. 23, 1897), 1198; VI (Jan. 12, 1899), 28; (July 6, 1899), 628; (July 13, 1899), 651–52; VII (Apr. 19, 1900), 364; and XVII (Apr. 21, 1910), 243; *Present Day Papers*, I (May 1914), 124–25; OYM Mins., Apr. 2, 1915, pp. 249–50.

15. *American Friend*, I (July 19, 1894), 4; II (Feb. 14, 1895), 145–46; V (Mar. 10, 1898), 219–20; and VI (May 18, 1899), 459–60; Rufus Jones to George Newman, Aug. 7, 1907, and Apr. 7, 1913, and Samuel Morris to Jones, Feb. 7, 1904, Jones Papers; Jones, *Middle Years*, pp. 43–44; Philadelphia *Public Ledger*, Jan. 14, 1908.

16. J. Henry Scattergood to Rufus Jones, Feb. 3, 1901; J. Passmore Elkinton to Jones, Mar. 15, 1914; Acton Griscom to Jones, Jan. 12, 1914; Alfred Lowry, Jr., to Jones, Feb. 9, 1918, all in Jones Papers; for a chronological list of works by Jones, see Caffrey, "Affirmation Mysticism of Rufus Matthew Jones," pp. 262–65.

17. *American Friend*, I (Oct. 4, 1894), 269, and VI (May 25, 1899), 483; Jones, *Middle Years*, pp. 5–9, 116, 119; Hopkins, *Rise of the Social Gospel*, pp. 205–14, 302–17; Henry H. Bonnell to Rufus Jones, Jan. 5, 1914, and Virgil N. Johnson to Jones, Aug. 1, 1914, and Sept. 7, 1914, Jones Papers.

18. Jacob Elfreth, Diary, Apr. 20, 1908; Elfreth Family Papers; OMS Mins., June 19, 1908, pp. 466–67, and Dec. 18, 1908, pp. 16–17; Handy, ed., *Social Gospel in America*, p. 12.

19. *Friend*, LXXXIV (July 28, 1910), 25; (Sept. 8, 1910), 73; and LXXXVII (Aug. 7, 1913), 61; *Friends' Intelligencer*, LXIV (Nov. 9, 1907), 712; HYM Mins., May 19, 1911, p. 35, and May 17, 1912, p. 99; OYM Mins., Apr. 24, 1914, p. 200, and Apr. 2, 1915, p. 249; AMM Women's Mins., Dec. 24, 1914, p. 186.

20. Wiebe, *Search for Order*, pp. 145–55; *American Friend*, IV (Oct. 28, 1897), 1007–10; HYM Mins., May 15, 1912, pp. 86–87; May 12, 1913, p. 109; May 15, 1917, pp. 374, 377; RMM Mins., May 20, 1914, p. 122; OMS Mins., Mar. 15, 1918, pp. 381–83; and Apr. 19, 1918, pp. 397–98; AMM Mins., May 20, 1918, pp. 189–90.

21. North House, *Annual Reports*, 1908–09, 1909–10, 1910–11, 1915–17, HSP; Disbrow, "Progressive Movement," pp. 199–206; TMM Mins., Apr. 15, 1908, p. 58.

22. Friends' Neighborhood Guild, *Reports*, 1901, 1914, 1917, Neighborhood Guild MSS., FHL; Bosworth, *Story of the Friends' Neighborhood Guild*, pp. 1–27; HYM Mins., May 15, 1906, pp. 333–34, and May 9, 1910, p. 470; Penn Sewing School, Mins., 1894–1906, Northern Association Papers.

23. North House, *Annual Reports*, 1908–09, 1910–11, 1911–12, 1917–18; Friends' Neighborhood Guild, *Reports*, 1907 and 1914, Neighborhood Guild MSS., FHL; Bosworth, *Guild*, p. 29.

24. TMM Mins., Mar. 17, 1909, p. 111; OYM Mins., Apr. 2, 1920, p. 203.

25. *Friend*, LXXXVII (Dec. 4, 1913), 265; Davis, *Spearheads for Reform*, p. 86.

26. Davis, *Spearheads for Reform*, pp. 94–102; Handy, *Christian America*, pp. 174–75, 179–85.

27. OMS Mins., Dec. 30, 1904, p. 374, and Aug. 14, 1919, pp. 23–25; Disbrow, "Progressive Movement," p. 301; *Friend*, LXXXV (Sept. 7, 1911), 73; *Friends' Intelligencer*, LXVIII (Sept. 9, 1911), 569–70; ICY, Managers' Mins., May 21, 1918; HYM Mins., May 13, 1919, p. 61, and May 12, 1920, pp. 116–17.

28. HYM Mins., May 13, 1887, pp. 322–24; May 18, 1888, pp. 356–57; May 10, 1897, pp. 276–77; May 10, 1898, p. 314; May 15, 1911, p. 7; May 11, 1915, p. 230; and May 15, 1916, p. 305; Patterson, *Martha Schofield*, pp. 23–24, 30–31; *Friends' Intelligencer*, LIV (Feb. 6, 1897), 91–92; (Apr. 17, 1897), 279–80; (May 8, 1897), 333–34; and LV (Mar. 12, 1898), pp. 188–89.

29. Friends' General Conference, *Proceedings, 1910*, p. 92; *ibid., 1912*, pp. 54–58; *ibid., 1916*, p. 62; Disbrow, "Progressive Movement," p. 301.

30. Cornelia Hancock to Henry C. Lea, Jan. 14, 1904, and Jan. 15, 1906, Lea Papers; Friendly Settlement Association, Minutes, 1905, Neighborhood Guild MSS., FHL; Spring Street Settlement, Journal, 1906–9, pp. 11–12, and Annual Meeting, Mins., 1910–16, pp. 16–20, 66, 110, Spring Street Settlement Papers; Johnson, *Under Quaker Appointment*, pp. 59–65.

31. Meier, *Negro Thought*, pp. 171–84; *Friend*, LXXXV (Sept. 7, 1911), 73; *Friends Intelligencer*, LXVIII (Feb. 18, 1911), 106–7, and LXX (Aug. 2, 1913), 493; Armstrong Association, *6th Annual Report, 1914* and *7th Annual Report, 1915*.

32. TMM Women's Mins., Oct. 19, 1919, pp. 63–66; Spring Street Settlement, Annual Meetings Mins., 1910–16, pp. 43, 51, FHL; ICY, Managers' Mins., Apr. 16, 1913; AMM Mins., Sept. 28, 1916, p. 104.

33. *Friends' Intelligencer*, LXX (Aug. 2, 1913), 493; Armstrong Association, *6th Annual Report, 1914* and *9th Annual Report 1917; Survey*, XXXVIII (Apr. 7, 1917), 27; HYM Mins., May 15, 1917, pp. 385–86, and May 14, 1918, p. 9; Spring Street Settlement, Annual Meeting Mins., 1910, p. 20.

34. HYM Mins., May 14, 1918, p. 9, and May 13, 1919, p. 56; Spring Street Settlement, Annual Meetings Mins., 1910–16, pp. 19, 21.

35. HYM Mins., May 17, 1912, p. 99.

36. *American Friend*, V (Jan. 12, 1899), 28.

Chapter 9. The Anvil of War

1. Brock, *Pacifism*, pp. 713–64; RMM Mins., Oct. 17, 1866, pp. 496–97; AMM Mins., Feb. 21, 1867, pp. 191–92; TMM Mins., Jan. 17, 1866, pp. 55–56; OMS Mins., Sept. 15, 1865, pp. 259–60; HRC Mins., May 13, 1867, p. 77.

2. HRC Mins., Dec. 13, 1872, and Jan. 24, 1873, pp. 146–49; HYM Mins., May 17, 1882, p. 180; May 19, 1882, p. 187; and May 14, 1897, p. 280; OMS Mins., Jan. 17 and Mar. 21, 1873, pp. 452–56; Dec. 19, 1873, pp. 12–13; Apr. 1, 1887, pp. 398–401; Jan. 3, 1896, p. 170; Feb. 8, 1897, p. 198; and Mar. 25, 1898, pp. 225–26.

3. Marchand, *American Peace Movement and Social Reform*, pp. 30–31, 39–73; HYM Mins., May 17 and 19, 1899, pp. 355, 366–69; OMS Mins., June 17, 1887, p. 409; Sept. 16, 1887, pp. 411–19; Apr. 18, 1890, pp. 457–59; June 16, 1896, pp. 179–86; May 9, 1899, pp. 257–58; Dec. 15, 1899, pp. 263–64; *City and State*, IV (June 2, 1898), 618; VI (Mar. 23, 1899), 180, and (May 25, 1899), pp. 343–44; XIV (Jan. 15, 1903), 53; and XVI (Apr. 28, 1904), 265; *Friends' Review*, XLVII (Dec. 7, 1893), 309; *American Friend*, IV (Dec. 16, 1897), 1174; V (July 7, 1898), 628–29; and X (Nov. 12, 1903), 772; "To Members of the Monthly Meeting of Friends of Philadelphia for the Western District . . . ." May 1898, printed letter in TMM Minute Book, DR.

4. OMS Mins., Mar. 16, 1900, pp. 265–74; May 11, 1900, pp. 287–95; Sept. 27, 1901, p. 321; Apr. 12, 1907, p. 436; Nov. 26, 1909, pp. 34–36; Jan. 6, 1911, pp. 63–65; Mar. 21, 1913, pp. 145–46; and Nov. 28, 1913, p. 174; HYM Mins., May 15, 1906, p. 334, and May 14, 1909, p. 456; HRC Mins., Mar. 17, 1911, p. 171.

5. Brock, *Pacifism*, pp. 871–76; Friends' Institute, Programs, 1903–7; Jones, *Later Periods*, II, 756–57; Marchand, *Peace Movement*, pp. 74–119, 138.

6. Marchand, *Peace Movement*, pp. 144–81; TMM Women's Mins., Oct. 21, 1914, p. 19; OMS Mins., Sept. 25, 1914, pp. 202–4, and Nov. 27, 1914, pp. 206–7. The Orthodox renamed the Meeting for Sufferings the Representative Meeting in 1914.

7. OMS Mins., Jan. 18, 1915, pp. 211–14, and Mar. 19, 1915, pp. 234–40; HRC Mins., Mar. 12, 1915, pp. 233–34; Sept. 17, 1915, p. 245; and Dec. 17, 1915, pp. 247–48; HYM Mins., May 14, 1915, p. 284; TMM Mins., July 21, 1915, p. 129; RMM Mins., Oct. 20, 1915, p. 209.

8. Marchand, *Peace Movement*, pp. 370–74; Chatfield, *For Peace and Justice*, pp. 19–21, 31, 38–41; HYM Mins., May 16, 1916, p. 321; OYM Mins., Mar. 29, 1917, p. 322.

9. HYM Mins., pp. 315–25.

10. Marchand, *Peace Movement*, pp. 182–212; 223–48, 266–87, 347–64.

11. Abrams, *Preachers Present Arms*, pp. 145–48, 162–66; Marchand, *Peace Movement*, pp. 212–22, 248–65, 287–322, 365–70; cf. Handy, *Christian America*, pp. 151–53.

12. OMS Mins., Apr. 27 and June 15, 1917, pp. 340–44, and June 20, 1917, pp. 346–48; Brock, *Pacifism*, pp. 368–70.

13. OYM Mins., Mar. 29, 1918, pp. 399–400; Rufus Jones, "The Quaker Peace Position," *Survey*, XXXIV (Apr. 3, 1915), 22–23.

14. OMS Mins., June 15, 1917, p. 344; June 20, 1917, p. 348; Aug. 16, 1917, p. 350; Oct. 19, 1917, pp. 352–53; Nov. 9, 1917, 356–59; Jan. 18, 1918, pp. 376–78; Apr. 19, 1918, pp. 399–401; June 21, 1918, pp. 403–6; and Nov. 1, 1918, pp. 412–15; Abrams, *Preachers*, p. 140; Chatfield, *Peace and Justice*, pp. 68–73.

15. OMS Mins., June 20, 1917, pp. 346–47; *Literary Digest*, LVII (May 11, 1918), 31, and (June 1, 1918), 43.

16. Rufus Jones to Violet Hodgkin, Oct. 20, 1914, and July 26, 1917, Jones Papers; Jones, *Service of Love*, pp. 1–16; Jones, *Trail of Life in the Middle Years*, pp. 203–4.

17. Jones, *Service of Love*, pp. 17–27, 60–76, 144–72, 209–26; RMM Mins., Feb. 19, 1919, pp. 407–8; OYM Mins., Mar. 28, 1918, p. 389.

18. Jones, *Service of Love*, pp. 77–84; *American Friend*, XVII (Oct. 6, 1910), 631.

19. Earl D. Fowler to Rufus Jones, May 24, 1915, and Dec. 23, 1915; Felix Morley to Jones, Oct. 9, 1915; Frank Morley to Jones, May 23, 1915; J. Clayton Strawbridge to Jones, Nov. 16, 1917; Davis Forsythe to Jones, Mar. 30, 1918; Joseph Stokes, Jr., to Jones, June 14, 1918; Norman Thomas to Jones, May 22 and 28, 1918, and Aug. 1, 1918, all in Jones Papers; *Survey*, XXXIV (Apr. 3, 1915), 22–23; Marchand, *Peace Movement*, p. 379.

20. HRC Mins., Apr. 20, 1917, p. 8; HYM Mins., May 18, 1917, pp. 434–41; RMM Mins., Feb. 13, 1918, pp. 334–36; Aug. 21, 1918, pp. 366–69.

21. *Advocate of Peace*, LXXX (May 1918), 146–47; Philadelphia *Public Ledger*, Nov. 6, 1918, p. 9; Henry Ferris to J. Henry Scattergood, May 3, 1918, Jones Papers; HYM Mins., May 15, 1919, p. 79; Hirst, *Quakers in Peace and War*, p. 520; clipping from the Philadelphia *Inquirer*, June 15, 1917, Ferris MSS.

22. Asa S. Wing to Rufus Jones, Sept. 13, 1918, Jones Papers; Philadelphia *Public Ledger*, Oct. 12, 1918; Oct. 13, 1918, p. 4; Oct. 15, 1918, p. 8; and Oct. 18, 1918, pp. 1, 11; "Committee Recommendation of the Haverford College Board of Managers," n.d., MS. in Brown Papers; Henry J. Cadbury to Rufus Jones, Jan. 1, 1919, and Jones to J. Rendel Harris, Jan. 21, 1919, Jones Papers.

23. Abrams, *Preachers*, pp. 187–88; *Advocate of Peace*, LXXX (May 1918), 146–47.

24. Davis, "Welfare, Reform, and World War I"; Hutchison, *We Are Not Divided*, pp. 175–92.

25. OMS Mins., Mar. 17, 1916, pp. 306–7; Apr. 19, 1918, p. 397; Feb. 28, 1919, p. 444; and June 16, 1920, pp. 43–45; HYM Mins., May 18, 1917, p. 444; OYM Mins., Apr. 2, 1920, p. 185.

26. OYM Mins., May 15, 1918, p. 23; Mar. 28, 1918, pp. 394–95; and Apr. 4, 1919, p. 59; Norman Thomas to Rufus Jones, Oct. 28 and Nov. 21, 1918, Jones Papers; OMS Mins., Jan. 28, 1919, pp. 438–39; Aug. 4, 1919, p. 23; HRC Mins., Mar. 14, 1919, pp. 34–36.

27. Jones, *Service of Love*, pp. 227–65; Howard H. Brinton to Rufus Jones, July 29, 1919, and M. Carey Thomas to Jones, Apr. 30, 1920, Jones Papers; OYM Mins., Apr. 4, 1919, pp. 53–56; Apr. 2, 1920, p. 183. On the twenties see Miller, *American Protestantism and Social Issues*, and Carter, *Decline and Revival of the Social Gospel*.

28. *Friends' Intelligencer*, LXXIII (Oct. 7, 1916), 614; Herbert W. Horwill, "A Quaker Socialist Movement," *Nation*, VII (Sept. 14, 1918), 291–93; Marchand, *Peace Movement*, pp. 376–78.

29. OYM Mins., Mar. 28, 1917, p. 312, and Mar. 30, 1917, p. 350; HYM Mins., May 15, 1919, p. 79; OSOC Mins., Apr. 9, 1917.

30. AMM Mins., June 28, 1917, p. 142; OSOC Mins., Apr. 24, 1917, and Oct. 13–14, 1917; HYM Mins., May 15, 1919, p. 77.

31. OSOC Mins., May 8 and 22, 1917.

32. *Ibid.*, June 5, 1917; June 14, 1918; Oct. 4–6, 1918; and Dec. 9, 1918.

33. OYM Mins., Mar. 26, 1917, p. 312; OSOC Mins., Apr. 9, 1918; Jan. 13, 1919; Feb. 10, 1919; Nov. 10, 1919; and Apr. 20, 1920; Vogel, *Precision, People and Progress*, pp. 38–48; OMS Mins., Jan. 17, 1919, p. 428.

Bibliography

The Bibligraphy is divided into three sections. The first describes the membership sample on which much of the text discussion is based. The other two list unpublished and published sources.

Membership Sample

From the membership records of three Center City Philadelphia Monthly Meetings—Arch Street, Twelfth Street, and Race Street —we selected the names of all Friends born between 1840 and 1849 and between 1860 and 1869. This division into generations was purposeful. Those born in the forties reached their years of active adulthood in the late nineteenth century. Those born in the sixties reached that stage after the turn of the century. The generational distinction afforded us opportunities to examine changes taking place in the membership between 1880 and 1920 with regard to a host of variables. To avoid a sample of unwieldly proportions, we eliminated those whose membership was not of sufficient duration to allow them to become active adult participants in their Meeting's activities: those who left their Meeting before the age of forty, those who did not have at least ten consecutive years of membership, and those who did not become Meeting members by 1895 for those born in the forties and by 1915 for the sixties generation. The remaining Quakers in the sample constituted the most stable segment of the membership.

The uniform application of these criteria produced a sample of 710 Friends. The total membership of the three Meetings at the turn of the century was 2,781. The sample therefore includes approximately a quater of the entire "universe" it was designed to represent. To have reduced it further would have made unreliable the statistics for the small Arch Street Meeting, which was represented by only 66 of the 710 total.

Printed directories issued by the Meetings made it possible to trace the residential history of each subject during the years of his membership. Where records were available, each subject's Meeting memberships were traced back to his birth. We were able then to distinguish between birthright Friends, those received in their youth at their parents' request, and convinced adults. Examination of the school and college alumni catalogs for Quaker institutions in the Philadelphia area produced helpful data on the educational experience of many of the subjects, as well as their children. City directories for the years 1870 through 1920 yielded occupational information for the subjects living in Philadelphia.

The Registry of Wills offices for Philadelphia, Bucks, Chester, Delaware, and Montgomery counties in Pennsylvania, and Camden and Burlington counties in New Jersey offered data with respect to bequests, property ownership, and financial resources for a large number of the subjects. We consulted Philadelphia newspapers for obituaries, which gave general biographical information not found elsewhere: membership in clubs, voluntary associations, and boards of directors. The Philadelphia Social Register from 1891 to 1920, a directory of business directorships, lists of supporters for political reform movements, and annual reports of philanthropic agencies were helpful in developing the profiles.

The minutes of each of the Meetings yielded further data on the subjects' participation in the institutional work of the Society. Lists of all appointments to standing committees from 1870 to 1920 were checked. Meetings also assigned members to special committees to deal with single problems or programs. Individuals were appointed to receive newcomers transferring from other Meetings, to prepare certificates for those transferring out, to inquire as to possible violations of the Discipline, to inquire into the "clearness" of a couple to marry, and to attend marriages in an official capacity. We examined the minutes with an eye to the appointment of Friends in the sample to such responsibilities. This produced institutional participation profiles for each subject, in which two points were assigned for each year's service on a standing committee or as an overseer, minister, elder, or clerk.

A single point was assigned for each of the other miscellaneous activities to which the subjects were assigned. These data were used in determining the typology of Friends.

While research turned up a considerable amount of information on some of the 710, it did not remove from obscurity all of the subjects. For a few, even occupational status could not be determined. The lack of uniformity of information left with the Registry of Wills offices in Pennsylvania and the partial estate records preserved in New Jersey limited the return for this variable to but half the subjects. Data on education in smaller Quaker institutions and in the public schools was sparse; information on voluntary association membership was uneven. These variables could provide only limited insights as a result. In spite of these limitations, sufficient data was available to provide a solid basis for comparing financial, occupational, and social status with religious commitment.

We began to collect data on the occupational status of the fathers of all subjects. But this proved to be an uncertain venture. City directories earlier in the nineteenth century provided information on some of those subjects who had been raised in the city. Name duplication and lack of precise information precluded thorough data collecting. Without comparable sources for fathers living outside Philadelphia, the information we did find would have produced biased conclusions. For this reason, we have omitted from consideration in Chapter 3 the matter of intergenerational mobility which a more thorough compilation of data on fathers' occupations would have produced. What information we did obtain was used to determine the ascribed occupational status of unemployed, unmarried women in the sample.

From the institutional participation profiles we developed a typology of Friends. "Weighty" Friends were those whose Monthly Meeting activity participation scores totalled more than 100 or whose participations per year were above 3.5, who had been appointed a minister, elder, clerk, or overseer by their Monthly Meeting, or who had been appointed to several Yearly Meeting Committees, but had not been active in their Monthly Meeting. "Practicing" Friends were those who left a record of Monthly Meeting activity but had not qualified as Weighty, nonparticipators in Meeting activity who left significant bequests to Quaker institutions, or nonparticipators who sent their children to Quaker schools and colleges almost exclusively. The "Nominal" Friends were all others. Essentially, Weighty Friends were those who accepted a major share of the assignments to perform Meeting business. Nominal Friends left no written record of participation in or support of Quaker institutions.

When data compiled in the biographical profiles of the 710 subjects is used in the text, we have not footnoted the detailed sources for the individuals discussed. These source citations are on file with the profiles themselves, which have been deposited in the Quaker Collection of the Haverford College Library and can be consulted there.

Unpublished Sources

Baily, Joshua L. Papers. Quaker Collection, Haverford College, Haverford, Pa.

Beehive School. Minutes, 1865–88. Department of Records of Philadelphia Yearly Meeting, Philadelphia, Pa.

Bettle Family. Papers. Friends' Historical Library, Swarthmore College, Swarthmore, Pa.

Brown, T. Wistar. Papers. Quaker Collection, Haverford College, Haverford, Pa.

Chase, Thomas. Papers. Quaker Collection, Haverford College, Haverford, Pa.

Elfreth Family. Papers. Quaker Collection, Haverford College, Haverford, Pa.

Elkinton Family. Papers. Friends' Historical Library, Swarthmore College, Swarthmore, Pa.

Evans, William Bacon, comp. Dictionary of Quaker Biography. Quaker Collection, Haverford College, Haverford, Pa.

Eyre, Isaac. Papers. Friends' Historical Library, Swarthmore College, Swarthmore, Pa.

Ferris, Henry. Papers. Friends' Historical Library, Swarthmore College, Swarthmore, Pa.

Friends' Freedmen Association, Minutes and Letterbooks, 1864–1920. Department of Records of Philadelphia Yearly Meeting, Philadelphia, Pa.

Friends' Institute. Programs Held at the Institute, 1903–7. Department of Records of Philadelphia Yearly Meeting, Philadelphia, Pa.

Friends' Neighborhood Guild. Papers. Friends' Historical Library, Swarthmore College, Swarthmore, Pa.

Garrett, John B. Papers. Quaker Collection, Haverford College, Haverford, Pa.

Green, Albert L. Papers. Friends' Historical Library, Swarthmore College, Swarthmore, Pa.

Hall, Prescott. Papers. Houghton Library, Harvard University, Cambridge, Mass.

Hartshorne, Henry. Papers. Quaker Collection, Haverford College, Haverford, Pa.

Indian Aid Association. Papers. Friends' Historical Library, Swarthmore College, Swarthmore, Pa.

Institute for Colored Youth [later Cheyney Training School for Teachers]. Managers' Minutes, 1865–1920. Department of Records of Philadelphia Yearly Meeting, Philadelphia, Pa.

Jenkins, Charles F. Papers. Friends' Historical Library, Swarthmore College, Swarthmore, Pa.

Jones, Rufus M. Papers. Van Pelt Library, University of Pennsylvania, Philadelphia, Pa.

Leeds, Josiah. Papers. Quaker Collection, Haverford College, Haverford, Pa.

Lightfoot, Thomas and Mary. Papers. Friends' Historical Library, Swarthmore College, Swarthmore, Pa.

Lytle, John J. "Some Account of Philadelphia Yearly Meeting—1856." Department of Records of Philadelphia Yearly Meeting, Philadelphia, Pa.

Masters, Rebecca K. Journal. Friends' Historical Library, Swarthmore College, Swarthmore, Pa.

Mitchell Family. Papers. Quaker Collection, Haverford College, Haverford, Pa.

Morris-Sansom. Papers. Quaker Collection, Haverford College, Haverford, Pa.

Mott, Lucretia. Papers. Friends' Historical Library, Swarthmore College, Swarthmore, Pa.

Northern Association. Papers. Friends' Historical Library, Swarthmore College, Swarthmore, Pa.

Penn Sewing School. History, 1868–88. Friends' Historical Library, Swarthmore College, Swarthmore, Pa.

Philadelphia Meeting for Sufferings [called Philadelphia Representative Meeting after 1913] (Orthodox). Meeting Minutes. Department of Records of Philadelphia Yearly Meeting, Philadelphia, Pa.

Philadelphia Monthly Meeting [Arch Street]. Membership Records. Department of Records of Philadelphia Yearly Meeting, Philadelphia, Pa.

——. Men's and Women's Meeting Minutes [Orthodox]. Department of Records of Philadelphia Yearly Meeting, Philadelphia, Pa.

Philadelphia Monthly Meeting [Race Street]. Membership Records. Friends' Historical Library, Swarthmore College, Swarthmore, Pa.

——. Men's and Women's Meeting Minutes [Hicksite]. Friends' Historical Library, Swarthmore College, Swarthmore, Pa.

Philadelphia Monthly Meeting [Twelfth Street]. Membership Records. Department of Records of Philadelphia Yearly Meeting, Philadelphia, Pa.

Philadelphia Monthly Meeting for the Western District [Twelfth Street]. Men's and Women's Meeting Minutes [Orthodox]. Department of Records of Philadelphia Yearly Meeting, Philadelphia, Pa.

Philadelphia Yearly Meeting. Census, 1881. Friends' Historical Library, Swarthmore College, Swarthmore, Pa.

Philadelphia Yearly Meeting [Hicksite]. Meeting Minutes. Friends' Historical Library, Swarthmore College, Swarthmore, Pa.

——. Representative Committee Minutes. Friends' Historical Library, Swarthmore College, Swarthmore, Pa.

Philadelphia Yearly Meeting [Orthodox]. Meeting Minutes. Department of Records of Philadelphia Yearly Meeting, Philadelphia, Pa.

——. Social Order Committee Minutes. Department of Records of Philadelphia Yearly Meeting, Philadelphia, Pa.

Registry of Wills. Offices in the following counties were consulted for the wills of Friends in the sample of membership: Bucks County, Doylestown, Pa.; Burlington County, Mount Holly, N.J.; Camden County, Camden, N.J.; Chester County, West Chester, Pa.; Delaware County, Media, Pa.; Montgomery County, Norristown, Pa.; Philadelphia County, Philadelphia, Pa.

Sharpless, Isaac. Papers. Quaker Collection, Haverford College, Haverford, Pa.

Spring Street Settlement. Papers. Friends' Historical Library, Swarthmore College, Swarthmore, Pa.

Welsh, Herbert. Papers. Historical Society of Pennsylvania, Philadelphia, Pa.

Whitson, Benjamin F. Journals. Friends' Historical Library, Swarthmore College, Swarthmore, Pa.

Yearly Meeting Tea Fund. Treasurer's Account, 1911–20. Department of Records of Philadelphia Yearly Meeting, Philadelphia, Pa.

Published Sources

Abell, Aaron I. *The Urban Impact on American Protestantism, 1865–1900.* Cambridge, Mass., 1943.

Abernathy, Lloyd M. "Insurgency in Philadelphia, 1905," *Pennsylvania Magazine of History and Biography*, LXXXVII (Jan. 1963), 3–20.

——. "The Progressive Campaign in Pennsylvania, 1912," *Pennsylvania History*. XXIX (April 1962), 175–92.

Abrams, Ray H. *Preachers Present Arms.* Philadelphia, 1933.

Ahlstrom, Sidney E. *A Religious History of the American People.* New Haven, Conn., 1972.

Alderson, William T., Jr. "The Freedman's Bureau and Negro Education in Virginia," *North Carolina Historical Review*, XXIX (Jan. 1952), 64–90.

Alsop, Gulielma Fell. *History of the Woman's Medical College, Philadelphia, Pennsylvania, 1850–1950.* Philadelphia, 1950.

The American Friend. 1895–1913.

An Appeal to Friends and Others on Behalf of the Destitute Freedmen of the South. Philadelphia, 1863.

Appel, John C. "The Significance of the Quakers in Public Education in Pennsylvania, 1801–1860." Unpub. Master's thesis, University of Maryland, 1943.

Armstrong Association. *Annual Reports.* 1908–20.

Ashbrook, William S. *Fifty Years: The Provident Life and Trust Company of Philadelphia, 1865–1915.* Philadelphia, 1915.

Association for the Care of Colored Orphans. *Annual Reports.* 1867–1920.

Association of Friends for the Free Instruction of Adult Colored Persons. *Annual Reports.* 1862–65.

Atkinson, Wilmer W. *An Autobiography.* Philadelphia, 1920.

Axelrod, Morris. "Urban Structure and Social Participation," *American Sociological Review,* XXI (Feb. 1956), 13–18.

Babbidge, Homer D., Jr. "Swarthmore College in the Nineteenth Century: A Quaker Experience in Education." Unpub. Ph.D. diss., Yale University, 1953.

Bacon, Margaret H. *History of the Pennsylvania Society for Promoting the Abolition of Slavery.* Philadelphia, 1959.

———. *The Quiet Rebels: The Story of the Quakers in America.* New York, 1969.

Ballinger and Richard's Denver City Directory. 1894.

Baltzell, E. Digby. *Philadelphia Gentlemen: The Making of a National Upper Class.* Glencoe, Ill., 1958.

The Banker's Directory: Blue Book, January 1900. Chicago, 1900.

Barbour, Hugh. *The Quakers in Puritan England.* New Haven, Conn., 1964.

Barnard, John. *From Evangelism to Progressivism at Oberlin College, 1866–1917.* Columbus, Ohio, 1969.

Bentley, George R. *A History of the Freedman's Bureau.* Philadelphia, 1955.

Berkhofer, Robert F., Jr. *Salvation and the Savage: An Analysis of Protestant Missions and American Indian Response, 1787–1862.* Lexington, Ky., 1965.

Berthoff, Rowland. *An Unsettled People: Social Order and Disorder in American History.* New York, 1971.

Billington, Ray Allen. *The Protestant Crusade, 1800–1860: A Study of the Origins of American Nativism.* Chicago, Quadrangle paperback ed., 1964.

Bispham, David. *A Quaker Singer's Recollections.* New York, 1920.

Blankenburg, Lucretia. *The Blankenburgs of Philadelphia.* Philadelphia, 1928.

Blodgett, Geoffrey. *The Gentle Reformers: Massachusetts Democrats in the Cleveland Era.* Cambridge, Mass., 1966.

Board of Public Education, First School District of Pennsylvania, comprising Philadelphia. *72nd Annual Report.* 1891.

Bosworth, Francis. *The Story of the Friends' Neighborhood Guild.* Philadelphia, 1950.

Boyd's Philadelphia City Directory. 1912–20.

Bradley, Edward S. *Henry Charles Lea: A Biography.* Philadelphia, 1931.

A Brief Narrative of the Struggle for the Rights of the Colored People in the City Railway Cars; and a Defence of William Still. Philadelphia, 1867.

A Brief Sketch of the Schools for Black People and Their Descendants Established by the Religious Society of Friends in 1770. Philadelphia, 1867.

Brinton, Anna D., ed. *Then and Now.* Philadelphia, 1960.

Brinton, Howard H., *Friends for 300 Years.* Wallingford, Pa. Pendle Hill paperback ed., 1965.

——. *Prophetic Ministry.* Wallingford, Pa., 1954.

——. *Quaker Education in Theory and Practice.* Wallingford, Pa., 1940.

——. *Seventy-five Years of Quakerism, 1885–1960.* Philadelphia, [1960].

Brock, Peter. *Pacifism in the United States: From the Colonial Era to the First World War.* Princeton, 1968.

Bronner, Edwin B., ed. *American Quakers Today.* Philadelphia, 1966.

Brown, Ira V. "Pennsylvania and the Rights of the Negro, 1865–1887," *Pennsylvania History,* XXVIII (Jan. 1961), 45–57.

Bruchey, Stuart. *The Roots of American Economic Growth, 1607–1861: An Essay in Social Causation.* New York, 1965.

Bryce, James. *The American Commonwealth.* 2 vols. New York, 1911.

Bryn Mawr College. *Alumnae Catalog.* 1920.

——. *President's Reports.* 1884–1920.

Buffalo City Directory. 1892.

Bullock, Henry Allen. *A History of Negro Education in the South: 1619 to the Present.* Cambridge, Mass., 1967.

Burgess, George H., and Miles Kennedy. *Centennial History of the Pennsylvania Railroad Company.* Philadelphia, 1946.

Burt, Nathaniel. *The Perennial Philadelphians: The Anatomy of an American Aristocracy.* Boston, 1963.

Cadbury, Henry J. "Negro Membership in the Society of Friends," *Journal of Negro History,* XXI (Apr. 1936), 151–213.

Caffrey, Augustine J., S.J. "The Affirmation Mysticism of Rufus Matthew Jones." Unpub. Ph.D. diss., Catholic University of America, 1967.

Canby, Henry S. "The People Called Quakers," *The Century,* LXXXIV (June 1912), 266–79.

Caplow, Theodore. *The Sociology of Work.* Minneapolis, 1954.

Carter, Paul A. *The Decline and Revival of the Social Gospel: Social and Political Liberalism in American Protestant Churches.* Ithaca, N.Y., 1962.

Cross, Robert D., ed. *The Church and the City, 1865–1910.* Indianapolis and New York, 1967.

Curti, Merle, et al. "Anatomy of Giving: Millionaires in the Nineteenth Century," *American Quarterly,* XV (Fall 1963), 416–35.

Darlington, Charles. *Memoirs of Charles Darlington.* 2 vols. Philadelphia, 1966.

Davis, Allen F. *Spearheads for Reform: The Social Settlements and the Progressive Movement, 1890–1914.* New York, 1967.

—— and Mark H. Haller, eds. *The Peoples of Philadelphia: A History of Ethnic Groups and Lower-Class Life, 1790–1940.* Philadelphia, 1973.

—— and John Sutherland. "Reform and Uplift among Philadelphia Negroes: The Diary of Helen Parrish," *Pennsylvania Magazine of History and Biography,* XCIV (Oct. 1970), 496–517.

Davison, Robert A. *Isaac Hicks: New York Merchant and Quaker, 1767–1820.* Cambridge, Mass., 1964.

Dewees, Watson, *A Century of Westtown History.* Westtown, Pa., 1899.

Diamond, Sigmund. *The Reputation of the American Businessman.* Cambridge, Mass., 1955.

Dickinson, Joan Younger. "Aspects of Italian Immigration to Philadelphia," *Pennsylvania Magazine of History and Biography,* XC (Oct. 1966), 445–65.

Diffenbacher's Pittsburgh City Directory. 1885, 1889, 1892, 1901.

Disbrow, Donald W. "The Progressive Movement in Philadelphia, 1910–1916." Unpub. Ph.D. diss., University of Rochester, 1956.

——. "Reform in Philadelphia under Mayor Blankenburg, 1912–1916," *Pennsylvania History,* XXVII (Oct. 1960), 379–96.

Doherty, Robert W. *The Hicksite Separation: A Sociological Analysis of Religious Schism in Early Nineteenth Century America.* New Brunswick, N.J., 1967.

Donald, Henderson, *The Negro Freedman: Life Conditions of the American Negro in the Early Years after Emancipation.* New York, 1952.

Douglass, H. Paul. *1000 City Churches.* New York, 1926.

Drake, Richard B. "Freedman's Aid Societies and Sectional Compromise," *Journal of Southern History,* XXIX (May 1963), 175–86.

Drake, Thomas E. *Quakers and Slavery in America.* New Haven, 1950.

DuBois, William E. B. *The Philadelphia Negro: A Social Study.* Philadelphia, 1899.

Dudden, Arthur P. "Lincoln Steffens' Philadelphia," *Pennsylvania History,* XXXI (Oct. 1964), 449–57.

Dusinberre, William. *Civil War Issues in Philadelphia, 1856–1865.* Philadelphia, 1965.

Elkinton, Joseph. *The Doukhobors: Their History in Russia, Their Migration to Canada.* Philadelphia, 1903.

——. *Selections from the Diary and Correspondence of Joseph S. Elkinton, 1830–1905.* Philadelphia, 1913.

Elson, Ruth Miller. "American Schoolbooks and 'Culture' in the Nineteenth Century," *Mississippi Valley Historical Review,* XLVI (Dec. 1959), 411–34.

Emlen, John T. "Movement for the Betterment of the Negro in Philadelphia," *The Annals of the American Academy of Political and Social Science,* XLIX (Sept. 1913), 81–92.

Faith and Practice (Orthodox Discipline). Philadelphia, 1926.

Farish, Hunter D. *The Circuit Rider Dismounts: A Social History of Southern Methodism, 1865–1900.* Richmond, 1938.

Ferm, Vergilius, ed. *The American Church of the Protestant Heritage*. New York, 1952.

Fichter, Joseph H., S.J. *Social Relations in the Urban Parish*. Chicago, 1954.

Fletcher, Robert S. *A History of Oberlin College*. Oberlin, Ohio, 1943.

Flexner, Eleanor, *Century of Struggle*. Cambridge, Mass., 1959.

Forbush, Bliss. *Elias Hicks, Quaker Liberal*. New York, 1956.

Fredrickson, George. *The Black Image in the White Mind: The Debate on Afro-American Character and Destiny, 1817–1914*. New York, 1971.

The Freedman's Friend (Cambria, Va.) 1867–1910.

The Friend. 1865–1920.

Friends' Association of Philadelphia and Its Vicinity for the Relief of Colored Freedmen. *Annual Reports*. 1864–74, 1887–88, 1899–1900.

Friends' Association of Philadelphia for the Aid and Elevation of the Freedmen. *Annual Reports*. 1864–72.

Friends' Central School. *Alumni Register*. 1921.

Friends' Freedmen Association. *An Appeal to Friends and Others on Behalf of the Destitue Freedmen of the South*. Philadelphia, 1863.

——. *Circular: To Teachers and Others Engaged by the Association of Friends of Philadelphia . . . for the Relief of Colored Freedmen, in the Care of Their Schools*. Philadelphia, 1866.

——. *Dear Friend: The Urgent Needs of the Freed People. . . .* Philadelphia, 1865.

——. *Statistics of the Operations of the Executive Board . . . Together with a Joint Report of Samuel R. Shipley . . . of his Visit to the Camps of the Freedmen on the Mississippi River*. Philadelphia, 1864.

Friends' General Conference. *Proceedings*. Philadelphia, 1910–16.

The Friends' Intelligencer. 1865–1920.

The Friends' Review. 1865–94.

Friends' Union for Philanthropic Labor. *Proceedings*. Philadelphia, 1896.

Fritz, Henry E. *The Movement for Indian Assimilation, 1860–1890*. Philadelphia, 1963.

Fuess, Claude M. *Amherst: The Story of a New England College*. Boston, 1935.

[Garrett, Martha]. *Memories of Philadelphia in the Nineteenth Century*. N.d.

Garrett, Philip C. "Immigration to the United States," *Proceedings of the Fifteenth National Conference on Charities and Correction*. Buffalo, 1888.

——. *Party Politics in Great Cities*. Philadelphia, 1882.

George School. *Alumni Directory*. 1935.

Ginger, Ray. *The Age of Excess: The United States from 1877 to 1914*. New York, 1965.

Glaab, Charles N., ed. *The American City: A Documentary History*. Homewood, Ill., 1963.

Glazier, Willard. *Peculiarities of American Cities*. Philadelphia, 1885.

Goldstein, Sidney, et al. *The Norristown Study: An Experiment in Interdisciplinary Research Training*. Philadelphia, 1961.

Goodchild, Frank M. "The Social Evil in Philadelphia," *Arena*, XV (March 1896), 574–86.

Gopsill's Philadelphia City Directory. 1870–1905.

Gordon, Milton M. *Assimilation in American Life: The Role of Race, Religion, and National Origins*. New York, 1964.

——. *Social Class in American Sociology*. Durham, N.C., 1958.

Gusfield, Joseph R. *Symbolic Crusade: Status Politics and the American Temperance Movement*. Urbana, Ill., 1963.

Gutman, Herbert G. "Protestantism and the American Labor Movement: The Christian Spirit in the Gilded Age," *American Historical Review*, LXXII (Oct. 1965), 74–102.

Hagan, William T. *American Indians*. Chicago, 1961.

Haines, Joseph E. *A History of Friends' Central School, 1845–1893*. Overbrook, Pa., 1938.

Hallowell, Anna D. *James and Lucretia Mott: Life and Letters*. Boston, 1884.

Handy, Robert T. *A Christian America: Protestant Hopes and Historical Realities*. New York, 1971.

——. ed. *The Social Gospel in America, 1870–1920*. New York, 1966.

Harbeson, William. "Philadelphia Victorian Architecture, 1860–1890," *Pennsylvania Magazine of History and Biography*, LXVII (July 1943), 254–71.

Hatt, Paul K., and A. J. Reiss, Jr., eds. *Reader in Urban Sociology*. New York, 1951.

Haverford College. *Biographical Catalog of the Matriculates*. 1922.

——. *Bulletin*. 1901–20.

——. *Reports of the Corporation*. 1888–1901.

——. *Reports of the Managers*. 1865–85.

——. [Library.] *Quaker Necrology*. 2 vols. Boston, 1961.

Hays, Samuel P. "The Politics of Reform in Municipal Government in the Progressive Era," *Pacific Northwest Quarterly*, LV (Oct. 1964), 157–69.

Higham, John. *Strangers in the Land: Patterns of American Nativism, 1860–1925*. New Brunswick, 1955.

Hilton, George W., and John F. Due. *The Electric Interurban Railways in America*. Palo Alto, Calif., 1960.

Hinshaw, William Wade, ed. *Encyclopedia of Quaker Genealogy*. 6 vols. Richmond, Ind., 1936–50.

Hirshson, Stanley P. *Farewell to the Bloody Shirt: Northern Republicans and the Southern Negro*. Bloomington, Ind., 1962.

Hirst, Margaret E. *Quakers in Peace and War*. London, 1923.

History of the Association of Friends for the Free Instruction of Adult Colored Persons. Philadelphia, 1890.

Hodgson, William. *The Society of Friends in the Nineteenth Century: A Historical View of the Convulsions and Schisms Therein during That Period.* 2 vols. Philadelphia, 1875.

Hofstadter, Richard. *The Age of Reform: From Bryan to F.D.R.* New York, Vintage paperback ed., 1955.

Hole, Helen G. *Westtown through the Years, 1799–1942.* Westtown, Pa., 1942.

Hoogenboom, Ari. *Outlawing the Spoils: A History of the Civil Service Reform Movement.* Urbana, Ill., 1961.

Hopkins, Charles H. *The Rise of the Social Gospel in American Protestantism, 1865–1915.* New Haven, Conn., 1940.

Horwill, Herbert W. "A Quaker Socialist Movement," *The Nation*, VII (Sept. 14, 1918), 291–93.

Hostetler, John A. *Amish Society.* Rev. ed. Baltimore, 1968.

Howe's Camden City Directory. 1885, 1891, 1893–94, 1900.

Huggins, Nathan I. *Protestants against Poverty: Boston's Charities, 1870–1900.* Westport, 1971.

Hunt, Everett L. *The Revolt of the College Intellectual.* New York, 1963.

Hutchinson, William R., ed. *American Protestant Thought: The Liberal Era.* New York, 1968.

Hutchison, John A. *We Are Not Divided: A Critical and Historical Study of the Federal Council of Churches of Christ in America.* New York, 1941.

Immigration Restriction League (Boston). *Reports of the Executive Committee.* 1895.

Isichei, Elizabeth. *Victorian Quakers.* London, 1970.

Jackson, Luther P. "The Educational Efforts of the Freedman's Bureau and the Freedman's Aid Societies in South Carolina, 1862–1872," *Journal of Negro History*, VIII (Jan. 1923), 1–40.

Jaher, Frederic Cople, ed. *The Age of Industrial Capitalism: Essays in Social Structure and Cultural Values.* New York, 1968.

James, Sydney V. *A People among Peoples: Quaker Benevolence in the Eighteenth Century.* Cambridge, Mass., 1963.

Janney, Samuel M. *An Examination of the Causes Which Led to the Separation of the Religious Society of Friends in America, 1827–28.* Philadelphia, 1868.

Jaquette, Henrietta S., ed. *South after Gettysburg: The Letters of Cornelia Hancock, 1863–1868.* New York, 1956.

Johnson, Emily Cooper. *Under Quaker Appointment: The Life of Jane P. Rushmore.* Philadelphia, 1953.

Jones, Rufus M. "The Churches in 1899: Principal Events of the Year: Society of Friends," *The Independent*, LII (Jan. 4, 1900), 31.

——. *Haverford College: A History and an Interpretation.* New York, 1933.

——. *The Later Periods of Quakerism.* 2 vols. London, 1921.

——. *Quakers in the American Colonies.* London, 1911.

——. *A Service of Love in War Time: American Friends' Relief Work in Europe, 1917–1919.* New York, 1920.

——. *The Trail of Life in College.* New York, 1929.

——. *The Trail of Life in the Middle Years.* New York, 1934.

Kane, John J. "The Irish Immigrant in Philadelphia, 1840–1880: A Study in Conflict and Accommodation." Unpub. Ph.D. diss., University of Pennsylvania, 1950.

Katzenstein, Caroline. *Lifting the Curtain: The State and National Woman Suffrage Campaigns in Pennsylvania as I Saw Them.* Philadelphia, 1955.

Kelsey, Rayner W. *Friends and the Indians, 1655–1917.* Philadelphia, 1917.

Keystone State Bazaar in Aid of the Pennsylvania Woman Suffrage Association, February 25, 26, 1915. N.p., 1915.

King, Moses. *Philadelphia and Notable Philadelphians.* New York, 1902.

Kirkland, Edward C. *Dream and Thought in the Business Community, 1860–1900.* Ithaca, N.Y., 1956.

Kirlin, Joseph L. J. *Catholicity in Philadelphia.* Philadelphia, 1909.

Kraditor, Aileen. *The Ideas of the Woman Suffrage Movement, 1890–1920.* New York, 1965.

Krone, Henrietta L. "Dauntless Women: A Story of the Woman Suffrage Movement in Pennsylvania, 1910–1920." Unpub. Ph.D. diss., University of Pennsylvania, 1946.

Lain's Brooklyn City Directory. 1890.

Lakeside Directory of Chicago. 1886, 1901.

Lief, Alfred. *Family Business: A Century in the Life and Times of Strawbridge and Clothier.* New York, 1968.

List of Organizations Managed Wholly or in Part by Members of the Society of Friends in Philadelphia Yearly Meeting [Orthodox]. Philadelphia, 1897.

Litwak, Eugene. "Geographical Mobility and Extended Family Cohesion," *American Sociological Review,* XXV (June 1960), 385–94.

Logan, Frenise A. *The Negro in North Carolina, 1876–1894.* Chapel Hill, 1964.

Lubell, Samuel. *Revolt of the Moderates.* New York, 1956.

McClure, Alexander K. *Old Time Notes of Pennsylvania.* 2 vols. Philadelphia, 1905.

McFarland, Gerald W. "The New York Mugwumps of 1884: A Profile," *Political Science Quarterly,* LXXVIII (Mar. 1963), 40–58.

McKelvey, Blake. *The Urbanization of America, 1860–1915.* New Brunswick, N.J., 1963.

Mackey, Philip E. "Law and Order, 1877: Philadelphia's Response to the Railroad Riots," *Pennsylvania Magazine of History and Biography,* XCVI (Apr. 1972), 183–202.

McLachlan, James S. *The American Boarding School: A Historical Study.* New York, 1970.

——. "The Genteel Reformers, 1865–1884." Unpub. Master's thesis, Columbia University, 1958.

McPherson, James M. "Grant or Greeley? The Abolitionist Dilemma in the Election of 1872," *American Historical Review*, LXXI (Oct. 1965), 43–61.

——. *The Struggle for Equality: Abolitionists and the Negro in the Civil War and Reconstruction*. Princeton, 1964.

——. "White Liberals and Black Power in Negro Education, 1865–1915," *American Historical Review*, LXXV (June 1970), 1357–86.

Magill, Edward H. *Educational Institutions in the Religious Society of Friends*. Philadelphia, 1893.

——. *Twenty-five Years in the Life of a Teacher, 1841–1906*. Boston, 1907.

Marchand, C. Roland. *The American Peace Movement and Social Reform, 1898–1918*. Princeton, 1972.

Marietta, Jack D. "Delinquency among Colonial Pennsylvania Quakers." Unpub. paper.

Marot, Helen. "Labor and the Flag." *The Masses*, VIII (June 1916), 20.

Marshall, Clara. *The Woman's Medical College of Pennsylvania: An Historical Outline*. Philadelphia, 1897.

Matlack, Chalkley, comp. *Brief Historical Sketches Concerning Friends' Meetings of Past and Present*. 2 vols. Moorestown, N.J., 1938.

May, Henry F. *The End of American Innocence: A Study of the First Years of Our Own Time, 1912–1917*. New York, 1959.

——. *The Protestant Churches and Industrial America*. New York, 1949.

Mead, Sidney E. *The Lively Experiment: The Shaping of Christianity in America*. New York, 1963.

Meier, August. *Negro Thought in America, 1880–1915*. Ann Arbor, 1963.

Meigs, Cornelia. *What Makes a College? A History of Bryn Mawr*. New York, 1956.

Miller, John A. *Fares Please: From Horse Cars to Streamliners*. New York, 1941.

Miller, Robert Moats. *American Protestantism and Social Issues, 1919–1939*. Chapel Hill, 1958.

Miller, William, ed. *Men in Business: Essays on the Historical Role of the Entrepreneur*. New York, Harper Torchbook ed., 1962.

Mills, C. Wright. *Power, Politics, and People: The Collected Essays of C. Wright Mills*. Ed. Irving Horowitz. New York, Ballantine paperback ed., n.d.

Moberg, David O. *The Church as a Social Institution*. Englewood Cliffs, N.J., 1962.

Mohr, Walter H., David B. Stafford, and Ernest F. Seegers. *History of George School, 1893–1943*. Bucks Co., Pa. 1943.

Monthly Register of the Society for Organizing Charity. 1879–89.

Morais, Henry S. *The Jews of Philadelphia: Their History from the Earliest Settlements to the Present time*. Philadelphia, 1894.

Morgan, H. Wayne, ed. *The Gilded Age: A Reappraisal*. Syracuse, 1963.

Morley, Christopher. *Travels in Philadelphia*. Philadelphia, 1920.

Morrow, Ralph. *Northern Methodism and Reconstruction*. East Lansing, Mich., 1956.

Morton, Richard L. " 'Contrabands' and Quakers on the Virginia Penin-sula," *Virginia Magazine of History and Biography*, LXI (Oct. 1953), 419–29.

Municipal League of Philadelphia. *Annual Reports of the Board of Managers*. 1894–95.

Murdock's Boston City Directory. 1901.

Murray, Andrew E. *Presbyterians and the Negro: A History*. Philadelphia, 1966.

Nash, Gary B. *Quakers and Politics: Pennsylvania, 1681–1726*. Princeton, 1968.

Niebuhr, H. Richard. *Christ and Culture*. New York, 1951.

——. *The Social Sources of Denominationalism*. New York: Meridian paperback ed., 1957.

Norris, George W. *Ended Episodes*. Philadelphia, 1937.

North House. *Annual Reports*. 1906–20.

Norwood, Alberta S. "Negro Welfare Work in Philadelphia, Especially as Illustrated by the Career of William Still, 1775–1930." Unpub. Master's thesis, University of Pennsylvania, 1931.

Olmstead, Clifton E. *History of Religion in the United States*. Englewood Cliffs, 1960.

O'Neill, William L. *Everyone Was Brave: The Rise and Fall of Feminism in America*. Chicago, 1969.

Osofsky, Gilbert. "Progressivism and the Negro: New York, 1900–1915," *American Quarterly*, XVI (Summer 1964), 153–68.

Parrish, Edward. *An Essay on Education in the Society of Friends*. Philadelphia, 1866.

Patterson, Mary S. *Martha Schofield: Servant of the Least, 1839–1916*. [Wallingford, Pa.], 1944.

Pearson, Elizabeth W., ed. *Letters from Port Royal: Written at the Time of the Civil War*. Boston, 1906.

Pennell, Elizabeth Robins. *Our Philadelphia*. Philadelphia, 1914.

Peterson, George E. *The New England College in the Age of the University*. Amherst, Mass., 1964.

Peterson, H. C., and Gilbert Fite. *Opponents of the War, 1917–1918*. Madison, 1957.

Philadelphia Association of Friends for the Instruction of Poor Children. *Annual Reports*. 1868, 1873, 1877.

Philadelphia Bulletin. 1934–40.

Philadelphia Civic Club. *Civic Club Digest of Educational and Charitable Institutions and Societies in Philadelphia*. Philadelphia, 1895.

——. *A Directory of the Charitable, Social Improvement, Educational and Religious Associations and Churches of Philadelphia*. Philadelphia, 1903.

Philadelphia Committee of 70. *Proceedings of the Town Meeting Held in the Academy of Music, Thursday Evening, January 18th, 1906* [Philadelphia], 1906.

——. *Report of the Executive Board*. 1905, 1912.

Philadelphia Directory of Directors. 1905, 1912.

Philadelphia Home for Aged and Infirm Colored Persons. *Annual Reports.* 1866, 1871, 1892.

Philadelphia Home for Destitute Colored Children. *Annual Reports.* 1861, 1866, 1869.

Philadelphia Inquirer. 1936–63.

Philadelphia Institute for Colored Youth. *Annual Reports.* 1860–1901.

Philadelphia Monthly Meeting [Arch Street]. *Members.* 1915.

Philadelphia Monthly Meeting [Race Street]. *Members.* 1876, 1888, 1894, 1904, 1909, 1913, 1924.

Philadelphia Monthly Meeting for the Western District [Twelfth Street]. *Members.* 1878, 1885, 1892, 1897, 1903, 1907, 1912, 1918, 1926.

Philadelphia Public Ledger, 1880–1936.

Philadelphia Yearly Meeting. *List of Organizations Managed Wholly or in Part by Members of the Society of Friends in Philadelphia Yearly Meeting* [Orthodox]. Philadelphia, 1897.

——. *Remonstrance against Prohibiting the Immigration of Colored People* [Orthodox]. Philadelphia, 1863.

——. *Rules of Discipline of the Yearly Meeting of Friends for Pennsylvania, New Jersey, and the Eastern Part of Maryland* [Orthodox]. 9 vols. [1873, 1880, 1884, 1888, 1890, 1893, 1903, 1907, 1910]. Philadelphia, 1873–1910.

——. *Rules of Discipline of the Yearly Meeting of Friends Held in Philadelphia* [Hicksite]. 6 vols. [1869, 1877, 1883, 1886, 1894, 1906]. Philadelphia, 1869–1906.

Pivar, David J. "The New Abolitionism: The Quest for Social Purity, 1876–1900." Unpub. Ph.D. diss., University of Pennsylvania, 1965.

——. "Theocratic Businessmen and Philadelphia Municipal Reform, 1870–1900," *Pennsylvania History,* XXXIII (July 1966), 289–307.

Polk's Indianapolis City Directory. 1887.

Pratt, Caroline. *I Learn from Children.* New York, 1948.

Pratt, Richard Henry. *Battlefield and Classroom: Four Decades with the American Indian, 1867–1904.* Ed. Robert M. Utley. New Haven, Conn., 1964.

Present Day Papers. 1914–16.

Priest, Loring B. *Uncle Sam's Stepchildren: The Reformation of United States Indian Policy, 1865–1887.* New Brunswick, N.J., 1942.

Proceedings of the Seventh Annual Meeting of the Lake Mohonk Conference of Friends of the Indians. Mohonk, N.Y., 1889.

Reform Club of Philadelphia. *Constitution, By Laws, Charter, Rules, Officers and Members.* Philadelphia, 1875.

Report of the Committee Appointed for the Purpose of Securing to the Colored People in Philadelphia the Right to the Use of the Street Cars. Philadelphia, [1867].

Republican Club Book, 1904: Pennsylvania Edition. Philadelphia, 1904.

Reynolds, John S. *Reconstruction in South Carolina, 1865–1877.* Columbia, S.C., 1905.

Rhoads, Charles. *Business Ethics in Relation to the Profession of the Religious Society of Friends.* Philadelphia, 1882.

Ringer, Benjamin. "The Parishioner and His Church." Unpub. Ph.D. diss., Columbia University, 1956.

Rischin, Moses, ed. *The Gospel of Success: Individualism and Beyond.* Chicago, 1965.

Robinson, Rowland E. "Recollections of a Quaker Boy," *Atlantic,* LXXXVIII (July 1901), 100–105.

Robson, Walter. *An English View of American Quakerism.* Ed. Edwin B. Bronner. Philadelphia, 1970.

Rose, Willie Lee. *Rehearsal for Reconstruction: The Port Royal Experiment.* Indianapolis and New York, 1964.

Rosenberg, Carroll Smith. *Religion and the Rise of the American City: The New York City Mission Movement, 1812–1870.* Ithaca, N.Y., 1971.

Ross, Dorothy. "The Irish Catholic Immigrant, 1880–1900: A Study in Social Mobility." Unpub. Master's thesis, Columbia University, 1959.

Russell, Elbert. *The History of Quakerism.* New York, 1942.

Sampson's Boston City Directory. 1890.

Sanville, Florence. "Social Legislation in the Keystone State," *Survey,* XXXIII (Feb. 6, 1915), 481–86, and XXIV (Feb. 24, 1915), 84–86.

Schackleton, Robert. *The Book of Philadelphia.* Philadelphia, 1918.

Scharf, J. Thomas, and Thompson Westcott. *History of Philadelphia, 1609–1884.* 3 vols. Philadelphia, 1884.

Schlesinger, Arthur M., Sr. *The Rise of the City, 1878–1898.* New York, 1933.

Sears, Irwin. "Growth of Population in Philadelphia: 1860 to 1910." Unpub. Ph.D. diss., New York University, 1960.

Sharpless, Isaac. "Pennsylvania Quaker Boy," *Atlantic,* C (Oct. 1907), 536–41.

——. "The Quaker Boy at School," *The Independent,* LXV (Sept. 3, 1908), 543–46.

——. *A Quaker Experiment in Government.* Philadelphia, 1898.

——. *Quakerism and Politics: Essays.* Philadelphia, 1905.

——. *The Story of a Small College.* Philadelphia, 1918.

Simkins, Francis B., and Robert H. Woody. *South Carolina during Reconstruction.* Chapel Hill, 1932.

Singleton, Gregory H. "Mere Middle-Class Institutions: Urban Protestantism in Nineteenth-Century America," *Journal of Social History,* VI (Summer 1973), 489–504.

Smith, Logan Pearsall, ed. *Philadelphia Quaker: The Letters of Hannah Whitall Smith.* New York, 1950.

——. *Unforgotten Years.* Boston, 1949.

The Social Register: Philadelphia. 1891, 1893, 1900, 1910, 1920.

Solomon, Barbara Miller. *Ancestors and Immigrants: A Changing New England Tradition.* Cambridge, Mass., 1956.

Speakman, Thomas H. *Divisions in the Society of Friends.* 3rd enlarged ed. Philadelphia, 1896.

——. *Reply to the Epistle of the Yearly Meeting of Orthodox Friends Held at Fourth and Arch Streets, Philadelphia, Fourth Month, 1897.* Philadelphia, 1899.

Spiers, Frederic W. *The Street Railway System of Philadelphia: Its History and Present Condition.* Baltimore, 1897.

Sproat, John G. *The Best Men: Liberal Reformers in the Gilded Age.* New York, 1968.

Steffens, Lincoln. *Shame of the Cities.* New York, 1957.

Stein, Maurice. *Eclipse of Community: An Interpretation of American Studies.* Princeton, 1960.

Stewart, Frank M. *A Half Century of Municipal Reform: The History of the National Municipal League.* Berkeley and Los Angeles, 1950.

Sutherland, John. "A City of Homes: Philadelphia Slums and Reformers, 1880–1920." Unpub. Ph.D. diss., Temple University, 1973.

Swarthmore College. *Alumni Register.* 1935, 1940.

——. *Annual Catalogue.* 1869–1901.

——. *Annual Meeting of Stockholders.* 1894–95.

——. *Bulletin.* 1902–20.

Swift, David E. *Joseph John Gurney: Banker, Reformer, Quaker.* Middletown, Conn., 1962.

Swint, Henry L. *The Northern Teacher in the South.* Nashville, 1941.

Tatum, George B. *Penn's Great Town: 250 Years of Philadelphia Architecture.* Philadelphia, 1961.

Tatum, Laurie. *Our Red Brothers and the Peace Policy of President Ulysses S. Grant.* Lincoln, Neb., 1970.

Taylor, Airutheus A. *The Negro in the Reconstruction of Virginia.* Washington, D.C., 1926.

Taylor, Francis. "The Development of the Activities of the Yearly Meeting (1827–1927)," *The Friend,* CI (Oct. 13, 1927), 191–93.

Thernstrom, Stephan, and Peter R. Knights. "Men in Motion: Some Data and Speculation about Urban Population Mobility in Nineteenth-Century America," *Journal of Interdisciplinary History,* I (Autumn 1970), 7–35.

Thirty Schools Tell Their Story. New York, 1943.

Thomas, Allen C. "Congregational or Progressive Friends: A Forgotten Episode in Quaker History," *Bulletin of the Friends' Historical Association,* X (Nov. 1920), 21–31.

Thomas, Richard, and Allen Thomas. *A History of Friends in America.* Rev. ed. Philadelphia, 1905.

Timberlake, James H. *Prohibition and the Progressive Movement.* Cambridge, Mass., 1962.

Tindall, George B. *South Carolina Negroes, 1877–1900.* Columbia, S.C., 1952.

Tolles, Frederick B. *Meeting House and Counting House: The Quaker Merchants in Colonial Philadelphia, 1682–1783.* Chapel Hill, N.C., 1948.

——. *Quakers and the Atlantic Culture.* New York, 1960.

Trow's New York City Directory, 1887–88, 1908.

Trueblood, Benjamin. "Mohonk and Its Conferences," *New England Magazine,* XVI (June 1897), 447–64.

Trueblood, D. Elton. *The People Called Quakers.* New York, 1966.

Union League of Philadelphia. *Annual Reports of the Executive Board.* 1886, 1895.

U.S. Bureau of the Census. *Religious Bodies: 1916.* Washington, D.C., 1919.

—— *Thirteenth Census of the United States, 1910: Population.* Washington, D.C., 1911.

——. *Twelfth Census of the United States, 1900: Population.* Washington, D.C., 1901.

U.S. Department of Interior. *Negro Education: A Study of the Private and Higher Schools for Colored People in the United States.* Bureau of Education Bulletin 1916, No. 38. 2 vols. Washington, D.C., 1917.

U.S. Immigration Commission (1907–10). *Immigrants in Cities.* Vol. XXVI of *Reports of the Immigration Commission.* Washington, D.C., 1911.

The Unity of Spirit: Proceedings and Papers of the National Federation of the Religious Liberals. Boston, [1909].

University of Pennsylvania. *Biographical Catalog of the Matriculates.* 1894, 1917.

Upington's Brooklyn City Directory. 1901.

Urban Traffic and Transportation Board. *History of Public Transportation in Philadelphia.* Philadelphia, 1955.

Van Dusen, John G. "The Exodus of 1879," *Journal of Negro History,* XXI (Apr. 1936), 111–29.

Vickers, George. *The Fall of Bossism: A History of the Committee of One Hundred and the Reform Movement in Philadelphia and Pennsylvania.* Philadelphia, 1885.

Vining, Elizabeth Gray. *Friend of Life: The Biography of Rufus M. Jones.* Philadelphia, 1958.

Vogel, William P. *Precision, People and Progress: A Business Philosophy at Work.* Philadelphia, [1949].

Walton, George A. and J. Bernard Walton, comps. *Diaries and Correspondence: Margaretta Walton, 1829–1904.* N.p., 1962.

Wargny, Frank. "Education of the Freedmen by Philadelphia and Baltimore Quakers during the Civil War and Reconstruction Period." Unpub. Master's thesis, The Johns Hopkins University, 1947.

Warner, Sam Bass, Jr. *The Private City: Philadelphia in Three Periods of Its Growth.* Philadelphia, 1968.

Warner, Strafford A. *Yardley Warner: The Freedman's Friend.* Didcot, [1957].

Weaver, W. Wallace. *West Philadelphia: A Study of Natural Social Areas.* Philadelphia, 1930.

Weinberg, Allen, and Dale Fields, comps. *Ward Genealogy of the City and County of Philadelphia.* Philadelphia, n.d.

Weisenburger, Francis P. *Ordeal of Faith: The Crisis of Church-Going America, 1865–1900.* New York, 1959.

Welsh, Herbert. "The Degradation of Pennsylvania Politics," *The Forum,* XII (Nov. 1891), 330–45.

Westtown School. *Catalog of Students.* 1945.

Weygandt, Cornelius. *Philadelphia Folks: Ways and Institutions in and about the Quaker City.* New York, 1938.

White, Morton, and Lucia White. *The Intellectual versus the City.* Cambridge, Mass., 1962.

White, Theo. B., ed. *Philadelphia Architecture in the Nineteenth Century.* Philadelphia, 1953.

Whittner, Lawrence S. *Rebels against War: The American Peace Movement, 1941–1960.* New York, 1969.

Wiebe, Robert H. *Businessmen and Reform: A Study of the Progressive Movement.* Cambridge, Mass., 1962.

Wiggins' Columbus City Directory. 1901.

Willcox, Mildred Sylvia. "A History of the Friends' Central School System." Unpub. Master's thesis, Temple University, 1935.

William Penn Charter School. *Alumni Catalog.* 1962.

Wilson, Warren H. *Quaker Hill.* New York, 1907.

Wolf, Edwin, II, and Maxwell Whiteman. *A History of the Jews of Philadelphia from Colonial Times to the Age of Jackson.* Philadelphia, 1957.

Woman's Medical College, Alumnae Association. *Transactions.* 1900–1901.

Wood, Gordon S. "The Massachusetts Mugwumps," *New England Quarterly,* XXXIII (Dec. 1960), 435–51.

Woodcock, George, and Ivan Avakumovic. *The Doukhobors.* Toronto, 1968.

Woodruff, Clinton R. "The Municipal League of Philadelphia," *American Journal of Sociology,* XI (Nov. 1905), 336–58.

——. "The Philadelphia Campaign against 'Machine Rule,'" *Review of Reviews,* XXIV (Nov. 1909), 558–61.

Woods, Robert A., and Albert J. Kennedy. *The Zone of Emergence.* Abr. and ed. Sam B. Warner, Jr. Cambridge, Mass., 1962.

Woodward, C. Vann. *Origins of the New South, 1877–1913.* Baton Rouge, 1951.

——. *The Strange Career of Jim Crow.* New York, Galaxy paperback ed., 1957.

Woodward, George. "A Triumph of the People," *Outlook,* LXXXI (Dec. 2, 1905), 811–15.

Wright, Richard R., Jr. *The Negro in Pennsylvania: A Study in Economic History.* Philadelphia, 1908.

Yarnell, Stanley R. *Quaker Contributions to Education in Philadelphia and Vicinity.* Philadelphia, 1926.

Yinger, J. Milton. *Religion in the Struggle for Power.* Durham, N.C., 1946.

Zilversmit, Arthur. *The First Emancipation: The Abolition of Slavery in the North.* Chicago, 1967.

Index